Praise for *Vedic Astrology*

There are many new books out relating to Eastern philosophies and Indian Astrology, but this one has many qualities which make it inviting for the Western mind. . . . What really stands out about this book are tidbits not found elsewhere. For example, her chapter on "The Role of the Astrologer" is not only informative to the reader, but also demonstrates the author's grasp of the role astrology plays in India, as well as the demands put on Indian astrologers. —Marion D. March, *Aspects*

The first thing I learned when I opened this book was that Ronnie Dreyer *knows* astrology! . . . This incredibly clear and complete book takes us through the history of Eastern astrology and helps us interpret our own charts. It is a solid foundation for any student of India's predictive arts.
—Matthew Herman, *Magical Blend*

Add this title to the still pitifully small number of easy-to-understand books on the astrology of India. . . . Readers thinking about taking a dip in the ocean of Vedic Astrology will find this book an excellent place to wade in. Vedic veterans will benefit from Ronnie's valuable new material on planetary combinations.
—Linda Johnsen, *Mountain Astrologer*

Vedic Astrology is a pioneering work that serves to bridge the gulf between East and West. . . [and] has been written with the western astrologer in mind. . . . The author clears a path through the maze of cultural influences that have lent themselves to creating the foundations of the Vedas, and leaves the reader with a clearer understanding of some of the spiritual ideas that permeate this ancient tradition, and which are inseparable from the practise of astrology. . . . This is a book that I would recommend to anyone who is thinking of learning Vedic astrology. Congratulations Ronnie, on a job well done!!
—Andrew Smith, *Dublin Astrologer*

Ronnie covers all the fundamentals of Vedic astrology in a well thought out manner. Her writing style and examples are clear and easy to follow with plenty of cross-references. . . . I would recommend this book to the newcomer to Vedic astrology, particularly those from a western astrology background. This book is a worthy contribution to the limited, although expanding, number of Vedic books by authors from the West.

—Neville Lang, *FAA Journal*

A dazzling, tour-de-force on a topic that needs elucidation for Western astrologers. —*Welcome to Planet Earth*

This is a solid book, well thought-out and very clear in presentation. It will allow you to systematically immerse yourself in Vedic astrology and compare a known chart (your own of course) to its sidereally offset image in the Jyotish reflection. Then you can use the *bhuktis* and *dasas* listed to see if they related to significant parts of your life. What more could you ask?

—Mary Downing, *Geocosmic Magazine*

In *Vedic Astrology*, Ronnie Dreyer gets straight to the heart of what Jyotish is, how to use it, how not to use it, how this kind of astrology works for the Hindu culture, and how it doesn't work for the American who thinks that life has a predilection for kindness and benevolence. . . . *Vedic Astrology* is an impressive contribution to any personal or professional astrology reference shelf. —*Midwest Book Review*

This is the book to get whether you're exploring the riches of Vedic astrology as a new student or desiring to add to your knowledge as one already into this study. Highly recommended.

—Todd Collard, *Mercury Hour*

VEDIC ASTROLOGY

A Guide to the Fundamentals of Jyotish

Foreword by
James Braha

Ronnie Gale Dreyer

SAMUEL WEISER, INC.

York Beach, Maine

First published in 1997 by
Samuel Weiser, Inc.
P. O. Box 612
York Beach, ME 03910-0612

Library of Congress Cataloging-in-Publication Data
Dreyer, Ronnie Gale.
  [Indian astrology]
  Vedic astrology : a guide to the fundamentals of jyotish / Ronnie
Gale Dreyer.
     p. cm.
  Includes bibliographical references and index.
  Originally published: Indian astrology. London : Aquarian Press,
1990.
  ISBN 0-87728-889-5 (pbk. : alk. paper)
  1. Hindu astrology. 2. Vedas—Criticism, interpretation, etc. I. Title.
BF1714.H5D74 1997
133.5'9445—dc21   97-5620
                                                        CIP

ISBN 0-87728-889-5
EB

Typeset in 10.5 Sabon

Printed in the United States of America

04 03 02 01 00 99
10 9 8 7 6 5 4 3 2

*To Ken who made the circle of my life full and complete.
After all is said and done, the center is what holds.*

TABLE OF CONTENTS

LIST OF ILLUSTRATIONS

List of Tables

FOR TWO THOUSAND YEARS, Hindu predictive astrology was virtually unknown in the Western world. During the mid-1980s a handful of pioneering astrologers traveled separately to India and brought this profound knowledge home, changing the situation forever. Ronnie Gale Dreyer was one of these individuals to whom Western astrologers shall be eternally indebted. She is also the first American woman astrologer to complete a comprehensive text on the subject—a subject that, in the East, is generally, though not absolutely, dominated by men.

Vedic Astrology is a major contribution; remarkably complete, exceptionally clear, and profoundly satisfying for those hungry for the knowledge of *Jyotish* or "the science of light," as it is called in India. Although the enormity and complexity of this vast subject nearly always seems overwhelming to beginners, Ronnie Dreyer has purposely organized the material in a way that is clear, understandable, and accessible to all. It is no small benefit that the author, an expert in the Eastern system, happens also to be schooled in Western astrology. This enables her to fathom exactly the perplexities and pitfalls that veteran Western astrologers new to Eastern astrology are likely to encounter. Throughout the text, there are warnings and hints that guide astrologers in the proper direction, protecting them from the interpretive disasters and calamities experienced by generations of forebears who have tried, and consistently failed, to learn *Jyotish* from Indian texts.

As a practicing *Jyotishi* (Hindu astrologer), Ronnie Dreyer has paid her dues many times over, not merely by professionally analyzing thousands of horoscopes, lecturing at astrology conferences worldwide, and writing two authoritative astrology texts, but especially by having learned *Jyotish* in India with an Indian mentor. The benefit of this, as any astrologer who has studied in the East will immediately recognize, cannot be overemphasized. *Jyotish* is an integral part of an unparalleled mystical and spiritual culture. In order to really grasp the art of this profound ancient knowledge, not merely with one's mind but with heart and soul and deep consciousness, nothing compares to immersing oneself in the culture of India and attuning one's intellect to the peculiar mindset of a masterful Eastern astrologer.

We Westerners are trained to think in a linear fashion, organizing and categorizing data so that it may be easily processed and assimilated. Indians, raised in a society where spirit is of the essence, live in a world of abstractions, instincts, and intuitive notions; in short, a world that routinely transcends boundaries, limitations, logic, and reasoning. Although attuning one's mind to an Indian astrologer's is at times a harrowing experience, the rewards for doing so are great. Indeed, the clarity, precision, and fine organization that make the information in this text so accessible are a direct result of Ronnie Dreyer's willingness to temporarily relinquish her own mental strategies in favor of her cultural opposite Indian mentor.

Those who find the material in this book demanding should consider the fact that you are learning *Jyotish* the easy way. Make no mistake, Ronnie Dreyer has done the rigorous work for you. She has analyzed and digested the Eastern thought process underlying *Jyotish* in order to present the material in a way our logical, Western minds can comprehend. If this seems obvious or irrelevant, consider a few tormenting experiences a Westerner is very likely to encounter at the feet of a *Jyotishi*: When studying a horoscope of a friend or loved one with your mentor, the *Jyotishi* makes some startlingly accurate prediction using a technique completely outside the realm of the system he or she has just taught you. For some inexplicable reason you are not told about the technique. The conversation goes something like this:

Jyotishi: This woman must be an actress.
Confused Westerner: She is! But how can you tell?
Jyotishi: Saturn is in the 12th house from Venus (i.e., Saturn occupies the 6th house and Venus occupies the 7th house, or Saturn is in the 3rd and Venus is in the 4th).
Confused Westerner: What!
Jyotishi: Yes . . .

Confused Westerner: But what do you mean? What does Saturn occupying the 12th house from Venus have to do with being an artist?

Jyotishi: Yes . . . . (long pause) Is it not true? Is she not an actress?

Confused Westerner: She is. But why?

Jyotishi: Yes.

The conversation now turns to a completely different subject, with no satisfaction in sight. Some weeks or months later, depending on the Westerner's luck, he or she learns from a different source that the *Jyotishi* was in fact incorporating an astrological technique from either *Jaimini* or *Tajaka*, two entirely different systems of *Jyotish*. (The system taught in this book is called *Parasara*, named after the great ancient Indian Seer. It is by far the most popular system, and is the one explained in all the books written by Westerners so far.) In this case, the logic behind the technique in question is that if Saturn (a natural career indicator) occupies the house preceding Venus (the planet of art) the person would likely be an artist, assuming the birth chart in other general ways indicates artistic talent. This is because if Saturn occupies the house preceding Venus, the first transit Saturn makes after birth is a conjunction to Venus. As to how the astrologer knew the woman was an actress rather than a singer or dancer, a rational explanation is not in order. The intuition needed to make that deduction is considered simple for an experienced Indian astrologer.

Another mind-bending experience for a Westerner occurs when your *Jyotishi* has trained you to use one particular house system (explaining that it is the most accurate one) and one day out of the clear blue makes a remarkably accurate statement about a person's life using a different house system than the only one he or she has taught you! Of course your mentor does not mention using a different house system. The conversation goes like this:

Jyotishi: This person has problems with his mother. Saturn is in the 4th house.

Westerner: Yes, that's true. His mother has a difficult life and the relationship between mother and son is strained.

The following day—the same chart
Jyotishi: He will have few children. Or he will have problems with them.
Confused Westerner: Why?
Jyotishi: Saturn is in the 5th house.
Massively Confused Westerner: Saturn is not in the 5th house, it occupies the 4th house!
Jyotishi: Yes, it is in the 4th house, but still . . . Is it not true? Does he have any children?
Resigned Westerner: None.
Jyotishi: See.

Some time later, perhaps in the quiet of the night before falling asleep, the realization is made that the astrologer was using a different house system for that single prediction. It then becomes glaringly obvious that many astrologers who make the most accurate predictions use two (or perhaps more—who knows since this is India?) different house systems simultaneously.

Ronnie Dreyer's approach and presentation of *Jyotish* is one that can be fully trusted. She employs ancient traditional techniques, but is bound only by what actually produces accurate results. This is no small matter, since there are literally thousands upon thousands of scriptural rules and precepts in this centuries old astrology, which are decidedly unequal in their efficacy. Many scriptural principles quickly guide the astrologer to great predictive accuracy, while others seem to work only fifty percent, or less, of the time (traditional explanations of *vargottama* planets, exalted retrograde planets, fallen retrograde planets, and *neechabhanga raja yoga* fall very short in my experience). Fortunately, Ronnie Dreyer, as you will soon realize, is an astrologer who relies on experience, not dogma.

She also confidently contributes her own powerful insights. Indeed, some of the best material in this book is contained in the highly original chapter titled Ascendant Combinations. The explanations are accurate, reliable, and not to be found in any other basic *Jyotish* text I have seen. While some Western practitioners of *Jyotish* who have never visited India might complain about the non-traditional nature of this chapter, the work is precisely what Indian astrology is all about. Although the basic techniques of the *Parasara* system of *Jyotish* are specific and unequivocal, a certain amount of license is granted to every practicing astrologer *who produces accurate results*. One of the most fascinating and enchanting features about the practice of *Jyotish* is the fact that Indian astrologers, and the techniques they use, often differ dramatically from town to town in India. While this can be a source of frustration to Westerners, Indians are concerned only with what works. As you will soon see, ascendant combinations, as described by Ronnie Dreyer, work.

Ronnie Dreyer also does a marvelous job of removing the confusion and mystery of this age-old astrology through her down to earth, factual delineations of planets in houses. Much of the reason Hindu astrology remained a shrouded secret in the West for so long was because of the cryptic, often heavy-handed writings of ancient Indian seers. Consider, for example, a few typical scriptural explanations of planets in houses. From *Phaladeepika* by Mantreswara (one of my favorite texts): "If Mars be in the second house, the person concerned will be ugly faced, devoid of learning and wealth, and will be dependent on bad people." Or, "If Saturn should be posited in the fifth house, the person born will be roaming about, will have lost his reason, will be bereft of children, wealth and happiness, will be perfidious and evil-minded." Such explanations burn the ears of Westerners, and further, when taken literally, simply ring false.

The point of such explanations, as far as can be reasoned, was to make extremely dramatic statements concerning the general significations of the houses and planets involved. For example, Mars, as a malefic planet in the 2nd house (the face, education, and money) could make a person "ugly faced, devoid of learning," etc., etc. Saturn, as a malefic planet, in the 5th house (the mind, children, etc.) could make a person "lose his reason, be bereft of children, be evil-minded" etc. But these kinds of delineations strain credibility for Western astrologers. Fortunately, the explanations of planets in houses in this text are far more moderate and accurate. Readers gain a reliable sense of what to expect and what to predict based on each and every example the author gives.

Vedic Astrology is a text to be analyzed and studied over and over again. Astrologers who are technically-minded or interested in the intricacies of Hindu calculation methods will be wonderfully pleased. Those who quickly become confused by technical material can, for now, simply rely on computers for such needs, and focus on Ronnie Dreyer's excellent interpretive material. The most pressing problem facing Westerners intent on learning *Jyotish* today is the lack of experienced teachers in local vicinities. Therefore, one should read and study not only this book, but every respectable text on the subject written by Westerners. Within a very short time, even the books by Indians will begin to make great sense. Most importantly, students should read, as carefully as possible, the comprehensive horoscope examples in this text, as this is where the author puts all the pieces together. Ronnie Dreyer has done a masterful job in presenting everything an astrologer needs to learn the art of accurate prediction. Laudably, she has left her ego at the door, put astrological pet peeves aside, written clearly and succinctly, and paved the way for a whole generation of astrologers to master a previously unapproachable mystical science.

ACKNOWLEDGMENTS

IT IS NOT VERY OFTEN that an author is afforded the opportunity to revise and reissue a first book which, in retrospect, always seems as if it could have been better written or contained more information. I am extremely fortunate and extend my heartfelt thanks to Donald Weiser, Betty Lundsted and the staff of Samuel Weiser for giving me that rare second chance to resurrect *Indian Astrology* as the new and improved *Vedic Astrology*. Their kindness and encouragement coupled with Betty's guiding editorial hand and author-friendly approach has made working on this project an absolute joy.

There are of course countless others without whom this book would never have taken off the ground and to whom I owe a debt of gratitude. First, as always, to the late Dr. Muralil Sharma, Professor of Jyotish at Sanskrit University, who, twenty years ago, tutored me simply because I had traveled so far in search of knowledge; and to my second teacher, Pandit Deoki Nandan Shastri, who chanted the *slokas* (stanzas) of *Phaladeepika* in Sanskrit and entrusted me with his very rare translated copy. To Lee Lehman, Diana Rosenberg, Diana Blok, and Karen Dreyer for their early support and enthusiastic words. To Ken and Joan Negus and the Astrological Society of Princeton, who gave me my first opportunity to present this material, and encouraged me to continue doing so. To Dennis Harness, David Frawley, and Stephen Quong who invited me to speak at the first International Symposium on Vedic Astrology, where I met fellow Jyotishis and discovered that Jyotish was alive and well in the United States. Thanks to the efforts of Dennis and David in forming the American Council of Vedic Astrology (ACVA), this ancient art has been revitalized and widely accepted by the astrological community. To Charles and Darlene Druttman of C&D Scientific Software for allowing me to generate Tables 9.5 and 9.6 from their Visual Jyotish software, and for their support of my work. To my friends, family, colleagues, and clients who have been my greatest teachers, as well as "Annemarie" and "Barbara," who graciously donated their charts and hours of recollections. But most importantly, I must gratefully acknowledge the astrology groups, conference attendees, and, of course, my students and clients, whose overwhelmingly positive response to this strange-sounding, potentially intimidating material showed me precisely how to make Jyotish completely accessible to a Western audience.

To Ken Bowser, who generously took time out of his busy schedule to critique chapters 1 and 2, and without whom serious errors may have gone completely unnoticed. Although we fought over the usage of language, I am forever indebted to his critical eye, marvelous scholarship and persistence in convincing me that he was ultimately correct. To Rob Hand for his unselfish endorsement and constant enouragement of my work. To Ken Irving, who valiantly constructed the diagrams used throughout this book, as well as for his editorial skills, loving support and unyielding confidence in my abilities. Without the sound of his voice to begin each day, this project wouldn't have been half as easy or pleasant to complete. Finally, to James Braha whose keen insights, compassion, and generosity of spirit serve to make him the excellent astrologer that he is. If not for his first book, *Ancient Hindu Astrology for the Modern Western Astrologer*, the doors to India's ancient wisdom might still remain under lock and key. I am proud to call him a colleague and friend.

On a personal note, I wish to thank my family and friends for always standing by me, and last, but not least, Fran Dreyer, my mother, friend, and firmest supporter, who came through for me once again in my moment of need. After discovering that the original disks had vanished, she saved the day by retyping, editing and proofing the entire book. For that, and for so much more which I could never repay, nor express in mere words, I am and always will be eternally grateful.

INTRODUCTION

IN THE AUTUMN OF 1976, I was fortunate enough to travel overland to India where I had the rare opportunity to study Jyotish (Hindu or Vedic astrology) in Benares, first with Dr. Muralil Sharma, a Professor of Jyotish at Sanskrit University, and later with Pandit Deoki Nandan Shastri, a practicing astrologer. It was an exceptional time, as many Westerners both young and old had embarked on the same quest for Eastern knowledge and culture to bring back home to Europe and America. Starting out from Athens, our tour bus with its 22 passengers journeyed through eastern Greece, Turkey, Iran, Afghanistan, and Pakistan before reaching its final destination: India. My memories of the mosques of Istanbul, the city of Teheran torn between the Shah of Iran's modernization and its traditional Islamic culture, the expansive barren deserts and wild-eyed nomads of Afghanistan, and the Golden Temple of the Sikhs in Amritsar, India (later used as a fortress during their internal strife with the Hindus) bring back images that are as vivid and clear today as they were when I first encountered them. Looking back, I feel lucky that I was able to travel through Asia during this historically unique period when there was still the chance to view firsthand Iran and Afghanistan—countries that have since been transformed and will never again be the way they once were.

When we finally arrived in India, my first reaction to this strange land was, to say the least, one of total disorientation and complete cultural shock. While I had expected India to be consummately different from both Europe and America, never in my wildest dreams had I envisioned the overwhelming pandemonium which I encountered there. Everywhere I looked I saw cows—deemed holy by the Hindus—freely roaming the streets, seeming at times more human than the homeless beggars whose frail bodies dotted every street corner. The cyclists and rickshaw drivers, not unlike the motorists and taxi drivers of any Western metropolitan city, added to the chaos by obstructing and tying up traffic. To add to the confusion, tea shops, clothing stores, and perfume stands were all wedged together waiting to be patronized by the crowds of exotic Indian men and women dressed in their kortas and saris. The styles and materials of these garments have not been altered by the passage of time and seem to parallel Jyotish, whose basic principles can be found in ancient and definitive texts written as far back as the fifth and sixth centuries A.D. The application of the rules of Jyotish to the lives of contemporary Indians evinces their adherence to the tenets of Hinduism—a centuries-old religion—and contributes to the cohesiveness of a society virtually untouched by modern life.

In the capital city of New Delhi, the endpoint of the bus ride, I inquired as to where I could learn Hindu astrology to supplement my knowledge of Occidental astrology. I was told to go to Benares,[1] a city in the north-central province of Uttar Pradesh, which houses Benares Hindu University, one of the largest and most diverse centers of learning in India. In addition to the University's matriculated Indian population, its enrollment boasts a huge cross-section of international students whose education is conducted in English. In Benares, where I lived for the next six months, I met many Europeans and Americans who were studying subjects such as religion, philosophy, Indian music, Hindi and Sanskrit both at the University and/or with a private tutor. None of them, however, were familiar with anybody studying or teaching Jyotish, the actual term for the mathematical and astronomical principles which are the foundation of what is now more popularly called Vedic astrology. I learned that Jyotish was taught at Sanskrit University, located at the opposite end of the city. However, there was one drawback. Instruction at Sanskrit University was conducted using Sanskrit texts, the ancient written language of India.

By chance (if there is such a thing), Dr. Muralil Sharma, a Professor of Jyotish, was in the Mathematics Department office at Sanskrit University at the precise moment of my inquiry and

---

[1] Benares is also called Varanasi, and people from all over India travel there just to swim in the blessed waters of the Ganges River, which runs through the city.

promptly offered to tutor me for one hour every day. Furthermore, his English was impeccable. When I brought up the question of payment, his reply was simple: Because I had traveled such a long distance in search of knowledge, it was his professional obligation to teach me whatever he could for the duration of my stay. This attitude exemplifies the Hindu conviction of predestination to fulfill a particular task. Dr. Sharma was grateful that the gods had entrusted him with their wisdom and, by passing it on to others, he was repaying them for granting him that knowledge.

In order to take notes from Dr. Sharma for one hour each morning, I bicycled crosstown faithfully each day to the Sanskrit University campus, braving the intense heat, the freely roaming cows, and the aggressive rickshaw drivers. Dr. Sharma instructed me to wear a traditional Indian sari so as not to distract the young Indian men on campus, and it was imperative that I prepare for my daily lesson by reciting what I had learned the previous day. Because Dr. Sharma knew that the length of my stay in India was limited to six months, he gave me a crash course in Jyotish by enlightening me about the ancient scriptural writings most relevant to modern life. He defined the nature of the Sidereal Zodiac, Tithis, Nakshatras, and other astronomical principles unique to Jyotish and explained those fundamental interpretive techniques which required the least complicated mathematical calculations. In order to illustrate the intrinsic relationship between astrology and Hinduism, Dr. Sharma also pointed out the horoscopic indications of an individual's patron god or goddess, caste, previous incarnations, and other religious principles which could affect him or her.

Soon afterward, I met my second astrology teacher, Pandit Deoki Nandan Shastri, whose impressive reading of a friend's horoscope led to our introduction. From his commercial storefront practice located in the heart of the bazaar—tourist shops, boutiques, temples and tea shops best described as an Indian shopping mall—he had become quite well versed in interpreting charts for foreign clients. Whereas Dr. Sharma excelled in teaching theory and astronomical principles, Pandit Shastri's forte was the art of interpretation. He introduced me to Shad Bala, the complicated numerical system used by Hindu as-

xxii 》 Vedic Astrology

trologers to evaluate character traits and to determine whether ensuing periods would be auspicious or inauspicious. He also taught me how to calculate the different types of charts which are constructed for various aspects of life, such as education, marriage, journeys, illness, etc. Since there were no computers available, many of these charts required hour-long mathematical calculations. I spent my mornings with Dr. Sharma and my afternoons with "Guru-ji" (as I referred to Pandit Shastri), who recited to me in Sanskrit the verses of the ancient text, *Phaladeepika*, followed by their English translations. I left India with translated copies of the scriptures, notebooks containing a wealth of information but, most of all, with a heart filled with gratitude for all the kindness shown me not only by my teachers but by all the Indian families and other friends I met along the way.

• • •

When I returned to the United States during the summer of 1977, I considered writing an astrology book which would combine ancient Hindu principles with modern Western methods of interpretation. The United States and England were at the height of the "Me Generation" and the popular mode of the day was the Human Potential Movement which expounded theories such as "we have total control over everything that happens—past, present, and future" and "nothing is ever left to chance." Humanistic astrology, whose philosophy was adapted from humanistic psychology as pioneered by Alfred Adler, Abraham Maslow, and Fritz Perls, was in vogue and I could not find a publisher interested in producing an astrology book pertaining to ancient fatalistic principles translated into a modern context. The tide has since turned 180 degrees, and not only has Jyotish been experiencing a renaissance, but people have grown dissatisfied with the fact that they have not been able to take as complete control of their lives as they had thought possible. Once again, people are turning to ancient, more event-oriented systems of thought to provide the answers which have not been available through modern psychological methodology. In addition to the "awareness" or control they have developed over their lives, they now accept that there will always be certain elements from their past or in their environment which are beyond their grasp. It is in this contemporary mode that the idea of transforming ancient beliefs into contemporary philosophy could begin to be embraced.

In 1986, nine years after returning from India, I was approached to write a book about Hindu astrology for a Western audience and thus the first incarnation of this present edition emerged as *Indian Astrology: A Western approach to the ancient Hindu art* (Aquarian Press, 1990). Whereas that book was addressed to an audience who could utilize Jyotish alongside Occidental astrological techniques, this new and completely revised edition allows the reader to employ Vedic astrology in its own right without comparing it to the tropical horoscope. In writing this book, however, I have been able to relive those six months in India and recall quite vividly my two Indian astrology teachers—the academic Dr. Sharma and the mercantile Pandit Shastri.

What follows, therefore, is a combination of material taken from the translations of the ancient astrological scriptures and techniques which my teachers imparted to me—many of which were passed down to them by their own teachers. Due to the popularity of Jyotish in the last few years, my teachers have come to include Dr. B. V. Raman, Dr. K. S. Charak, and K. N. Rao, who visit the United States regularly to share their knowledge. Most important, I have incorporated the practical techniques which I have utilized most in my own astrological practice over the years and which I have found to actually work.

Because the astrological scriptures were written by adherents of Vedic, or Hindu, philosophy and because the earliest proof that the stars were used to mark rituals are found in the Vedas, the terms "Hindu Astrology" and "Vedic Astrology" have been used interchangeably. Throughout this book, however, I most often use the term "Jyotish"—the actual Sanskrit term for the astronomical, mathematical, and interpretive principles which constitute the astrology practiced in India.

Since this book is merely an introduction to the basic principles of Hindu astrology, I have extracted from the scriptures practical and nonreligious concepts which can be utilized comfortably by a Western audience. Although I have omitted references to past and future lives or classifications by caste, I have included nonsecular Hindu principles for the insight they provide into Indian lifestyles. On many occasions, I have transposed archaic expressions into modern Western terminology and have condensed complicated methods of interpretation into concise easy-to-use formulas. In other instances, I have quoted directly from the scriptures to illustrate the authenticity of the language used.

I do not attempt to prove the complete accuracy of Vedic astrology and I do not recommend that Western astrologers or students of astrology necessarily replace their present systems with it. I also advise very firmly against inserting Vedic astrological definitions into the Western horoscope and vice versa. What I do recommend, however, is using each system independently, since both provide a completely different focus. It is important to remember that, while Jyotish may be a feasible means of prediction for the follower of Hinduism who does not have complete autonomy over life, its formulas are not always applicable to Westerners who enjoy so many available choices. To this end, I have consciously omitted scriptural methods of foretelling illness and death, and I advise anyone researching Jyotish to ignore these aspects of it since they are often not pertinent to modern life and can be dangerous and misleading.

Because these pages contain new and strange-sounding material, I recommend that this book not be devoured, but instead be digested chapter by chapter over an extended period of time. I hope that, in addition to providing a methodical means for understanding and perhaps using Jyotish, this book will convey the significant role that astrology plays in uniting the Hindu community, whose religion still dictates most of its activities. Finally, my wish is for this work to serve as one more link between East and West—if only because the roots of both our astrological systems lie in ancient Babylonia and Greece—and as one more way of saying that despite different cultural, religious, and national identities, we are all synchronized with the universal rhythm of life.

Part I
Structure

CHAPTER 1

HISTORY OF INDIAN ASTROLOGY

TO TRACE THE EARLIEST roots of astrology in India, it is helpful to go back to the third and fourth millennia (between 4000 and 2000 B.C., the approximate dates of the Age of Taurus) when there were four major Eastern civilizations whose communities centered around fertile river valleys. The locations of these thriving cultures were the Nile Valley in Egypt, the valley between the Tigris and Euphrates Rivers in Sumer, or Southern Mesopotamia, the Hwang Ho Valley in China, and the Indus Valley in India. Due to advanced irrigation techniques, agriculture flourished and food was abundant in these valleys. Sailors and merchants from India and Sumer traded profitably with each other, and these two areas were introduced to the other's cultural and natural resources. What each of these agrarian cultures ultimately had in common was their commitment to self-sufficiency, maximum productivity, and economic stability—qualities of the sign of Taurus from which this era derives its name.

These early farming communities depended upon seasonal changes and meteorological conditions to stimulate their crops, and they adjusted their planting methods accordingly. By directly observing the patterns in the sky, they came to understand how certain configurations affected weather conditions and, in turn, their harvest. They were soon able to predict auspicious times for planting based not only on the seasonal changes but on the prominence of the Sun and the phases of the Moon. In Sumer, China, and India, the Sun was viewed as a destructive entity due to its intense heat which scorched the earth and left the land parched. The Moon, on the other hand, was revered as a creative power which brought the cool night air and promoted growth. Planting during the waxing phase of the Moon was common among the farmers of these cultures and is practiced even today. In fact, it is still said that a project should begin during the waxing moon, but never during a waning moon.

Between approximately 3500 B.C. and 1750 B.C., Southern Mesopotamia (present-day Iraq) was populated by the Sumerians who probably migrated there from the East. When Semitic tribes from southern Arabia known as Akkadians (named for their Semitic dialect) settled the region around 2350 B.C., the area was initially renamed Sumer-Akkad to designate the cohabitation and cooperation between these two cultures. The Akkadians proved to be the stronger power, however, and they eventually took over the region. The great civilization of Babylonia was inaugurated around 1848 B.C., with Babylon as its capital, replacing Nippur, the former capital of Sumer-Akkad. Northern Mesopotamia (present-day northern Iraq and Turkey), inhabited by Indo-European tribes who hailed from the Russian steppes and dispersed throughout England, Rome, Greece, Iran, and, eventually, India, was taken over by the Semitic Assyrians around 1400 B.C.

The Babylonian Empire gained prominence throughout the ancient world for its intellectual and scientific advances, including astrology. In their role as soothsayers, Babylonian priests developed an extensive method of divination linking certain events and growing patterns to earthquakes, floods, wind directions, thunder, lightning, and other meteorological phenomena which they thought to be manifestations of the divine will. These conditions guided Babylonian farmers in the timing of their harvest, the king as to when he could travel, and merchants and sailors in planning their voyages. Precision and attention to detail made the priests impeccable record keepers and many of their omens were recorded on clay tablets as early as 1750–1500 B.C. By studying the heavenly bodies, however, the Babylonian priests soon found the luminaries to be superior omens from which they could efficiently anticipate natural phenomena and their accompanying significant events.

Within the hierarchy of Babylonian society, the priests were the scientists and, as such, the most educated class. They were given access to the libraries and observatories, where they spent countless solitary hours observing the sky using the most advanced instruments of their day. In Babylonia, as well as in Greece, India, and China, these early observations of the Sun, the Moon, and the planets were made with the gnomon, a vertical stick which measured astronomical distances by the length and direction of the shadow it cast. By methodically studying planetary configurations, Babylonian priests were able to time planetary cycles, estimate astronomical distances, and observe celestial relationships. In time, they developed a more advanced method of prediction by which they could chart recurring configurations such as eclipses, phases of the moon, and the positions of the most prominent "stars"—The Moon, the Sun, Jupiter, Venus, Saturn, Mercury, and Mars.[1] These phenomena were coupled with what appeared to be coinciding events, growing patterns, or meteorological condition. With this knowledge, they were soon able to predict, with amazing regularity, weather patterns, auspicious planting times, and whether the ensuing period would bring peace or hostility. Though all ancient civilizations were aware of the correlations between the timing of celestial movements and mundane conditions, the Babylonians methodically logged this information and are thus credited with creating the first recorded astrological system.

The Babylonians methodically recorded the movements of the planets with their accompanying celestial occurrences as early as 1701 B.C. with the writing of the Venus Tablet of Amisaduqua, listing the cycles of Venus. But it was not until the Middle Babylonian Period (1000 B.C.) that the astronomical data for each planet, along with accompanying effects, was recorded onto thousands of cuneiform tablets and compiled in a volume called *Enuma Anu Enlil*. The most complete extant volume was excavated from the site of the palace of the Assyrian King Ashurbanipal at Nineveh (668–635 B.C.) and is presently stored at the British Museum. Cuneiform writing entailed scratching marks and symbols onto wet clay tablets with a pointed stick or reed stylus. By uncovering and translating these tablets, which had lain buried for thousands of years, archaeologists in the 19th century were not only able to decipher astronomical and astrological data, but to learn about life in Mesopotamia itself.

The desire to know beforehand when to expect certain climatic conditions, holidays, and other phenomena brought about the creation of a calendar and accurate scientific data to

---

[1] Franz Cumont, *Astrology Among the Greeks and Romans* (New York: Dover, 1960), pp. 7–8.

back up the calendrical listings. Since approximately 3000 B.C., the Egyptians had been using a completely solar calendar which based the year on successive heliacal risings of Sirius, the dog star, which average 365 days apart. The Babylonians, on the other hand, constructed a soli-lunar calendar which fit lunar months into the solar year by intercalating, or adding, an extra month every few years. The Egyptians had been dividing their year into three seasons of four months, each marked by distinct climatic changes; by contrast, the Babylonians divided their year, the way we still do today, by the spring (vernal) equinox, summer solstice, autumn equinox, and winter solstice—the four cardinal points. The months were marked off by the phases of the Moon and the days were divided by the appearance and disappearance of the Moon rather than by the rising and the setting of the Sun. The calendar also included planetary placements and conjunctions, phases of the Moon, and lunar and solar eclipses. It was with the gnomon that the equinoctial and solstitial points, along with other lunar measurements included on the calendar, were discovered.[2]

In the eyes of the priests, the celestial bodies were manifestations of their gods and goddesses. To this end, many religious holidays held in their honor were celebrated in accordance with the New Moon or Full Moon, whereas other pagan festivities occurred on one of the equinoxes or solstices. The Babylonians celebrated their New Year around the spring equinox, the time of reaping the harvest, whereas the Sumerians before them had celebrated their New Year around the autumn equinox, the time of sowing the crop. By marking off the holidays on their lunar calendar, the Babylonians knew in advance when to make the necessary preparations for these rites, which were such a vital part of the religious and social life of the community.

Influenced by the Persians, who conquered Babylonia in 539 B.C., the Babylonians continued to make great strides in the fields of both astronomy and astrology. These advances included the discovery of the astrolabe (an instrument used to measure altitudes), the perfection of lunar measurements, and the early use of the zodiac. Records of the period indicate that

---

[2] Council of Scientific and Industrial Research, *Report of the Calendar Reform Committee* (New Delhi: Government of India Publications, 1955), p. 188.

the oldest extant individual horoscope is dated 410 B.C. The earliest horoscopes were most probably the charts of kings and other royal personages whose destinies represented the fate of the nation. Until this time, the Babylonians had been concerned primarily with agricultural planning as well as political and economic forecasting.

The philosopher Herodotus and the mathematician Pythagoras were among the Greek intellectuals who visited Babylonia in the fifth century B.C. and brought back impressive astronomical data which included lunar measurements, the equinoctial and solstitial points, the constellations of the zodiac, and the construction of individual horoscopes. When Babylonia was finally conquered by the Greeks in 331 B.C., this information was transmitted intact to Greek scientists who combined Babylonian findings with their own astronomical theories. Unlike the combined field of Babylonian astronomy and astrology, Greek astronomy had been, up until this time, neither mathematically sophisticated nor religious. It was only when Babylonian astronomy was introduced into Greek culture that the planets took on qualities similar to those of the Greek gods and goddesses of Mount Olympus. Gradually, as in our own culture, two sciences developed side by side—astronomy and astrology. While astronomers mapped out the positions of the Sun, the Moon, and the planets which determined, among other things, the length of the year and the timing of the seasons, astrologers raised these physical bodies to the level of religious deities or other influential symbols.

The Greek astronomers Hipparchus and Ptolemy delved deeper than their Babylonian counterparts by calculating the rate of the movement of the equinoxes called precession. Likewise, Greek astrologers—whose philosophy emphasized the inherent dignity and self-determination of man—lifted the horoscope beyond its religious and mundane aspects in order to view the fate of the individual. These early Greek astrologers greatly influenced the way we approach astrological interpretation today.

As the Euphrates River changed direction, the canals could no longer transport water, and the once-fertile Mesopotamian Valley became dry and barren. With the water supply practically cut off, the great agrarian communities of the Middle East slowly disappeared and the population the region could support was drastically reduced. Egypt was conquered by Caesar in 44 B.C. and, by the time of the Christian Era, the Roman Empire ruled the ancient world. The Julian calendar, implemented throughout the Roman Empire, was not initially calculated according to Christian dates. Later on, however, the Christians introduced their own holidays, which were Hebrew in origin. Most of the ancient astrological cuneiform tablets were either destroyed or buried when Babylon was finally pillaged by the Romans in the first century A.D.

During the Christian era, astrology was rejected as heresy by the Church, and did not resurface in the Western world until the Renaissance, when it was once again taught in universities and revered as a science. Only since the ancient tablets were recovered during the 19th-century excavations in Iraq have we learned that it was not the Greeks who originated the astrology we use today—though they did indeed perfect it—but the Babylonians.

It is the consensus of most archaeologists and historians that astronomical and astrological knowledge was disseminated throughout the ancient world by sailors, merchants, and, most important, by conquering peoples. The Babylonian system of star gazing and time measurement was the forerunner of most modern astrological systems and it especially influenced the lunar-based system of India which is still used today. Though each culture used its own particular observations to develop an astrological system which best suited its religious and cultural needs, the origins of astrology, as we know it today, lie in ancient Babylonia.

The Development of Astrology in India[3]

2500–1600 B.C.

Contemporaneous with Egypt and Sumer, the progressive Harappan civilization located in the Indus River Valley was

---

[3] Due to scanty archeological evidence in India, there are disagreements as to Indian chronology. I have based these approximate dates on the findings of Dr. Stan-

named for its largest excavated cities, called Harappa and Mo-henjo-daro. Not much is known about these people except that their sailors and merchants most probably traveled to the Near and Middle East, where information as well as goods was shared. Like the Egyptians and the Sumerians, these Indians were adept at working with metals and bronze and were inno-vators in the arts and sciences. On the symmetrical avenues and streets of their well-planned cities stood architecturally ad-vanced buildings used for living quarters, government offices, and temples. There were courtyards, bathing facilities, and even advanced drainage systems. Irrigation techniques made them successful farmers, and their cities prospered and became great commercial centers. It has been surmised that the Indus River floods which occurred around 1700 B.C. devastated the land and destroyed many of the cities.

1500–1000 B.C.—Vedic Era

Sometime during the second millennium, India was, according to some scholars, inhabited by Indo-Aryan tribes from the Russian steppes who resettled the Indus River Valley and formed their own communities in the Ganges River Valley. In the same way that the Akkadians overran the Sumerians and conquered Southern Mesopotamia, the Indo-Europeans, more adventurous and aggressive than the early Indian farmers, are thought to have taken possession of the land, inherited their cities, and merged their two cultures.

This period is famous for the *Mahabharata* and *Ramayana*, two great epics of the earliest heroes of Hinduism.

> The Epics were passed on by word of mouth. . . . The longest of the two Epics is the Mahabharata, . . . the longest poem in the world. . . . It is the story of a great civil war in the region where now is located the city of Delhi. Its most famous portion is the Bhagavadgita. The

ley Wolpert, Professor of History at UCLA, in *A New History of India* (New York: Oxford University Press, 1993), and a description of events on the *Report of the Calendar Reform Committee*, published by the Council of Scientific and Industrial Research (New Delhi: Gov't. of India Publications, 1955).

second of the two great Epics, the Ramayana, tells the story of Rama, a heroic Aryan king of Vedic times. It relates the adventures of Rama as he undertakes to rescue his wife Sita, who had been kidnapped by a devil-king of Ceylon. . . . Originally the tales in the Epics were told to preserve the memory of the deeds of famous Aryan warriors. However, as the stories were passed down from generation to generation they began to take on religious significance. Many of the basic beliefs of modern Hinduism became embodied in the tales.[4]

These Indo-Aryans are also credited by some scholars with authoring the Vedas, the primary source of religious knowledge, which were probably composed and orally transmitted as early as 1400 B.C.[5] Considered to be the "Hindu Bible," the Vedas, a rich body of literature comprised of sacred hymns and poems, map out the basic creation myths and legends of the people. These scriptures outlined the original tenets of Hinduism, the religion of four-fifths of today's Indian population.

The Vedic hymns are said to have been revealed by the seven stars or planets, called *rishis,* literally meaning "to shine."[6] The priests who wrote the Vedas were called Brahmins and they dedicated the Vedas to their God, Brahma, the source of life. The Vedas, as well as other religious and astrological scriptures that followed, were written in Sanskrit, the original language of the Hindu people. The following passages from the Vedas illustrate some of the ideas which form the doctrine of Hinduism.

1) The essence of all things is one supreme energy which permeates every aspect of the universe. It is an impersonal, immaterial, unborn, and undying force. It is called Brahman.

---

[4] *Report of the Calendar Reform Committee,* p. 43.
[5] Although they were probably composed as early as 1400 B.C., the Rig Veda, the oldest of the four Vedic books, was not actually recorded until around 600 B.C., and the oldest extant copy dates from A.D. 1200.
[6] Christopher McIntosh, *Astrologers and their Creed* (London: Century Hutchinson, 1969), p. 49.

2) There are individual souls which are unbreakable and eternal parts of the universal soul. They are named Atman. Brahman and Atman are one and indivisible, yet the Atman living in the world of senses as nature, seems to exist apart from Brahman. . . . This apparent separateness is Maya or illusion.

3) Nature is the manifestation of the supreme energy . . . Brahman, and is in continuous evolution according to its immutable law.

4) So long as we live in illusion we place our faith in ever-changing things of nature. The effect of the fickle nature incites our pains and pleasures as experiences in our life. Only through the realization or reabsorption of oneself into Brahman can one become free from worldly sensations of pain and pleasure.

5) Activities are the incidence [sic] of life. Every person acts according to his soul, mind, and the senses and produces his destiny as misfortunes or fortunes. For there cannot be a result without action in the past. Thus each soul receives many experiences birth . . . after birth and gradually shakes off illusions of separateness and proceeds through self-purification toward oneness.[7]

Central to Hinduism is the law of karma, the idea that deeds in this lifetime are determined by the quality of other lifetimes. The Sanskrit word, *karma*, represents the accumulated actions, positive and negative, of former lifetimes that help to create a person's present *dharma*, or "assigned" duties in this lifetime.

The karma of the individual is the factor which determines the progress of the soul through its various incarnations. Karma appears in three aspects: Sanchita, the sum or result of acts committed in the previous incarnation; Prarabda, acts of the present incarnation which are subject both to the influence of the previous life and to the exercise of free will in the present one; and Agami, future, unrealized acts.

---

[7] Viswanath Deva Sharma, *Astrology and Jyotirvidya* (Calcutta: Viswa Jyotirvid Samgha, 1973), p. 13.

Thus the progress of the soul from one incarnation to another is conditioned by a mixture of free will, karma and
fate.[8]

Ever since Eastern religions and spirituality were introduced
into mainstream Western culture, much of the Sanskrit terminology has been misunderstood. Many Westerners loosely use
the word "karma" to describe anything that happens which
seems fated. If, for instance, we receive a gift from someone
soon after we bought a gift for someone else, we call it
"karma." We have, of course, lifted its meaning from the traditional definition which does, in fact, refer to the act of getting
back what we have given. What Hindus are referring to, however, are important acts which will have their consequences
throughout the course of many lifetimes.

Dr. B. V. Raman, one of India's foremost modern Hindu
astrologers, describes the laws of karma as follows:

> According to ancient texts when one dies, his soul which is
> enveloped in a subtle body and invested with the sum-total
> of good and bad Karma passes after some time into an-
> other body leaving off his gross body, as a man casts off
> worn-out clothes and puts on new ones. His reincarnation
> takes place in a physical body corresponding with the
> deeds done by him in his previous life. The processes of
> death and birth go on until the person concerned attains
> emancipation. The cardinal doctrine of Karma therefore is
> the law of cause and effect in accordance with the maxim
> 'as a man soweth so shall he reap'.[9]

As an illustration of life in India, the Vedas describe a society
consisting of priests, warriors, merchants, artisans, and slaves,
whose classification forms the descending class order which
eventually became the rigid Hindu caste system. These five categories are equivalent to the contemporary caste system of
Brahmins (priests and the well-educated), Kshatrias (rulers and

---

[8] McIntosh, *Astrologers and their Creed*, p. 49
[9] B. V. Raman, *Planetary Influences on Human Affairs* (Bangalore: IBH
Prakashana, 1982), pp. 29–30.

warriors), Vaishya (merchants), Shudra (farm laborers), and the lowest class, Harijans or Untouchables (outcasts) who do not work or own property and often support themselves by begging on the streets. Whereas the Brahmin caste once consisted only of priests, contemporary Brahmins—still the highest rung on the ladder—now include the well-educated and wealthy.

Although the caste system is not an aspect of Hinduism per se, and is considered almost universally to be politically unjust, it is still an accepted socio-economic division of the Hindu population. The Hindu accepts that a person's caste, the family he or she was born into, and the chosen profession (often the father's or father-in-law's) are derived from the soul's journey through previous lifetimes. If you committed sins, crimes, or were dishonorable in the last life, then you will pay for your indiscretions by being born into a lowly caste in this incarnation. If you were honorable, then you will reap rewards this time around. Moreover, obligations performed within a caste determine who and what a person will be in the next life.

> Hence a Brahmin in this life may be born as a Harijan in the next life; a rich man in this life may be born as a poor man in the next life and vice versa. Thus the station of life or the degree of wealth, etc., that one has attained in this life is mostly due to the Karma at his credit in the previous life.[10]

Though there are no definite astronomical rules set down in any of the four books comprising the Vedas, the numerous references to the Sun, the Moon, the months, and the seasons indicate that the authors were quite familiar with astronomy and astrology. The Atharvaveda, the last of the Vedic books, contains a detailed listing of the uniquely Indian Nakshatras, or lunar mansions, starting with Krittika, the asterism which was, at the time of this writing, heliacally rising at the vernal equinox. Principles of ayurvedic medicine, as well as rituals and sacrifices to be performed in conjunction with celestial occurrences, were also listed in the Atharvaveda.

---

[10] Raman, *Planetary Influences on Human Affairs*, p. 29.

Though it was the Babylonians who first used a lunar-based calendar and a thorough astrological system, we know from records of this period that the Indians, too, had developed a soli-lunar calendar and that their year was already being divided into 12 months. There are no names as such for these 12 months, but there is mention in the Rig Veda, the earliest of the four Vedic books, of a wheel of time divided into 12 parts.[11]

500 B.C.–A.D. 300—Vedanga Jyotish

The period extending from 500 B.C. until A.D. 300 was dominated by the Vedanga Jyotish, a separate body of work and an adjunct to the written laws of Vedic worship. In addition to containing the calendric and astronomical principles that were formulated and set down during the previous Vedic age, the Vedanga Jyotish also describes life in India at that time.

The Vedanga Jyotish is referred to as one of the six limbs of the Vedas, with "Vedanga" indicating anything relating to the Vedas and "Jyotish" meaning astronomy. Today Jyotish, as it is taught in the universities in India and practiced by professional astrologers, has come to include the study of mathematical, astronomical, and astrological principles. In this time period, however, it consisted solely of the precise mathematical rules affecting planetary movements, much of which was influenced by the discoveries of the Babylonians and the Greeks.

Due to foreign conquests and invasions from the Near and Middle East, there existed during this period a plethora of philosophies which not only modified the arts and sciences, but drastically changed life in general. After annexing Babylonia and Egypt, Alexander the Great extended his empire into India's northwest province of Punjab between 327–325 B.C. The Greek Empire, now incorporating Mesopotamian and Egyptian culture, became so powerful as it spread from Asia Minor to northwest India that Greek remained the predominant language throughout the entire East for quite some time.

---

[11] Council of Scientific and Industrial Research, *Report of the Calendar Reform Committee*, p. 283.

After the Greek Macedonian leadership was overthrown, the Maurya Dynasty (321–185 B.C.), formed as a coalition between the Indians and the Greek Seleucid leaders, witnessed remarkable contributions in the areas of religion, art, and literature. Despite their cultural flowering, the Indians' hostility toward the Greeks was especially prevalent under Buddhist King Asoka (262-232 B.C.), during whose reign a great portion of the population, adhering to Buddhist tenets, disavowed belief in predestination and, ultimately, astrology. Even those Hindu political leaders who were anti-Buddhist were opposed to astrology, as they felt it discouraged people from showing any personal initiative. The Indians accepted these condemnations and continued to reject astrology as a belief system.[12]

Just like Babylonian priests before them, monks in India were in a perfect position to carry out astronomical studies due to their solitude and access to materials and instruments. But because astronomical knowledge became confused with astrological omens, the cultivation of scientific astronomy was forbidden in monasteries throughout India. This thwarted the germination of astrological thought until Buddhism declined during the second century B.C., and the study of astrology, condemned by the Buddha, slowly found its way back into the mainstream of religious thought. The city of Ujjain, noted for its astronomical observatories, became a center where astrological ideas were disseminated and practitioners of astrology could combine Western ideas with Eastern methodology. Ujjain was, in fact, later adopted as the Indian "Greenwich" from which point east and west longitudes were recorded.

Between the appearance of the writings of the Greek astronomer, Hipparchus, in 100 B.C. and the publication of Ptolemy's astronomical treatise, *Tetrabiblos*, in A.D. 150, there was an enormous rise in horoscopic astrology throughout the West. The concept of the individual horoscope rapidly spread to the rest of the world and was reintroduced into India during the Saka and Kusana regime (100 B.C. to A.D. 200). The *Yavanajataka* (*Jataka* meaning "natal astrology" and *Yavana* meaning "Ionians," or "Greeks"), the oldest surviving text on

---

[12] *Report of the Calendar Reform Committee*, p. 235.

Jyotish written by Sphujidhvaja (A.D. 191) which synthesizes
Vedic principles with Greek astrological techniques, dates from
this era.

With the Greek influence on Hindu astrology and mythology (See Table 1.1, page 17), the Indian gods and goddesses
took on some of the characteristics of the Greek deities, and the
days of the week in India were soon named after the planets.
The qualities and names of the zodiacal signs were also retrans-
lated from the Greek into Sanskrit. But it was not until around
A.D. 400, the beginning of the Siddhantic period, that these
Greek techniques were fully utilized and assimilated into Indian
culture.

A.D. 400–1200—Siddhantic Period

This period, encompassing India's Golden Age (approx. A.D.
320–A.D. 700), was marked by the use of the Siddhantic calendar, which was based on the Siddhantas, five scientific astronomical treatises written around A.D. 400. One of the texts, the
Surya Siddhanta, was said to have been described by the Sun
God to Asura Maya, the architect of the gods, who then un-
veiled it to the Indian *rishis*, the same stars who revealed the
Vedas to the Brahmin priests. The *Surya Siddhanta*, still referred to today, describes the Hindu version of the creation of
the world, including the creation of the Sun, the Moon, and the
planets. The universe is taken to be geocentric and the planets
are listed in descending order according to their proximity to
the Earth. Ranging from farthest to closest planet, they are
recorded as follows: Saturn, Jupiter, Mars, Sun, Venus, Mercury, Moon.[13]

The Siddhantic calendar was a soli-lunar calendar which
incorporated the lunar calculations of the Babylonians, the zodiacal signs of the Greeks, plus the *tithi* and the *nakshatra*,
uniquely Indian lunar measurements.[14] The Indian lunar day,
called a *tithi*, is measured by the length of time it takes for the
Moon to travel 12°, one-thirtieth of a lunar month, or 360°.

---

[13] CSIR, *Report of the Calendar Reform Committee*, pp. 238–239.
[14] Nakshatras will be discussed in more detail in chapter 9.

Table 1.1. Different Names of Zodiacal Signs.*

BEGINNING AND ENDING OF THE SIGNS	NAMES OF THE SIGNS AND SYMBOL	ENGLISH EQUIVALENT	GREEK NAMES	VARAHA MIHIRA	INDIAN NAMES	BABYLONIAN NAMES
0°–30°	♈ Aries	Ram	Krios	Kriya	Mesha	Ku or Iku [Ram]
30°–60°	♉ Taurus	Bull	Tauros	Tāburi	Vrishaba	Te-te [Bull]
60°–90°	♊ Gemini	Twins	Didumoi	Jituma	Mithuna	Masmasu [Twins]
90°–120°	♋ Cancer	Crab	Karxinos	Kulīra	Kataka	Nangaru [Crab]
120°–150°	♌ Leo	Lion	Leon	Leȳa	Simha	Aru [Lion]
150°–180°	♍ Virgo	Virgin	Parthenos	Pathona	Kanyā	Ki [Virgin]
180°–210°	♎ Libra	Balance	Zugos	Jūka	Thula	Nuru [Scales]
210°–240°	♏ Scorpio	Scorpion	Scorpios	Kaurpa	Vrischika	Akrabu [Scorpion]
240°–270°	♐ Sagittarius	Archer	Tozeutes	Tauksika	Dhanus	Pa [Archer]
270°–300°	♑ Capricorn	Goat	Ligoxeros	Ākokera	Makara	Sahu [Goat]
300°–330°	♒ Aquarius	Water Bearer	Gdroxoos	Hṛdroga	Kumbha	Gu [Water carrier]
330°–360°	♓ Pisces	Fish	Ichthues	Antyabha	Meena	Zib [Fish]

*It can be easily inferred from the table that the names are of Babylonian origin, but their exact significance is not always known. It has been assumed that the symbols used to denote the signs have been devised from a representation of the figure of the animal or object after which the sign has been named, for example, the mouth and horns of the Ram, the same of the Bull, and so on. It is seen that Varahamihira's alternative names given in column 5 are simply Greek names corrupted in course of transmission and as adopted for Sanskrit. . . . the purely Sanskrit names given in column 6 are all translations of Greek names with the exceptions of: twins, which becomes Mithuna or "amorous couple," the archer; which becomes the "bow," the Goat, which becomes the crocodile, water bearer, which becomes the water pot. Some of them appear to have been translations of Babylonian names. The Babylonian names are given in the seventh column, with their meanings . . . it is thus seen that the names of the zodiacal signs are originally of Babylonian origin. They were taken over almost without change by the Greeks and subsequently by the Romans and the Hindus from Greco-Chaldean astrology (*Report of the Calendar Reform Committee*, p. 193).

Beginning with the New Moon—the conjunction of the Moon and the Sun—one tithi is completed when the waxing Moon moves ahead of the Sun by 12°. The tithis are numbered from 1 to 15, with the end of the fifteenth tithi, or 180°, being the Full Moon. Moving from Full Moon and back again to New Moon, the tithis of the waning Moon are also numbered from 1 to 15, with the end of the fifteenth tithi, or 360°, equaling the New Moon. This gives 30 tithis in a lunar month. By counting 30 lunar days from the New Moon or conjunction, the Moon has traveled 360° from New Moon to Full Moon and back again to New Moon, completing its monthly phases. The average lunar day, or the time it takes the tithi to travel 12°, is 23.62 hours, a little less than the solar day of 23 hours 56 minutes, measured from sunrise to sunrise. Because of the irregularity in the Moon's motion, the length of the individual tithi can vary from 20 to 26 hours.[15] Since Siddhantic times, the Hindu lunar calendar has been marked off by these tithis rather than by our solar days. Religious holidays, birthdays, weddings, and other rituals are still celebrated according to their tithi, and are listed in the almanac called the Panchang.

The individual days were also marked off according to which lunar mansion, or nakshatra, the Moon occupied during the evening. Since there is no mention of nakshatras on any of the thousands of Babylonian cuneiform tablets nor in the annals of Greek writers, it is the consensus of most that these lunar mansions are uniquely Indian. Due to the present method of accurately calculating the tithi and the nakshatra, the actual measurements have changed radically over the centuries. What remains constant is that they are as significant in Hindu timekeeping today as they were when first recorded in the Siddhantas.

The authors of the *Surya Siddhanta* supported the concept of the Tropical Zodiac, which uses the spring (vernal) equinox, or equinoctial point, to designate the symbolic first degree of Aries and the beginning of the astrological year. This was due to a phenomenon called the Precession of the Equinoxes, the retrograde movement of the vernal point through the constella-

---

[15] CSIR, *Report of the Calendar Reform Committee*, p. 221.

tions of the zodiac. The concept of precession was brought to India by the Greeks and was included in the writings of the *Surya Siddhanta*. By observing the shifting of the equinoctial and solstitial points due to the Precession of the Equinoxes, Hindu astronomers determined their own rate for this motion instead of utilizing the rate already determined by the Greek astronomer, Hipparchus.

Although these points were supported by the originators of the *Surya Siddhanta*, the writers of subsequent Hindu calendars rejected their usage. Instead of employing the equinoctial point to indicate the start of the astrological year, later Hindu calendar makers utilized the first degree of the actual constellation Aries to indicate when it commenced. This "fixed degree of Aries" formed the basis of the Sidereal, or Nirayana, Zodiac, the one still used by Hindus today. This constitutes the major difference between their system and ours.

It was during the Siddhantic period that the first Hindu astrologers began to emerge. Influenced by Greek horoscopy and Siddhantic mathematical rules, the astronomers in India discovered that, by drawing a map of the sky at the exact moment of birth, a picture of the person's character and life could be determined. For Hindu astrologers, the horoscope represented the stage a man's soul had reached and why his particular caste suited him. Different planetary configurations were indicative of character traits, accumulated past karma, and present dharma.

> Astrology reveals the result of our past karma, expressed probably in terms of what we crudely call planetary influences. Astrology reveals the consequence of our actions which we do not remember in this life and are untraceable in this birth. . . . planets, therefore, indicate the results of previous karma and hence there is nothing like fate or destiny in its absolute sense controlling us. . . . The future is a reflection of the past. The horoscope simply indicates the future.[16]

---

[16] Raman, *Planetary Influences on Human Affairs*, p. 21, 24, 34.

By applying concepts of karma and reincarnation, the horoscope illustrates how to fulfill our mission in this life based on the deeds performed in previous lives. Though horoscopic astrology was never mentioned in the Vedas, all Indian astrologers were adherents of Vedic thought. As a result, their astrology could not help but reflect tenets of Hinduism as well as the values of Indian society. What the Vedas and every other religious scheme ultimately have in common with astrology is a belief in the harmony of the universe. Astrologers expound this by simply regarding the stars as an extension of ourselves.

By basing their craft on Vedic principles, many astrologers attributed their knowledge to divine sources. After approximately A.D. 500, however, Indian astronomers ceased claiming divine authorship of their treatises and began to acknowledge their own writings. The earliest known Indian astrologers were Aryabhata (A.D. 476–523) and Parasara (fifth century A.D.), whose *Hora Sastra* was the first major astrological treatise to appear and the volume upon which all future writings were based. But the most revered astrologer was Varahamihira (A.D. 505-587), a student of Parasara and transmitter of the knowledge that Parasara was unable to convey to the public. Varahamihira, who practiced astrology at the court of King Vikramaditya, did for Jyotish what Ptolemy did for Greek astronomy and astrology. Varahamihira summarized all the astronomical and astrological knowledge available in India in a series of definitive books. In addition to his many astronomical works, which include *Daivajna-Vallabha* and *Brihat Samhita*, his masterwork, *Brihat Jataka*, is considered by some to be India's foremost astrological text. *Brihat Jataka*, literally "Great Natal Horoscopy," describes the planets, Moon's nodes, zodiacal signs, and houses in the light of Vedantic thought by explaining how their placements in the horoscope resulted from past deeds and influence present purpose.[17] It further elaborates on a variety of categories and techniques used to delineate character and forecast events. Varahamihira's methodical approach gave Jyotish its scientific status and influenced generations of practitioners in this field. Other astrological works influenced by the

---

[17] I have omitted religious interpretations and associations and, instead, have concentrated on astrological interpretation and forecasting.

teachings of Varahamihira and still used by modern astrologers are Kalyana Varma's treatise, *Saravali,* thought to have been written in the sixth century A.D., and Mantreswara's *Phaladeepika,* written during the 13th century A.D. These books are similar in form and content to *Brihat Jataka* with certain variations due to the different authorship. Included in *Phaladeepika* were new Arabic-influenced astrological techniques which were brought over during Muslim rule. (I will be using these works as points of reference throughout this book.)

Although a fatalistic approach to astrology is anathema to our concept of free will, the horoscope's validation of present deeds based on past actions is certainly one reason why astrology has remained a vital part of Indian life. Even those Indians who do not consult astrologers respect its legitimacy as an art and a science and recognize the astrologer as an influential figure within the Hindu community.

1200–1757—Muslim Rule

The Siddhantic calendar, minus the implementation of the precession of the equinoxes, continued to be used as India's official calendar until A.D. 1200, when India fell under Islamic domination. Throughout Muslim rule from 1200 to 1757, the completely lunar Hejira calendar was introduced and used for civil and administrative affairs. Hindu communities throughout India managed to maintain their independence and retained their calendars for religious purposes. These calendars were, however, mathematically incorrect since so many Indian observatories had either been destroyed by Turkish armies or simply abandoned by their astronomers. This left the task of calendar making solely in the hands of regional astrologers who had little knowledge of actual astronomy, yet depended on direct observations and unscientific ancient treatises for their calculations.[18]

Due to a complete lack of uniformity, and to disagreement over which starting year to use for the calendar and the precise positioning of the first degree of Aries, almost every region in

---

[18] CSIR, *Report of the Calendar Reform Committee,* p. 2.

India developed its own soli-lunar calendar with its own unique cultural and historical tradition. Holidays and religious festivities were celebrated on different days throughout India because of the variable date and time of the first degree of Aries, the first day of the New Year. As a result, all regional calendars conflicted with regard to epoch, New Year's Day, and the naming of the months.[19]

1757–Present

With the advent of British rule in 1757, the Christian Gregorian calendar[20] replaced the Muslim calendar as the official calendar of India. The Gregorian calendar uses the Egyptian solar year of 365-1/4 days, the length of time it takes for the Earth to revolve around the Sun. The four cardinal points determine the seasons and the length of the year; the extra quarter day is made up with the inclusion of a leap year every fourth year. The Gregorian calendar was used for official timekeeping, civil and administrative matters, and anything else linking India to the rest of the world. Throughout each governmental regime, however, every religious community always retained its own regional calendar. This applied not only to Hindu communities but also to Muslim communities, which continued to use their medieval Hejira calendar, and the Buddhists, Jains and Christians, each of whom had their individual calendars and timekeeping methods.

By the time India gained its independence in 1947 under the rulership of Pandit Jawaharlal Nehru, there were still two types of calendars in use—the official Gregorian solar calendar and the regional religious lunar calendars. While weeding out remnants of the bureaucracy left behind by the British, the Government found this practice of varying calendars much too disconcerting. In 1952, five years after the last British troops left India, the Government of India appointed the Calendar Reform Committee to rectify "the Hindu calendar problem."

---

[19] Apurba Kumar Chakravarty, *Origin and Development of Indian Calendrical Science* (Calcutta: Indian Studies Past and Present, 1975), p. 49.
[20] The Gregorian calendar is used for official functions by all Christian countries and most non-Christian countries.

The actual purpose of the Calendar Reform Committee was to investigate whether the Christian Gregorian calendar, the international calendar, should be upheld as the official time-keeper of India since it had been imposed by the British from whom they were now independent, and whether there should be one unified religious calendar which would service all the practicing Hindu communities and meet the Committee's requirements for holidays to be uniformly celebrated. In 1955, their recommendations were published in the *Report of the Calendar Reform Committee*. In answer to the first question, the Committee recommended the retention of the Gregorian calendar as the only official calendar in India. Because it had been successfully utilized for so many years, the Committee felt the Gregorian calendar was vital to ensure that timekeeping in India would keep pace with the rest of the world.

In response to the second, more complicated, question, the Calendar Reform Committee felt that there should be only one religious calendar used throughout the country. Because each region disagreed about the precise calculation of the first degree of the actual constellation Aries, holidays tended to fall on different days throughout the country. In addition, due to the Precession of the Equinoxes, that first degree of Aries (the first day of the New Year) was slowly but consistently moving so that certain holidays would ultimately fall in seasons different from those originally intended. It is not unusual—according to the Chinese or Hebrew lunar calendar—for religious holidays to coincide with the New and Full Moon rather than on the same dates every year. It *is* uncommon, however, for those events to be celebrated progressively later each year.

Though the Hindu population seemed quite comfortable with their diverse calendars, these inconsistencies nonetheless presented the Committee with a dilemma. In response, the Calendar Reform Committee recommended setting up a yearly "official Indian ephemeris and nautical almanac" published by the Government of India, which would list the positions of the Sun, the Moon, the planets, and other heavenly bodies.[21] The almanac would include listings of the tithi and the nakshatra

---

[21] CSIR, *Report of the Calendar Reform Committee*, p. 8.

and, most important, one unified civil and religious calendar, called the National Calendar, to be used throughout India. The Indian New Year would commence on the vernal equinox, the Tropical Zodiac's 1st degree of Aries, as was originally set down in the Siddhantas. Since this ephemeris would be published by the Government, the listings of tithis and nakshatras would be astronomically correct and celebrations could be held on the "correct" day throughout India. The Calendar Reform Committee further recommended that the calendar be implemented on March 21, 1956. The Ayanamsa would be Lahiri's Ayanamsa of 23°15' and there would be six seasons divided by climatic changes: summer (grisma), rains (varsa), autumn (sarat), late autumn (hemanta), winter (susna), and spring (vasanta).

The Government of India soon realized that Hindu communities would be hard-pressed to accept the recommendations of the Calendar Reform Committee and as impossible a task as getting all Indians to speak one language. This became especially evident when the government declared that the 1963 Durga Puja Festival, in honor of the Goddess Durga, be celebrated at a designated date and time. Since India is a country comprised of diverse languages, traditions, and even different patron gods and goddesses, the Hindus used their regional dates and completely ignored the date and time set by the government.[22]

The government decided that, even if no attention was being paid to their recommendations, they could at least supply correct astronomical data. An official almanac was to be published each year containing "an ephemeris showing the true planetary positions and other relevant information leaving the preparation of the religious calendar to the persons most qualified for the work."[23] The planets are listed in the Indian ephemeris according to their positions at sunrise (an arbitrary hour), as opposed to our ephemeris which lists the planets at either noon or midnight (fixed times). The city of Ujjain provides the central time zone from which the listings in the ephemeris

[22] Chakravarty, *Origin and Development of Indian Calendrical Science*, pp. 56–57.
[23] Chakravarty, *Origin and Development of Indian Calendrical Science*, pp. 56–57.

emanate, equivalent to the way Greenwich, England is used to convey 0° longitude. The day is not divided into hours and minutes but into *ghatis* and *vighatis*. There are 2-1/2 ghatis in an hour and 60 ghatis in a day. Each ghati is further divided into 60 vighatis. By supplying data, the government ensured the availability of mathematically accurate calculations, with the rest left to each Hindu community.

Since the development of the calendar went hand in hand with the development of religious and astrological thought in India, some of the recommendations of the Calendar Reform Committee affected astrological timekeeping as well. The official ephemeris became a reference book astrologers could use for calculating the positions of the planets according to the Sidereal Zodiac. Like the calendar, the astrology of India has always remained both solar and lunar, combining the influence of the Greco-Chaldean school with their own unique calculations and philosophy of life. Many modern Indian astrologers still use techniques dating from Siddhantic times, synthesized with more modern methods used in the West. The bulk of their teachings, however, can still be traced back to the earliest astronomers and astrologers and, most important, to the Hindu Vedic tradition, indicating how steadfast Jyotish has actually remained.

CHAPTER 2

SIDEREAL ASTROLOGY VERSUS
TROPICAL ASTROLOGY

ONE OF THE UNIQUE features of Jyotish is its use of the fixed, sidereal (*nirayana*) zodiac instead of the symbolic, tropical (*sayana*) zodiac. Although this distinction was briefly mentioned in the previous chapter, it is important to review the technical differences between the two zodiacs in more detail.

By the time Babylonia was annexed by Alexander the Great in 331 B.C., its strictly mundane astrology had begun to develop into a primitive horoscopic astrology under the Persians, who had conquered Mesopotamia in 539 B.C. Through their own conquest of Babylonia, the Greeks inherited an astrological legacy that included the prediction of celestial events such as eclipses and the heliacal risings and settings of the planets, the creation of the earliest individual horoscopes, and the division of the sky into twelve star groupings which were named according to their various shapes and sizes. These groupings eventually became the twelve signs of the zodiac— the imaginary belt the signs seem to form around the constellations. This circular belt measures 360° and each zodiacal sign consists equally of 30°.

In the fixed Sidereal Zodiac of the Babylonians, the location of the familiar 12 equal 30° divisions was determined in relation to certain stars, especially the Aldebaran-Antares axis at 15° of Taurus and Scorpio, respectively, in the Babylonian scheme. By contrast, Hindu astronomers (5th–6th century A.D.) designated the beginning of the astrological year with individual stars in either the asterism of Revati, which spans 16° sidereal Pisces 40' to 0° Aries, or Aswini, which spans 0° Aries to 13° Aries 20', whereas modern astronomers like Lahiri utilize the opposite point of Spica, which lies at 0° Libra.

In contrast to modern Western astrology, and the Greek astrology of Ptolemy and his followers, neither the Babylonians nor the Indians[1] measured their divisions from the vernal

---

[1] As stated in chapter 1, the Siddhantic Calendar utilized the vernal equinox to begin the new year, but this was later rejected.

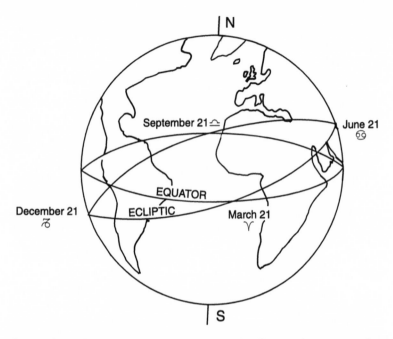

Figure 2.1. The equinoxes and the ecliptic. The equinoxes are the points at which the equator intersects with the ecliptic, the apparent path the Sun takes traveling through the zodiac. According to the tropical zodiac, the vernal equinox always marks 0° Aries.

equinox, and thus 0° Aries in their zodiac did not coincide with the place where we would find the Sun on the first day of spring. The vernal equinox is the point at which the Sun in its annual journey crosses the celestial equator, moving from south declination to north declination, and vice versa. Because it is the Earth that actually revolves around the Sun, the Sun only *appears* to be moving through the signs of the zodiac, along the portion of the zodiacal belt known as the ecliptic (see figure 2.1). But since the Earth's rotational axis moves slowly in a circular precessional motion, the equinoctial point does not return to its exact starting place for 25,800 years. Instead, the vernal point moves in a retrograde manner through the zodiacal belt, increasing at a yearly precessional rate of 50.23 to 50.27 seconds per year, depending on whose calculations are used. This varies slowly over time. Known as the Precession of the Equinoxes, this slow and steady backward movement of the vernal equinox along the ecliptic is behind the concept of planetary "ages," as a new age is said to begin whenever the vernal equinox enters a new sign.

Employing an annual precessional rate of approximately 50.23 seconds, the figure with which we will work throughout this book, it would take approximately 71.67 years for the equinoctial point to advance 60 minutes, or one degree (71.67 × 50.23″ = 3600 seconds, or 60 minutes, or 1 degree). If we multiply 71.67 years (the time it takes for the equinox to advance 1 degree) by 30 degrees (one sign of the zodiac), the product is 2,150 years, the approximate time it takes for the vernal point to traverse an entire sign, thus constituting the length of a planetary era. According to these calculations, the Age of Aquarius cannot possibly begin until at least A.D. 2341 approximately 2,150 years after the vernal point embarked on its retrograde journey through the constellation of Pisces (thus defining the Piscean Era). At that time, the vernal point will begin its retrograde movement through the actual constellation of Aquarius. Since such calculations depend on the precise placement of the constellational boundary which demarcates 0° Aries, and on the rate of precession one uses, estimates among astrologers for the year when the Age of Aquarius actually begins range from at least 1787 to 2376.

The Indian system of epochs (known as *Yugas*), which has nothing to do with these planetary ages, is made up of four planetary eras which, when added together, comprise *Maha Yuga* (literally "great age"). Consisting of 4,320,000 years, Maha Yuga is divided into ratios of 4:3:2:1 as follows:

Krtia Yuga (Golden Age)	1,728,000 years	= 4
Treta Yuga (Silver Age)	1,296,000 years	= 3
Dvapara Yuga (Copper Age)	864,000 years	= 2
Kali Yuga (Earthen Age)	432,000 years	= 1
	4,320,000 years[2]	10

---

[2] Michael Baigent, Nicholas Campion, and Charles Harvey, *Mundane Astrology* (London: Aquarian Press, 1984), p. 124.

Maha Yuga represents a period of steady spiritual and material decline, starting from the Golden Age of Krtia Yuga and ending with Kali Yuga whose completion, according to Vedic scriptures, will signal the end of the world as we know it. Kali Yuga, the period of ultimate evil and destruction, is symbolized by Mata (Mother) Kali, the Goddess of Creation and Destruction, who is always pictured surrounded by serpents and with one foot on the body of her dead husband, Shiva, God of Creation and Destruction. The prevailing Kali Yuga began in 3102 B.C. when there was a grand conjunction of most of the planets. The number of years comprising Kali Yuga—432,000 years—is equivalent to the number of years in the Great Babylonian Year, making it quite plausible that this information was brought over to India from the Near East.[3]

• • •

The difference between our Tropical (Sayana) Zodiac and the Hindu Sidereal (Nirayana) Zodiac lies in the placement of the first degree of Aries, the beginning of the astrological year. The Tropical Zodiac is known as a symbolic or "movable" zodiac because the vernal equinox, which occurs on March 20th–21st in the Gregorian calendar, is always considered to be 0° Aries, despite the fact that the vernal point has not fallen on that constellational degree for about 1700 years. The Sidereal Zodiac, on the other hand, is a "fixed" zodiac because the beginning of the astrological year is always the first degree of the actual constellation of Aries. Due to the fact that the vernal point currently falls at approximately 6° Pisces 17′ on March 21st, the beginning of India's astrological year will actually be demarcated around April 14th, the actual first degree of Aries (see figure 2.2).

The difference in degrees between where the vernal equinox is actually placed sidereally (6° Pisces 17′ at present) and 0° Aries in the Sidereal Zodiac is called the *ayanamsa*, and this figure must be subtracted from tropical planetary positions in order to arrive at the sidereal positions. The precise calcula-

---

3 Michael Baigent, et al., *Mundane Astrology*, p. 124.

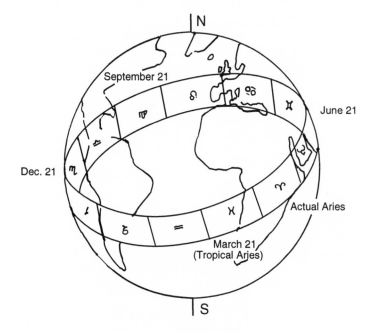

Figure 2.2. Sidereal versus Tropical Zodiac.

tion of the ayanamsa is also the focus of disagreement between Hindu and Western siderealists. The Ayanamsa used in this book is based on the calculations of the late astrologer, K. S. Krishnamurti, whose books and unique system were introduced to me by my first teacher, the late Dr. Muralil Sharma, Professor of Jyotish at Sanskrit University.

Krishnamurti's Ayanamsa, listed in Table 2.1 for the years A.D. 1900–2010 (see page 32), is based on the precessional rate of 50.2388 seconds per year, with the original year of the two coinciding zodiacs given as A.D. 291. Referring to Table 2.1, the actual degree of the vernal equinox (and the Tropical Zodiac's 0° Aries) is presently 6° Pisces 17′, or 0° Aries minus 1997's ayanamsa of 23°43′.

Table 2.1. The List of Ayanamsas between the Years 1900 and 2010, according to Krishnamurti.*

AYANAMSA			AYANAMSA			AYANAMSA		
YEAR	DEGREE	MINUTE	YEAR	DEGREE	MINUTE	YEAR	DEGREE	MINUTE
1900	22°	22′	1937	22°	53′	1974	23°	24′
1901	22°	23′	1938	22°	54′	1975	23°	25′
1902	22°	23′	1939	22°	54′	1976	23°	25′
1903	22°	24′	1940	22°	55′	1977	23°	26′
1904	22°	25′	1941	22°	56′	1978	23°	27′
1905	22°	26′	1942	22°	57′	1979	23°	28′
1906	22°	27′	1943	22°	58′	1980	23°	29′
1907	22°	28′	1944	22°	59′	1981	23°	30′
1908	22°	29′	1945	22°	59′	1982	23°	30′
1909	22°	30′	1946	23°	00′	1983	23°	31′
1910	22°	31′	1947	23°	01′	1984	23°	32′
1911	22°	32′	1948	23°	02′	1985	23°	33′
1912	22°	33′	1949	23°	03′	1986	23°	34′
1913	22°	33′	1950	23°	04′	1987	23°	35′
1914	22°	34′	1951	23°	04′	1988	23°	35′
1915	22°	35′	1952	23°	05′	1989	23°	36′
1916	22°	36′	1953	23°	06′	1990	23°	37′
1917	22°	37′	1954	23°	07′	1991	23°	38′
1918	22°	38′	1955	23°	08′	1992	23°	39′
1919	22°	38′	1956	23°	09′	1993	23°	40′
1920	22°	39′	1957	23°	10′	1994	23°	41′
1921	22°	39′	1958	23°	10′	1995	23°	41′
1922	22°	40′	1959	23°	11′	1996	23°	42′
1923	22°	41′	1960	23°	12′	1997	23°	43′
1924	22°	42′	1961	23°	13′	1998	23°	44′
1925	22°	43′	1962	23°	14′	1999	23°	45′
1926	22°	44′	1963	23°	15′	2000	23°	46′
1927	22°	44′	1964	23°	15′	2001	23°	47′
1928	22°	45′	1965	23°	16′	2002	23°	49′
1929	22°	46′	1966	23°	17′	2003	23°	50′
1930	22°	47′	1967	23°	18′	2004	23°	51′
1931	22°	48′	1968	23°	19′	2005	23°	52′
1932	22°	49′	1969	23°	20′	2006	23°	53′
1933	22°	49′	1970	23°	20′	2007	23°	54′
1934	22°	50′	1971	23°	21′	2008	23°	55′
1935	22°	51′	1972	23°	22′	2009	23°	56′
1936	22°	52′	1973	23°	23′	2010	23°	57′

*From K.S. Krishnamurti, *Casting the Horoscope*, Vol. 1 [Madras: Mahabala, 1971], p. 58.

The variety of ayanamsas can be attributed to the fact that astrologers disagree about the starting point of Aries, the exact annual rate of precession, and the year in which the vernal equinox actually coincided with 0° Aries. The ayanamsa most often used is that of Lahiri, Secretary of the Calendar Reform Committee and compiler of India's official ephemeris. Lahiri's ayanamsa is quite close to Krishnamurti's, as he calculated the rate of precession to be 50.27 seconds and the year of the two coinciding zodiacs as A.D. 285. Cyril Fagan, who championed the use of the Sidereal Zodiac here in the West, determined the starting year as A.D. 221, and Dr. B. V. Raman,[4] publisher of *The Astrological Magazine* and President of the Indian Council of Astrological Sciences, has determined yet another starting date and, as a result, has come up with his own ayanamsa. For 1997, the most commonly used ayanamsas are as follows:

Fagan-Bradley	24°42'
Lahiri	23°49'
K.S. Krishnamurti	23°43'
B.V. Raman	22°22'

A discrepancy of more than two degrees between the ayanamsas of Raman and Fagan can make a very marked difference, especially with planets that change signs according to different ayanamsas. A difference of one degree also accounts for a difference of about one year when calculating planetary periods.

Throughout this book we will be constructing charts according to the Sidereal Zodiac. To arrive at the nirayana (sidereal) position, we will be subtracting Krishnamurti's ayanamsa for the year of birth from the sayana (tropical) position of each planet. The Sanskrit word *Nir-ayana* simply means "without ayan or ayanamsa."

Using the charts of Annemarie and Barbara,[5] the following steps illustrate how to calculate the nirayana planetary posi-

---

[4] Dr. B. V. Raman's *The Astrological Magazine*, English language books, and astrology school in Bangalore have all aided in the dissemination of Indian astrology throughout the Western World.

[5] Throughout this book, the charts of two clients, Annemarie and Barbara, will be used to illustrate the calculation and interpretation of the Hindu chart known as the Rasi Chakra.

Table 2.2. Annemarie's Planets.

PLANETS*	TROPICAL OR SAYANA POSITION	SIDEREAL OR NIRAYANA POSITION
Ascendant	21° Scorpio 40′	28° Libra 34′
Sun	4° Capricorn 25′	11° Sagittarius 19′
Moon	5° Taurus 6′	12° Aries 00′
Mars	26° Aquarius 24′	3° Aquarius 18′
Mercury	14° Sagittarius 6′	21° Scorpio 00′
Jupiter	11° Taurus 8′	18° Aries 2′
Venus	18° Aquarius 14′	25° Capricorn 8′
Saturn	25° Libra 51′	2° Libra 45′
North Node	13° Aquarius 7′	20° Capricorn 01′
South Node	13° Leo 7′	20° Cancer 01′

*Throughout this book, the planets will be listed as they are in India—according to the order of the days of the week which they rule as follows: Sun, Moon, Mars, Mercury, Jupiter, Venus and Saturn.

tions using the appropriate ayanamsa. Let's begin with Annemarie, who was born on December 26, 1952 at 5:50 Greenwich Mean Time. The first step is to look at Table 2.1 (page 32) and find the year of Annemarie's birth with its corresponding ayanamsa. Because this date is so close to 1953, it is more accurate to use the 1953 ayanamsa of 23° 6′ rather than the ayanamsa from 1952.

The next step is to subtract the ayanamsa of 23° 6′ from the corresponding sayana placements of the Ascendant, planets, and Moon's Nodes at the exact moment of Annemarie's birth. Table 2.2 lists the corresponding tropical and sidereal positions in Annemarie's chart.

Barbara's chart follows. She was born on January 30, 1960 at 16:59 Greenwich Mean Time. Table 2.1 (page 32) indicates that, in 1960, the ayanamsa was 23° 12′. Table 2.3 displays the sidereal positions of Barbara's Ascendant, planets, and nodes, after the ayanamsa is subtracted from the tropical positions.

According to the Tropical Zodiac, Barbara has three planets in Capricorn and one planet in Sagittarius. Using the Side-

Table 2.3. Barbara's Planets.

PLANETS	TROPICAL OR SAYANA POSITION	SIDEREAL OR NIRAYANA POSITION
Ascendant	0° Gemini 21′	7° Taurus 9′
Sun	9° Aquarius 49′	16° Capricorn 37′
Moon	12° Pisces 14′	19° Aquarius 2′
Mars	12° Capricorn 17′	19° Sagittarius 5′
Mercury	12° Aquarius 43′	19° Capricorn 31′
Jupiter	24° Sagittarius 53′	1° Sagittarius 41′
Venus	4° Capricorn 17′	11° Sagittarius 5′
Saturn	12° Capricorn 53′	19° Sagittarius 41′
North Node	25° Virgo 26′	2° Virgo 14′
South Node	25° Pisces 26′	2° Pisces 14′

real Zodiac, however, she has four planets in Sagittarius and two planets in Capricorn. This will not represent a contradiction, however, since Jyotish is interpreted very differently from Western Tropical astrology.

Since they could not be seen with the naked eye, Uranus, Neptune, and Pluto (the trans-Saturnian planets) which were discovered in 1781, 1846, and 1930 respectively, were not included in the Vedic scriptures. Although these planets are utilized by some contemporary Vedic astrologers, their interpretation has, for the most part, been lifted from Western astrological texts. Because this is an introductory text, I have chosen not to include the outer planets in order to avoid any confusion.

There will always be disputes between the Tropical and Sidereal schools of astrology, as well as differences of opinion as to which ayanamsa is correct. Some will always insist on the superiority of a particular interpretive mode. Many skeptics and critics of astrology use the existence of two zodiacs to uphold their accusations that the subject is inconsistent, unreliable, and generally unfounded. Many astrologers, however, do not necessarily see this as an indication of astrological chaos and readily acknowledge the coexistence of two systems.

It is quite possible that, due to the simplicity of the Hindu chart and the fact that the Sidereal Zodiac is based on actual rather than symbolic planetary placements, it is tempting to interpret the Jyotish chart merely in terms of external factors, such as finances, education, profession, marriage, children, and health. Since Hindus are event-oriented and interested in fulfilling their dharma, concern with the aforementioned areas of life certainly suits the Sidereal zodiac.

Although the Tropical zodiac can lend itself to this type of interpretation if the consultant wishes to slant the reading in that direction, most Westerners are interested in these issues, as well as the personal psychology and attitudes behind the outcome, including longings, needs, fears, anger, hopes, and dreams. Although it appears to outsiders that Hindus are completely fatalistic, they are actually in agreement with interpreters of the Tropical zodiac that, with a thorough understanding of ourselves, we can make the most of the cards we are dealt.

Most Indians feel that, even if the chart is inbred with *upaye* (Sanskrit for "afflictions"), every problem has an antidote or solution. Hindus usually turn to prayer, mantras, propitiations, or gemstones directly related to the planetary afflictions. We tend to employ prayer, meditation, psychotherapy, or other self-help methods of our own choosing to resolve our problems. In my opinion, the difference between fatalistic and psychological interpretation depends on the astrologer more than whether a system is sidereal or tropical. The scriptures were written by astrologers whose art was influenced by their cultural and religious milieux and not by the type of zodiac they utilized.

In the end, much like different schools of psychological thought, each distinct astrological system should reach the same conclusions, although the methodology and focus of the readings may be very different indeed.

CHAPTER 3

CONSTRUCTING THE HOROSCOPE

THERE ARE FIVE AREAS into which Hindu astrology can be divided:

1. *Jataka* (Natal Horoscopy)—This type of horoscope is generally drawn up for a child at birth and includes the birth chart, divisional charts, predictive dasa system, etc.;

2. *Varshaphal* (Solar Return)—the annual chart drawn up for the precise moment the Sun returns to its natal sign and degree;

3. *Prashna* (Horary)—the chart drawn up for a particular moment, usually in answer to a specific question;

4. *Muhurtha* (Electional)—the event chart used to set up times for surgery, marriage, contract signing, etc., which especially utilizes the Moon's Nakshatras;

5. *Samhita* (Mundane)—the chart of a collective such as a country, weather conditions, epidemics, wars, calamities, etc.

For the purposes of this book, we will concentrate only on Jataka, the study of the individual horoscope. Tables 3.1 and 3.2 represent both the planets and the zodiacal signs used in Jyotish. Table 3.1 (page 38) consists of three columns and lists their anglicized names, corresponding Sanskrit names, and their transliteral pronunciation. Table 3.2 (page 38) is structured in the same manner with the addition of the planetary rulers of the zodiacal signs.

The Sanskrit word, *graha*, meaning "rotating body," can be applied to each of the nine heavenly bodies used in Jyotish—the Sun, the Moon, the five planets, and the Moon's Nodes, better known as Rahu (North Node) and Kethu (South Node). The Sun and the Moon, called the two "lights" in ancient cultures, are classified as planets in most astrological systems. The

Table 3.1. Planets.

PLANETS	GRAHAS	PRONUNCIATION*
The Sun	Ravi	RA-vi
	Surya	SUR-ya
The Moon	Chandra	CHAN-dra
	Soma	SO-ma
Mars	Kuja	Ku-JA
	Mangal	MAN-gal
Mercury	Budha	Bud-HA
Jupiter	Guru	Gu-RU
Venus	Sukra	SU-kra
Saturn	Sani	SA-ni
North Node	Rahu	RA-hu
South Node	Kethu	Ke'-TU

*Accented syllable is shown in capital letters.

Table 3.2. Signs of the Zodiac.

ZODIACAL SIGNS	RASIS	PRONUNCIATION*	PLANETARY RULER
Aries	Mesha	Me-SHA	Mars
Taurus	Vrishaba	VRISH-aba	Venus
Gemini	Mithuna	Mithu-NA	Mercury
Cancer	Kataka	Kata-KA	Moon
Leo	Simha	SIM-ha	Sun
Virgo	Kanya	Kan-YA	Mercury
Libra	Thula	Too-LA	Venus
Scorpio	Vrischika	VRISCH-ika	Mars
Sagittarius	Dhanus	DHA-nu	Jupiter
Capricorn	Makara	MA-kara	Saturn
Aquarius	Kumbha	Kum-BHA	Saturn
Pisces	Meena	MEE-na	Jupiter

*Accented syllable is shown in capital letters.

order of the Sun, the Moon, and the planets, in Jyotish, always corresponds with the order of the days of the week which they rule—Sunday (Sun) through Saturday (Saturn). In Sanskrit, English, and most European languages, the names of the days of the week are derived from the names of the planets.

Unlike the planets, Rahu and Kethu (Sanskrit for Dragon's Head and Dragon's Tail) are not physical bodies with shape or mass, but are the two intersecting points formed where the orbit of the Sun cuts the orbit of the Moon (see figure 3.1, page 40). They are always 180° apart, or in opposition to one another. The point formed after the Moon has traveled from south to north is called the Ascending or North Node, more commonly known as the Dragon's Head. The Dragon's Tail is the Descending or South Node and is the point formed after the Moon has moved in its course from North to South.[1]

Symbolically, Rahu and Kethu serve the same function as the planets in both the birth chart and in the planetary periods called dasas; they do not correspond to days of the week, nor can they ever rule a zodiacal sign or house. With some understanding of the Sidereal Zodiac behind us, let's move on to the construction of the Rasi Chakra, Sanskrit for horoscope. The word *horoscope* means "picture of the hour" and is derived from two Greek words—*hora* meaning "hour" and *scope* meaning "picture" or "vision." The Sanskrit term *Rasi Chakra* consists of *Rasi* meaning "constellation" or "zodiacal sign," and *Chakra* denoting "wheel." The Rasi Chakra is defined literally as a "zodiacal wheel."[2] Because of the Hindu belief in reincarnation, the description of a person's life as one spoke on the continuing wheel of many lifetimes epitomizes their concept of astrology. The wheel, however, does not apply to the diagram of the birth chart, which is constructed in the shape of a rectangle. Though the layout of the rectangular chart varies from region to region, the North Indian and the South Indian

---

[1] S. Kannan, *Fundamentals of Hindu Astrology*, (New Delhi: Sagar Publications, 1981), p. 300.

[2] The chakras are the seven energy centers of the body, and are described in C. W. Leadbeater's book, *The Chakras* (*Wheaton: Theosophical*, 1972), as "wheels of energy."

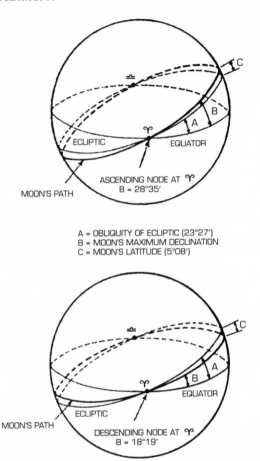

Figure 3.1. Moon's Nodes and inclination of orbit. Diagram reproduced from *The Astrologer's Astronomical Handbook*, by Jeff Mayo.

charts (See figure 3.2 on page 41) are the two most commonly
utilized. The calculations and basic interpretation of the chart,
however, remain the same throughout India.

To calculate the Rasi Chakra, we must first find the precise
degree of the *Lagna*, Sanskrit for "Ascendant," which can be
calculated by subtracting the ayanamsa from your own Ascendant according to the Tropical Zodiac, or by using Jyotish soft-

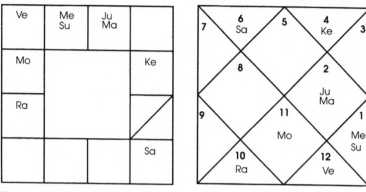

Figure 3.2. Left: South Indian chart; Right: North Indian chart.

ware (see Appendix). Because the sign of the Ascendant may be seen on the horizon at the moment of birth, it is sometimes called the rising sign. That is why the Ascendant of a person born around sunrise will inevitably be the same zodiacal sign as the Sun sign. Although the sign and degree will indicate the exact longitude of the Lagna, the 1st house is comprised of the entire zodiacal sign in which the ascending degree is placed. Even if the Ascendant falls on 29° Libra, for example, the 1st house will cover the entire sign of Libra.

Because Jyotish is a whole-sign house system, the horoscope is divided into twelve equilateral 30° Bhavas, or houses, each of which comprises an entire zodiacal sign which follows sequentially from the Ascendant. If, for example, the Lagna is 29° Libra, the first house would consist of the entire sign of Libra; the 2nd house would contain the entire sign of Scorpio; the 3rd house would be all of Sagittarius, etc. The planetary ruler or lord of each house, vital to horoscope interpretation, is defined as the ruler of the zodiacal sign found within that house.

As a result, there are only twelve possible combinations of the sign/houses—one for each Ascendant. It is for this reason that in India the rising sign is infinitely more meaningful than the Sun sign, which has just as much significance as any other planet. In fact, if somebody from India should ask "what is your sign," the response would be the rising, and not the sun, sign. Once the Lagna is revealed, it is immediately apparent which planet rules each house, which planet will be individually malefic and benefic, and which area of the chart will be affected by the transiting planets. (These factors will be discussed throughout the book.)

South Indian and North Indian Charts

The South Indian chart (see figure 3.2) was originally used in the southwestern coastal province of Kerala. The South Indian chart is sign-driven, as the signs are in stationary positions around the chart. Within the rectangle, the first sign of the zodiac, Aries, is placed second from upper left, with the signs following in clockwise fashion. The signs are stationary and are, therefore, always placed in the same boxes. The house occupied by the zodiacal sign of the Ascendant is usually filled in with a diagonal and the planets are then positioned in their respective signs and houses.

The North Indian chart (see fig 3.2) is the one I utilize in my own practice since I learned Jyotish in Benares (Varanasi), a city in the north central province of Uttar Pradesh. The North Indian chart is house-driven, in that the Ascendant and the houses remain in fixed positions around the chart. The Ascendant, always marked by the number of its corresponding sign, is placed in the upper central position. The subsequent signs are then placed in their sequential order counterclockwise around the chart. The Ascendant never changes its placement, just as in the chart from South India the signs never change their placements.

Each chart has its own strong features. As will become evident in the section on houses, the North Indian chart perfectly exemplifies the concept of the different types of houses: Kendra, or angular; Trikona, or trinal; and Dusthana (inauspicious), which are weaker and lie on the outer rims of the chart. The concept of angular houses, for instance, makes no sense with the South Indian model, since the house positions change from chart to chart. The South Indian chart is, however, a use-

Table 3.3. Annemarie's Planets.

GRAHAS	PLANETS	DEGREE	RASI	MINUTES	SIGN
Lagna	(Ascendant)	28	Thula	34	(Libra)
Ravi	(Sun)	11	Dhanus	19	(Sagittarius)
Chandra	(Moon)	12	Mesha	00	(Aries)
Kuja	(Mars)	3	Kumbha	18	(Aquarius)
Budha	(Mercury)	21	Vrischika	00	(Scorpio)
Guru	(Jupiter)	18	Mesha	02	(Aries)
Sukra	(Venus)	25	Makara	08	(Capricorn)
Sani	(Saturn)	2	Thula	45	(Libra)
Rahu	(North Node)	20	Makara	01	(Capricorn)
Kethu	(South Node)	20	Kataka	01	(Cancer)

ful tool for purposes of rectification, since a different Ascendant can be tested by merely readjusting the diagonal.

Using the North Indian chart as our model, let's construct the charts of Annemarie and Barbara. The first step is to take the nirayana positions of the Ascendant and planets of Annemarie's chart. Table 3.3 lists her nirayana planets (Grahas) and the Ascendant (Lagna).

Figure 3.3 on page 44 illustrates the steps that were taken to draw Annemarie's Rasi Chakra.

Constructing the Rasi Chakra

Step 1. Begin with a blank rectangle within which the planets will be placed (figure 3.3a). The rectangle is first filled in with an "X" drawn from corner to corner (figure 3.3b) and then with a diamond (figure 3.3c), dividing the rectangle into 12 sections which will become the 12 bhavas, or houses of the Rasi Chakra. The Lagna, or Ascendant, is then placed in the top center position, with the subsequent houses sequentially marked around the horoscope (figure 3.3d, p. 44). To indicate the sign of the Lagna within the chart itself, use the number which corresponds to its appropriate sign as follows:

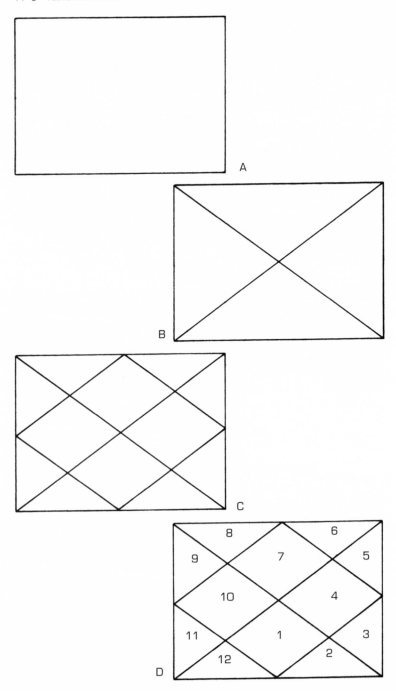

Figure 3.3. Constructing the Rasi Chakra.

Aries = 1   Libra = 7
Taurus = 2   Scorpio = 8
Gemini = 3   Sagittarius = 9
Cancer = 4   Capricorn = 10
Leo = 5   Aquarius = 11
Virgo = 6   Pisces = 12.

Insert the number 7—the number of Annemarie's Libra Ascendant—in the top central position to indicate that the entire 30° of Libra occupy the 1st house. The numbers of the zodiacal signs of the remaining eleven houses are then inserted in sequential order counterclockwise around the Rasi Chakra, if you are using the North Indian model. If you are using the South Indian model, simply draw a diagonal through the sign of the Lagna. The 2nd house comprises the entire eighth sign of Scorpio; the 3rd house is the entire sign of Sagittarius; etc. Each house, therefore, simply consists of the entire zodiacal sign.

Figure 3.4 (below, left) gives the North Indian version of Annemarie's chart after placing the planets in their proper

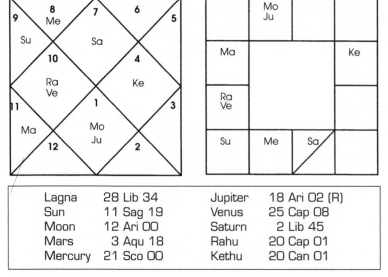

Lagna	28 Lib 34	Jupiter	18 Ari 02 (R)
Sun	11 Sag 19	Venus	25 Cap 08
Moon	12 Ari 00	Saturn	2 Lib 45
Mars	3 Aqu 18	Rahu	20 Cap 01
Mercury	21 Sco 00	Kethu	20 Can 01

Figure 3.4. Annemarie's chart (Rasi Chakra). Left: North Indian model; and Right: South Indian model. Born December 26, 1952, 5:50 A.M., GMT. Birthplace withheld for confidentiality. Source: Birth certificate.

signs/houses around the horoscope. Since the names of the planets are always written out in Sanskrit, they are written here in English. Glyphs are never used in Jyotish, as they are a Western invention. The exact degrees and minutes are listed alongside or beneath the Rasi Chakra.

Figure 3.4 (page 45, right) also shows how Annemarie's chart would look if constructed using the South Indian diagram. Simply place a diagonal in the sign/house of the Ascendant before placing the planets in their proper signs around the chart. Since the signs are always in the same place, refer to figure 3.2 (page 41) for their proper location.

Let's do the same with Barbara's chart. Her planets and Ascendant are as follows:

Table 3.4. Barbara's Planets.

GRAHAS	PLANETS	DEGREE	RASI	MINUTE	SIGN
Lagna	(Ascendant)	7	Vrishaba	9	(Taurus)
Ravi	(Sun)	16	Makara	37	(Capricorn)
Chandra	(Moon)	19	Kumbha	2	(Aquarius)
Kuja	(Mars)	19	Dhanus	4	(Sagittarius)
Budha	(Mercury)	19	Makara	31	(Capricorn)
Guru	(Jupiter)	1	Dhanus	41	(Sagittarius)
Sukra	(Venus)	11	Dhanus	5	(Sagittarius)
Sani	(Saturn)	19	Dhanus	41	(Sagittarius)
Rahu	(North Node)	2	Kanya	14	(Virgo)
Kethu	(South Node)	2	Meena	14	(Pisces)

Using a Taurus Ascendant, place the number 2 in the top central position and insert the remaining numbers counterclockwise around the chart. As with Annemarie's chart, the next step is to insert the planets in their proper signs/houses. Figure 3.5 represents Barbara's completed Rasi Chakra in the North and South Indian systems respectively.

The charts of these two women perfectly illustrate the way the Hindu horoscope, or Rasi Chakra, looks. The degrees and minutes of each planet may be listed either alongside the horoscope, inside the bhavas, or written on a separate piece of paper, according to the way an astrologer finds it most practical and/or aesthetically pleasing.

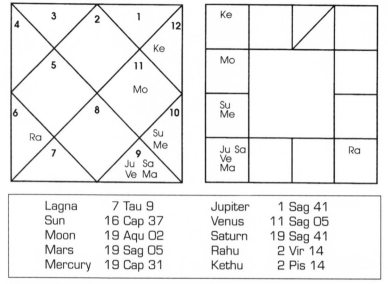

Lagna	7 Tau 9	Jupiter	1 Sag 41
Sun	16 Cap 37	Venus	11 Sag 05
Moon	19 Aqu 02	Saturn	19 Sag 41
Mars	19 Sag 05	Rahu	2 Vir 14
Mercury	19 Cap 31	Kethu	2 Pis 14

Figure 3.5. Barbara's chart (Rasi Chakra). Left: North Indian model; Right: South Indian model. January 30, 1960, 16:59, GMT. Birth place withheld for confidentiality. Source: Birth certificate.

The Rasi Chakra is visually more simple than its Western counterpart. A Western horoscope is usually drawn with many multi-colored aspect lines connecting the planets, in order to distinguish between the various aspects. These lines only make the Western horoscope *appear* more intricate than its Vedic counterpart. In reality, the interpretation of the Rasi Chakra is no more or less complex than that of the circular horoscope.

The Moon Chart (Chandra Lagna)

There are other types of charts that are constructed in the same manner as the Rasi Chakra, though used for different interpretive purposes. The Moon Chart, or *Chandra Lagna*, meaning "Moon as Ascendant" (see figure 3.6, and figure 3.7, page 48), is constructed by placing the Moon in the Ascendant position with the rest of the planets in their natal positions. The Moon

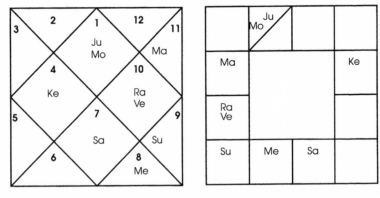

Figure 3.6. Annemarie's Moon chart (Chandra Lagna). Left: North Indian model; Right: South Indian model.

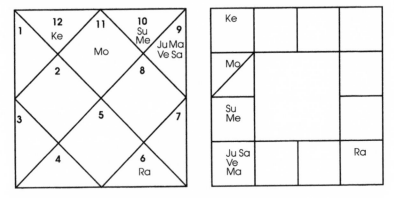

Figure 3.7. Barbara's Moon chart (Chandra Lagna). Left: North Indian model; Right: South Indian model.

Chart is interpreted by viewing the planets in relation to this most important heavenly body. The Chandra Lagna is always used as a supplementary chart where information can be obtained which is not always obvious from the birth chart alone. Conversely, the Chandra Lagna may verify conclusions already confirmed from the Rasi Chakra. When certain themes—positive or negative—appear in both charts, those tendencies are especially dominant throughout one's life. In fact, the nature of a particular planet is often assessed after it is viewed in relation to the Ascendant, the Moon, and the Sun. The Moon chart is also considered by some astrologers to be superior to the Rasi Chakra when describing a woman's emotional and physical make-up, or when assessing her propensity for childbearing.

It is very common in Jyotish to analyze any area of the chart by placing that particular house in the Ascendant position. For instance, to learn more about Annemarie's mother, the 4th house (which represents the maternal line) would be placed in the Ascendant position. The chart would then be interpreted in the same way as the birth chart.

Navamsa Chart

In Jyotish, there are 16 Varga (short for Shodasavarga) charts, formed by using a particular number to divide the Rasi. Used alongside the Rasi Chakra and the Moon Chart in horoscope analysis, the navamsa chart is the most significant varga chart and an extremely important interpretive device formed by dividing each Rasi of 30° into nine equal sections of 3-⅓° called navamsas. Table 3.5 (pages 50–52) illustrates this principle of division. Beginning with the first degree of Aries, the zodiacal degrees and signs are placed in columns A and B, their planetary rulers in column C, and their corresponding navamsa signs and planetary lords in columns D & E. As the table indicates, nine sub-zodiacs from Aries to Pisces of 40° each (360° ÷ 9) are thus formed.

In order to actually construct the navamsa chart, the natal Ascendant and planets must first be converted to their corresponding navamsa signs. (The varga charts are concerned with signs and not degrees.) Referring to Table 3.5, Annemarie's planets and their navamsa signs are identified as shown in Table 3.6 (page 53).

The navamsa chart is drawn precisely like the birth chart, by placing the Ascendant's navamsa sign in the 1st house position and the planets in their corresponding navamsa signs. Using Annemarie for an example, the corresponding navamsa sign of her Ascendant, 28 Libra 34, is Gemini with the other planets following suit. Figure 3.8 (page 53) is therefore An-

Table 3.5. Divisions of the Navamsa Chart.

DEGREES & MINUTES	SIGN	PLANETARY LORD	NAVAMSA SIGN	PLANETARY LORD
0.00–3.20	Aries	Mars	Aries	Mars
3.20–6.40			Taurus	Venus
6.40–10.00			Gemini	Mercury
10.00–13.20			Cancer	Moon
13.20–16.40			Leo	Sun
16.40–20.00			Virgo	Mercury
20.00–23.20			Libra	Venus
23.20–26.40			Scorpio	Mars
26.40–30.00			Sagittarius	Jupiter
0.00–3.20	Taurus	Venus	Capricorn	Saturn
3.20–6.40			Aquarius	Saturn
6.40–10.00			Pisces	Jupiter
10.00–13.20			Aries	Mars
13.20–16.40			Taurus	Venus
16.40–20.00			Gemini	Mercury
20.00–23.20			Cancer	Moon
23.20–26.40			Leo	Sun
26.40–30.00			Virgo	Mercury
0.00–3.20	Gemini	Mercury	Libra	Venus
3.20–6.40			Scorpio	Mars
6.40–10.00			Sagittarius	Jupiter
10.00–13.20			Capricorn	Saturn
13.20–16.40			Aquarius	Saturn
16.40–20.00			Pisces	Jupiter
20.00–23.20			Aries	Mars
23.20–26.40			Taurus	Venus
26.40–30.00			Gemini	Mercury
0.00–3.20	Cancer	Moon	Cancer	Moon
3.20–6.40			Leo	Sun
6.40–10.00			Virgo	Mercury
10.00–13.20			Libra	Venus
13.20–16.40			Scorpio	Mars
16.40–20.00			Sagittarius	Jupiter
20.00–23.20			Capricorn	Saturn
23.20–26.40			Aquarius	Saturn
26.40–30.00			Pisces	Jupiter

Table 3.5. Divisions of the Navamsa Chart (continued).

DEGREES & MINUTES	SIGN	PLANETARY LORD	NAVAMSA SIGN	PLANETARY LORD
0.00–3.20	Leo	Sun	Aries	Mars
3.20–6.40			Taurus	Venus
6.40–10.00			Gemini	Mercury
10.00–13.20			Cancer	Moon
13.20–16.40			Leo	Sun
16.40–20.00			Virgo	Mercury
20.00–23.20			Libra	Venus
23.20–26.40			Scorpio	Mars
26.40–30.00			Sagittarius	Jupiter
0.00–3.20	Virgo	Mercury	Capricorn	Saturn
3.20–6.40			Aquarius	Saturn
6.40–10.00			Pisces	Jupiter
10.00–13.20			Aries	Mars
13.20–16.40			Taurus	Venus
16.40–20.00			Gemini	Mercury
20.00–23.20			Cancer	Moon
23.20–26.40			Leo	Sun
26.40–30.00			Virgo	Mercury
0.00–3.20	Libra	Venus	Libra	Venus
3.20–6.40			Scorpio	Mars
6.40–10.00			Sagittarius	Jupiter
10.00–13.20			Capricorn	Saturn
13.20–16.40			Aquarius	Saturn
16.40–20.00			Pisces	Jupiter
20.00–23.20			Aries	Mars
23.20–26.40			Taurus	Venus
26.40–30.00			Gemini	Mercury
0.00–3.20	Scorpio	Mars	Cancer	Moon
3.20–6.40			Leo	Sun
6.40–10.00			Virgo	Mercury
10.00–13.20			Libra	Venus
13.20–16.40			Scorpio	Mars
16.40–20.00			Sagittarius	Jupiter
20.00–23.20			Capricorn	Saturn
23.20–26.40			Aquarius	Saturn
26.40–30.00			Pisces	Jupiter

Table 3.5. Divisions of the Navamsa Chart (continued).

DEGREES & MINUTES	SIGN	PLANETARY LORD	NAVAMSA SIGN	PLANETARY LORD
0.00–3.20	Sagittarius	Jupiter	Aries	Mars
3.20–6.40			Taurus	Venus
6.40–10.00			Gemini	Mercury
10.00–13.20			Cancer	Moon
13.20–16.40			Leo	Sun
16.40–20.00			Virgo	Mercury
20.00–23.20			Libra	Venus
23.20–26.40			Scorpio	Mars
26.40–30.00			Sagittarius	Jupiter
0.00–3.20	Capricorn	Saturn	Capricorn	Saturn
3.20–6.40			Aquarius	Saturn
6.40–10.00			Pisces	Jupiter
10.00–13.20			Aries	Mars
13.20–16.40			Taurus	Venus
16.40–20.00			Gemini	Mercury
20.00–23.20			Cancer	Moon
23.20–26.40			Leo	Sun
26.40–30.00			Virgo	Mercury
0.00–3.20	Aquarius	Saturn	Libra	Venus
3.20–6.40			Scorpio	Mars
6.40–10.00			Sagittarius	Jupiter
10.00–13.20			Capricorn	Saturn
13.20–16.40			Aquarius	Saturn
16.40–20.00			Pisces	Jupiter
20.00–23.20			Aries	Mars
23.20–26.40			Taurus	Venus
26.40–30.00			Gemini	Mercury
0.00–3.20	Pisces	Jupiter	Cancer	Moon
3.20–6.40			Leo	Sun
6.40–10.00			Virgo	Mercury
10.00–13.20			Libra	Venus
13.20–16.40			Scorpio	Mars
16.40–20.00			Sagittarius	Jupiter
20.00–23.20			Capricorn	Saturn
23.20–26.40			Aquarius	Saturn
26.40–30.00			Pisces	Jupiter

Table 3.6. Annemarie's Planets and Navamsa Signs.

PLANET	PLACEMENT	NAVAMSA SIGN
Ascendant	28 Libra 34	Gemini
Sun	11 Sagittarius 19	Cancer
Moon	12 Aries 00	Cancer
Mars	3 Aquarius 18	Libra
Mercury	20 Scorpio 00	Capricorn
Jupiter	18 Aries 02	Virgo
Venus	25 Capricorn 08	Leo
Saturn	2 Libra 45	Libra
North Node	20 Capricorn 01	Cancer
South Node	20 Cancer 01	Capricorn

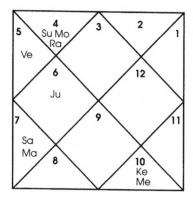 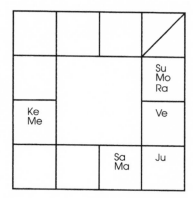

Figure 3.8. Annemarie's navamsa chart. Left: North Indian model; Right: South Indian model.

nemarie's navamsa chart drawn to completion when the planets are placed around the chart in their corresponding navamsa positions.

Barbara's planets and their corresponding navamsa signs are given in Table 3.7 (page 54) and Figure 3.9 (page 54) represents Barbara's navamsa chart when drawn to completion.

The navamsa chart is often considered the mirror of the birth chart, or the ultimate path which the individual takes.

Table 3.7. Barbara's Planets and Navamsa Signs.

PLANET	PLACEMENT	NAVAMSA SIGN
Ascendant	7 Taurus 09	Pisces
Sun	16 Capricorn 37	Taurus
Moon	19 Aquarius 02	Pisces
Mars	19 Sagittarius 05	Virgo
Mercury	19 Capricorn 31	Gemini
Jupiter	1 Sagittarius 41	Aries
Venus	11 Sagittarius 05	Cancer
Saturn	19 Sagittarius 41	Virgo
North Node	2 Virgo 14	Capricorn
South Node	2 Pisces 14	Cancer

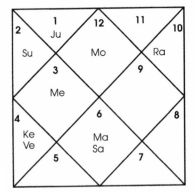
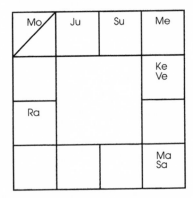

Figure 3.9. Barbara's navamsa chart. Left: North Indian model; Right: South Indian model.

Some astrologers feel that the navamsa chart will be more dominant than the birth chart later in life. Like the Chandra Lagna, the navamsa chart is primarily used in conjunction with the Rasi Chakra to obtain a more well-rounded, in-depth view of the individual. It is interpreted according to the same rules as the birth chart and any major themes of the navamsa chart will be incorporated into the interpretation of the Rasi Chakra. For example, Annemarie's navamsa chart has an emphasized 2nd house. The quest for money and possessions (2nd house themes) will be a strong aspect of her life, even though it may not be obvious from the Rasi Chakra alone. In addition, a theme which recurs in both the Rasi Chakra and the navamsa chart will become a dominant factor in the person's life.

The navamsa chart may also strengthen or weaken a particular planet. If a planet is exalted in the birth chart, but is debilitated in the navamsa chart, the area of life represented by that particular planet may not bring the results which may have been promised by the birth chart alone. Conversely, if a planet is in its fallen position in the Rasi Chakra, an exalted or rulership position in the navamsa chart could improve the area of life represented by that planet. In any event, a final judgment of the Rasi Chakra is reserved until the astrologer consults both the Moon and navamsa charts.

Besides the importance of the navamsa chart as a check and balance for the birth chart, each varga represents a specific area of life. The navamsa chart, in particular, is utilized to determine the most appropriate time to wed the partner one chooses and the quality of the marriage itself. Hindu astrologers use navamsa charts particularly to ascertain whether or not a couple is compatible. Comparing the navamsa charts of the prospective bride and groom to see whether the two charts are complementary is a method considered by some astrologers to be infinitely more reliable than comparing the two Rasi Chakras.

Shodasavargas

There are 16 vargas (degree divisional charts), including the Rasi Chakra and the navamsa, which are used in Jyotish.[3] The Rasi Chakra itself is considered to be a varga, because the Rasi is divisible by one unit while the navamsa chart is formed by dividing the Rasi into nine units.

---

[3] Mantreswara advocates using ten Varga charts, while Parasara utilizes the sixteen divisional charts listed here. Other divisional charts are used in other branches of astrology in India that do not exclusively follow the rules set down by Parasara.

The following is a list of the other divisional charts and the areas of life which they represent, according to Parasara's *Hora Sastra*.[4] These positions will be of utmost importance when determining planetary strength and weakness (see chapter 6).

1. Rasi Chakra—individual chart;
2. Hora—wealth;
3. Drekkana—happiness through siblings; effort;
4. Chaturthamsa—good luck and fortune;
5. Septamsa—children;
6. Navamsa—married life;
7. Dasamsa—career and status;
8. Dwadasamsa—parents, heredity;
9. Shodasamsa—happiness through conveyances and property;
10. Vimsamsa—spiritual life;
11. Chaturvimsamsa—academic achievements;
12. Bhamsa—strength and weakness;
13. Trimsamsa—good or bad luck;
14. Khavedamsa—auspicious and inauspicious effects;
15. Akshavedamsa—general indications;
16. Shastiamsa—general indications.[5]

Each of these charts represents a different phase of life and is used to gain added insight by uncovering many of the subtleties which cannot be readily seen from the Rasi Chakra alone. The most commonly used charts include hora (dividing the Rasi by 2), drekkana (dividing the Rasi into 3 parts of 10° each), septamsa (dividing the Rasi into 7 parts of 4°17′ each), dasamsa (dividing the Rasi into 10 parts of 3° each), and dwadasamsa (dividing the Rasi into 12 parts of 2°30′ each). The following tables provide examples of how the hora, drekkana, and septamsa charts are calculated.

---

[4] It is too complex to explain how each of these are calculated in this particular volume, however, every Jyotish software packet will plot out the planets' placements throughout the vargas.

[5] Parasara, *Hora Sastra* (New Delhi: Ranjan Publications, 1991), p. 92.

Table 3.8. Divisions of the Hora Chart.

DEGREES	SIGNS	HORA	DEGREES	SIGNS	HORA
1–15	Aries	Sun	1–15	Libra	Sun
16–30	Aries	Moon	16–30	Libra	Moon
1–15	Taurus	Moon	1–15	Scorpio	Moon
16–30	Taurus	Sun	16–30	Scorpio	Sun
1–15	Gemini	Sun	1–15	Sagittarius	Sun
16–30	Gemini	Moon	16–30	Sagittarius	Moon
1–15	Cancer	Moon	1–15	Capricorn	Moon
16–30	Cancer	Sun	16–30	Capricorn	Sun
1–15	Leo	Sun	1–15	Aquarius	Sun
16–30	Leo	Moon	16–30	Aquarius	Moon
1–15	Virgo	Moon	1–15	Pisces	Moon
16–30	Virgo	Sun	16–30	Pisces	Sun

Hora Chart

Unlike the Navamsa Chart, the hora is not constructed as a chart, per se, but is a list of whether each planet is posited in its strong or weak hora. Dividing the Rasi by two, each hora is comprised of 15°. The hora chart distinguishes whether each planet is in the hora of the Sun or the Moon. A planet is considered to be in the hora of the Sun if it is 0–15° of a masculine sign, namely Aries, Gemini, Leo, Libra, Sagittarius, and Aquarius, and 16–30° of a feminine sign, namely Taurus, Cancer, Virgo, Scorpio, Capricorn, and Pisces. A planet is deemed to be in the hora of the Moon if it is 0–15° of a feminine sign, and 16–30° of a masculine sign. It is said that the Sun, Mars, and Jupiter are stronger if placed in the hora of the Sun, while the Moon, Venus, and Saturn are more advantageous if placed in the hora of the Moon. Mercury is neutral.

Drekkana Chart

The Drekkana is derived by dividing each sign into the three signs of the same element. Table 3.9 illustrates these divisions.

Table 3.9. Divisions of the Drekkana Chart.

DEGREES	SIGNS	DREKKANA	ELEMENT
0–10	Aries	Aries	Fire
11–20	Aries	Leo	
21–30	Aries	Sagittarius	
0–10	Taurus	Taurus	Earth
11–20	Taurus	Virgo	
21–30	Taurus	Capricorn	
0–10	Gemini	Gemini	Air
11–20	Gemini	Libra	
21–30	Gemini	Aquarius	
0–10	Cancer	Cancer	Water
11–20	Cancer	Scorpio	
21–30	Cancer	Pisces	
0–10	Leo	Leo	Fire
11–20	Leo	Sagittarius	
21–30	Leo	Aries	
0–10	Virgo	Virgo	Earth
11–20	Virgo	Capricorn	
21–30	Virgo	Taurus	
0–10	Libra	Libra	Air
11–20	Libra	Aquarius	
21–30	Libra	Gemini	
0–10	Scorpio	Scorpio	Water
11–20	Scorpio	Pisces	
21–30	Scorpio	Cancer	
0–10	Sagittarius	Sagittarius	Fire
11–20	Sagittarius	Aries	
21–30	Sagittarius	Leo	
0–10	Capricorn	Capricorn	Earth
11–20	Capricorn	Taurus	
21–30	Capricorn	Virgo	
0–10	Aquarius	Aquarius	Air
11–20	Aquarius	Gemini	
21–30	Aquarius	Libra	
0–10	Pisces	Pisces	Water
11–20	Pisces	Cancer	
21–30	Pisces	Scorpio	

Septamsa Chart

The Septamsa is calculated by dividing the zodiac into seven
sub-zodiacs. Table 3.10 illustrates these divisions.

Table 3.10. Divisions of the Septamsa Chart.

DEGREES	SIGN	SEPTAMSA	DEGREES	SIGN	SEPTAMSA
0– 4°17	Aries	Aries	0– 4°17	Libra	Libra
4°17– 8°34		Taurus	4°17– 8°34		Scorpio
8°34–12°51		Gemini	8°34–12°51		Sagittarius
12°51–17°08		Cancer	12°51–17°08		Capricorn
17°08–21°25		Leo	17°08–21°25		Aquarius
21°25–25°42		Virgo	21°25–25°42		Pisces
25°42–30°00		Libra	25°42–30°00		Aries
0– 4°17	Taurus	Scorpio	0– 4°17	Scorpio	Taurus
4°17– 8°34		Sagittarius	4°17– 8°34		Gemini
8°34–12°51		Capricorn	8°34–12°51		Cancer
12°51–17°08		Aquarius	12°51–17°08		Leo
17°08–21°25		Pisces	17°08–21°25		Virgo
21°25–25°42		Aries	21°25–25°42		Libra
25°42–30°00		Taurus	25°42–30°00		Scorpio
0– 4°17	Gemini	Gemini	0– 4°17	Sagittarius	Sagittarius
4°17– 8°34		Cancer	4°17– 8°34		Capricorn
8°34–12°51		Leo	8°34–12°51		Aquarius
12°51–17°08		Virgo	12°51–17°08		Pisces
17°08–21°25		Libra	17°08–21°25		Aries
21°25–25°42		Scorpio	21°25–25°42		Taurus
25°42–30°00		Sagittarius	25°42–30°00		Gemini
0– 4°17	Cancer	Capricorn	0– 4°17	Capricorn	Cancer
4°17– 8°34		Aquarius	4°17– 8°34		Leo
8°34–12°51		Pisces	8°34–12°51		Virgo
12°51–17°08		Aries	12°51–17°08		Libra
17°08–21°25		Taurus	17°08–21°25		Scorpio
21°25–25°42		Gemini	21°25–25°42		Sagittarius
25°42–30°00		Cancer	25°42–30°00		Capricorn
0– 4°17	Leo	Leo	0– 4°17	Aquarius	Aquarius
4°17– 8°34		Virgo	4°17– 8°34		Pisces
8°34–12°51		Libra	8°34–12°51		Aries
12°51–17°08		Scorpio	12°51–17°08		Taurus
17°08–21°25		Sagittarius	17°08–21°25		Gemini
21°25–25°42		Capricorn	21°25–25°42		Cancer
25°42–30°00		Aquarius	25°42–30°00		Leo
0– 4°17	Virgo	Pisces	0– 4°17	Pisces	Virgo
4°17– 8°34		Aries	4°17– 8°34		Libra
8°34–12°51		Taurus	8°34–12°51		Scorpio
12°51–17°08		Gemini	12°51–17°08		Sagittarius
17°08–21°25		Cancer	17°08–21°25		Capricorn
21°25–25°42		Leo	21°25–25°42		Aquarius
25°42–30°00		Virgo	25°42–30°00		Pisces

Harmonics

Though an entire chapter could easily be devoted to both the philosophical and mathematical correlations between harmonics charts, as pioneered by British astrologer John Addey, and varga charts, it is a subject which will only be briefly mentioned. It is important to touch on this, however, to understand the extent to which Addey used the Hindu divisional charts as the basis of his theory.

In the same way that varga charts are formed by using different numerals to divide the Rasi (30°), harmonic charts are formed by using those same numerals to divide the zodiac (360°). The late John Addey perfected the system of harmonics by basing it on the same principles as Jyotish:

> [T]his old tradition in Hindu astrology of creating sub-cycle charts is really a practical application of the idea of harmonics. Each division of the circle into a subordinate number of cycles or circles has its own significance, derived from the symbolism of the number by which the division is made. By dividing up the original circle of the Zodiac into a number of lesser circles one is, in effect, considering the distribution of the natal positions within the sub-circle of a particular horoscope. It is true perhaps that the Indian astrologer may think of this technique as one in which each sign is divided by a particular number— in this case nine—but in point of fact, what he has done first and foremost is to divide the whole circle by nine, and then divide each of those nine divisions into a little Zodiac of twelve signs.[6]

Like the vargas, harmonic charts are sub-zodiacs used to identify character traits and subtle parts of the personality that are unnoticeable using the horoscope alone. By advocating the usage of harmonics charts based on multiples ranging from 2 to 12, Addey discovered more in-depth ways of interpreting the chart, in addition to using newer aspect combinations. He

---

[6] John Addey, *Harmonics in Astrology* (London, England: Urania Trust, 1996), p. 101.

found the most significant harmonics charts, however, to be the fifth harmonic, the seventh harmonic, and the ninth harmonic, which are comparable to the panchamsa, septamsa, and navamsa charts.

For example, the navamsa chart is formed by dividing the Rasi by nine, into divisions of 3⅓°. By dividing the entire zodiac by nine, each sub-zodiac from Aries to Pisces will span 40°. Since the novile aspect of 40° in a birth chart shows up as a conjunction or opposition in the Ninth Harmonic Chart, Addey concluded that this aspect emphasized certain talents which were not readily seen using traditional aspects. The same principle applies to the Fifth Harmonic Chart, wherein the conjunctions and oppositions form quintiles and bi-quintiles (72° and 144°), since the first 72° of the panchamsa chart comprises the first of five sub-zodiacs. Finally, in the Seventh Harmonic Chart the conjunctions and oppositions form septiles (51½°), while the first 51½° of the septamsa chart comprises the first of the seven sub-zodiacs.

Through Addey's work and persistence, aspects based on these divisions are often used today in Western astrology alongside the more traditional square, opposition, sextile, and trine (based on multiples of two and three and are seen as conjunctions and oppositions in the second and third harmonics charts).

But more important, John Addey hoped that the study of harmonics might lead to a new commitment toward a unification of Eastern and Western principles, based in part on the universality of numbers and the rhythms of the universe. In his own words:

> The picture that has so emerged is one of the harmonics, that is the rhythms and sub-rhythms, of cosmic periods, which can be demonstrated to provide the basis of all astrological doctrine both ancient and modern. . . . This is only one of the many ways in which the new approach to astrology in terms of harmonics promises a reunion of the Eastern and Western traditions in astrology and, indeed, seems likely to illuminate Indian astrology for Indians as much as Western astrology for Westerners.[7]

---

[7] John Addey, *Harmonics in Astrology*, pp. 13, 90.

.

Part II
Interpretation

CHAPTER 4

DEFINING THE PLANETS, SIGNS AND HOUSES

CHART INTERPRETATION SHOULD BEGIN with a definition of the planets, signs, and houses. When viewing the planets, it is most important to remember that each one represents a different quality—the capacity for love, intelligence, work, emotions—as well as adopting the identity of the house it rules. The expression of the planet is further modified by its relationship to the zodiacal sign in which it is placed, the house it occupies, and the aspects it receives. Interpretation of the horoscope, however, is ultimately dependent on how an astrologer synthesizes these elements and judges their influences.

The following descriptions include both authentic delineations taken from translations of ancient writings,[1] and modern interpretations of these texts. Some of these depictions cannot be applied to our lives, but have been included for the purposes of historical documentation. See Table 4.1, page 66.

The Planets (Grahas)

The following descriptions include both positive and problematic qualities. Whether they manifest as beneficial or difficult influences depends upon their association with the other elements in the chart. (It is interesting to note that the writers of the ancient scriptures endowed the planets with human characteristics.)

The Sun (Ravi, or Surya)

Ravi rules Leo (Simha), the day of the week is Sunday, the god is Shiva, the gemstone is ruby, garnet, or other red stones, and

---

[1] These delineations are taken from Parasara's *Hora Sastra* (New Delhi: Ranjan Publications, 1991), Varahamihira's *Brihat Jataka* (New Delhi: Sagar Publications, 1985), Kalyana Varma's *Saravali* (New Delhi: Ranjan Publications, 1983), and Mantreswara's *Phaladeepika* (Bangalore: K. Subrahmanyam, 1981).

Table 4.1. Characteristics and Associations of the Planets.*

PLANET	RULING SIGN	BODY PART	DAY	GEM	COLOR	SENSE	GOD(DESS)
Sun	Leo	Heart Spine	Sunday	Ruby	Copper	Soul	God Shiva
Moon	Cancer	Breasts	Monday	Pearl	White	Mind	Goddess Parvati
Mars	Aries Scorpio	Head	Tuesday	Coral	Red	Sight	God Kamara
Mercury	Gemini Virgo	Lungs	Wednesday	Emerald	Green	Smell	God Vishnu
Jupiter	Sagittarius Pisces	Thighs	Thursday	Topaz	Yellow	Hearing	God Brahma
Venus	Taurus Libra	Kidneys Eyes	Friday	Diamond	Multi-color	Taste	Goddess Lakshmi (Vishnu's Wife)
Saturn	Capricorn Aquarius	Bones Teeth	Saturday	Sapphire	Black	Touch	God Yama

*The components of this chart are compiled from different sources. For instance, the colors are taken from *Brihat Jataka*, while the gemstones, gods, and goddesses, are taken from *Phaladeepika*.

the color is copper. Parts of the body ruled by the Sun include the heart, spine, man's right eye, woman's left eye, mouth, spleen, throat, circulatory system, and brain. The associated profession may involve business inherited from the father, dealings in copper and gold, and government service. The Sun indicates executives, political figures, administrators, kings, dictators, and heads of state. Acquisition of wealth comes from fruit trees, medicine, wool, metals. The Sun is the soul.[2]

> The Sun has somewhat yellow eyes, is of the height of the length of the two arms stretched out, of bilious nature and with very little hair on his head.[3]

> The Sun is of bilious temperament, lord of bones, limited quantity of hair, dark red form, reddish brown eyes, red, square-built body, valiant, wrathful broad shoulders. He is a Shiva worshipper, doctor, minister, king, performer of sacrifice. It has to do with matters concerning the self, copper, gold, father, auspiciousness, happiness, dignity, power, glory, influence, health, vigor, fortune and the God Shiva.[4]

The Sun represents *prana*, Sanskrit for the "breath of life," and determines the level of confidence and vitality. It is common practice for Hindus to pray to the Sun to regain lost physical strength, and perform religious rites on holidays throughout the year celebrating its power. The Sun is the *karaka* (Sanskrit for "indicator") of the self, the father, and the career. The Sun gives activity, authority, steadiness, self-acquisition, strong will, executive position, self-employment, and good fortune. People with a powerful Sun in their horoscope will be excellent managers, overachievers, autocratic, bossy, aggressive, and outspoken. There may be, at times, too much preoccupation with status and recognition.

If the planet is well-placed there will be ambition, brilliance, command, dignity, energy, fame, generosity, health, individuality, optimism, royalty, success, vitality, and warmth.

---

[2] Mantreswara, *Phaladeepika*, p. 11.
[3] Varahamihira, *Brihat Jataka*, p. 19.
[4] Mantreswara, *Phaladeepika*, p. 14.

There will be a cheerful outlook on life, and spirituality will guide all that one does. If the planet is ill-placed there will be arrogance, dominance and egotism, jealousy, lavishness, over-ambition, irritability, and anger. Illnesses associated with the Sun include heart disease, backache, skin diseases, colds, and fever of undetermined sources.

The Moon (Chandra, or Soma)

Chandra rules Cancer (Kataka), the day of the week is Monday, the goddess is Parvati, the gemstone is pearl, moonstone, and other white stones, and the color is white. Other parts of the body include the breasts, left eye of the male, right eye of the female, stomach, esophagus, uterus, ovaries, lymphatic system, and bladder. Professions include healthcare givers, advertising, public relations, journalism, or anything that deals with the public. Work may also involve shipping, water products, pearls, corals, agriculture, cattle, clothes, or working with another woman. The Moon[5] represents both the mind and the body.[6]

> The Moon has a thin and round body, is of an exceedingly windy and phlegmatic nature, is learned and has a soft voice and beautiful eyes. . . .[7]

> The Moon has a huge body, is young and old, lean and white, has fine lovely eyes, black and thin hair, governs blood, is soft in speech, wears white, is yellowish in color, has wind and phlegm in his composition and is mild in temperament. It has to do with matters concerning mother, mental tranquility, fruits, tenderness, flowers, fame, pearls,

---

[5] Mercury rules speech and communication, whereas the Moon reflects how ideas are perceived and transmitted. Soma represents the concept that our emotional control and physical well-being is directly related to our ability to think, see things clearly, and take control of our lives. The scriptures say that if we are mentally unstable or our minds are restless and unfocused, then chances are we will not have inner peace and, as a result, never be productive.

[6] Mantreswara, *Phaladeepika*, p. 11.

[7] Varahamihira, *Brihat Jataka*, p. 19.

milk, sweet substances, women, bodily health, beauty, heart, understanding, and affluence. The Moon is female and is concerned with the sea.[8]

The Moon represents the personality which reflects the light of the Sun, or inner identity and essence, to the outside world. A watery planet, it promotes frequent changes of feeling, residences, and careers. It is receptive rather than initiating, and symbolizes the mother, the mind, and the body. The Moon is associated with family life, the home and clandestine affairs. Its placement in the horoscope reveals the conditions surrounding infancy and, in a woman's chart, the ability to conceive. An afflicted Moon may cause upset stomachs and frequent vomiting.

If the planet is well-placed there will be love of home and family, sensitivity, and the ability to make changes in one's life with relative ease. If the planet is ill-placed there may be changeability, vacillation, and indulgence with food and alcohol. Diseases are digestive disorders, eye diseases, and mental instability.

Mars (Kuja, or Mangal)

Kuja rules both Aries (Mesha) and Scorpio (Vrischika), the day of the week is Tuesday, the god is Kamara, the gemstone is coral and the color is red. Parts of the body ruled by Mars include the head, external sex organs, left ear, muscular system, blood, uterus, pelvis, and prostate. Professions are hunters, military personnel, dentists, surgeons, butchers, and barbers. Wealth is acquired through metals, battles, gold, cooking, acquisition of land, acts of oppression, and spying. Mars represents strength and the sense that it rules is sight.[9]

Mars has sharp and cruel eyes and a young body, is generous, of bilious nature, of unsteady mind, and has a narrow middle.[10]

---

[8] Mantreswara, *Phaladeepika*, p. 14.
[9] Mantreswara, *Phaladeepika*, p. 12.
[10] Varahamihira, *Brihat Jataka*, p. 19.

Mars has slender waist, curled and shining hair, fierce eyes, is bilious and cruel in nature, red, wrathful but generous. It rules matters pertaining to strength, products from the earth, brothers, war, courage, fire, enemies, attachment to females, mental dignity. It has to do with courage, disease, younger brothers, lands, foes, blood, paternal relations. He is a crook, and an arms bearer, a goldsmith and a thief.[11]

According to the scriptures, Mars is commander-in-chief of the celestial forces. It is a fiery, dry planet noted for both its constructive and destructive energy. As the karaka for siblings, Mars also represents the level of ambition, desires, sexuality, courage, mechanical ability, and physical strength. Mars-dominated people approach life with the utmost enthusiasm and tend to act before thinking. If afflicted, its influence may contribute to impulsiveness, drinking, violence, and aggression.

A well-placed Mars will bring self-confidence, endurance, heroism, strength, courage, combativeness, sharp wit, and a go-ahead spirit. There will also be mental activity and muscular strength, organizational ability, independence, strong determination, ambition, and leadership qualities. If the planet is ill-placed, there will be rashness, loss of temper, foolhardiness, a quarrelsome nature, and impetuousness. Illnesses include measles, mumps, bleeding infections, and a tendency toward colds, fever, and allergies.

Mercury (Budha)

Budha rules Gemini (Mithuna) and Virgo (Kanya), the body part is lungs, the day of the week is Wednesday, the god is Vishnu, the gemstone is emerald, tourmaline, and jade, and the color is green. Parts of the body include the lungs, nervous system, and solar plexus. Professions are salespeople, agents, orators, secretaries, writers, traders, and linguists. Wealth is acquired through poetry, scriptures, clerical work, astrology, Vedas, and mantras. Mercury is speech and the sense it rules is smell.[12]

---

11 Mantreswara, *Phaladeepika*, p. 15.
12 Mantreswara, *Phaladeepika*, p. 12.

Mercury has an impediment in his speech, is fond of joke, and is of a bilious, windy and phlegmatic nature . . .[13]

Mercury is green, full of nerves, pleasant in speech, red and broad eyes, and is fond of fun. It has to do with matters pertaining to learning, eloquence, skill in fine arts, dexterity in speech, maternal uncle, aptness for acquiring knowledge, cleverness and the mechanical arts. It has to do with relatives, discrimination, friends, speech and action. He is a cowhand, learned man, artisan, accountant.[14]

Mercury, the planet of communication, is indicative of one's level of intelligence. The karaka for cousins, it also describes one's speech patterns, restless energy, a tendency to travel, cleverness, and quick-wittedness. According to the scriptures, a good astrologer must have a prominent Mercury in order to understand and communicate the birth chart. There is moodiness and forgetfulness, along with logic, sharpness, and an ability to learn quickly. If this planet is prominent in the chart, there will be frequent short trips, since Mercury-dominated people are quite adaptable to new situations. There is a fondness for the occult sciences, versatility, mathematical and engineering skills.

If the planet is well-placed, there is an inquiring, analytical mind and the ability to grasp ideas quickly. If the planet is ill-placed, there will be lack of concentration, vacillation, and restlessness that must be tempered. There will be cunning, mischievousness, conceit, talkativeness, eccentricities, and general instability. Illnesses may include nervous ailments, eye disease, sore throat, anemia, and itchiness.

Jupiter (Guru, or Brihaspati)

Guru rules Sagittarius (Dhanus) and Pisces (Meena), the day of the week is Thursday, the god is Brahma, the gemstone is yellow sapphire, topaz, amber, and citrine, and the color is yellow. Parts of the body it rules include the thighs, hips, liver, gall bladder, and pancreas. Jupiter's condition will indicate the fat

---

[13] Varahamihira, *Brihat Jataka*, p. 20.
[14] Mantreswara, *Phaladeepika*, p. 15.

content in the body and there may be a tendency toward growths and cysts. Professions include lawyer, teacher, publisher, editor, actor, banker and priest. Wealth is acquired with the help of Brahmins, through morality, religion, or banking. Jupiter is knowledge and health.[15]

> Jupiter has a big body, yellow hairs and eyes, high intellectual powers, and a phlegmatic nature . . .[16]

> Jupiter has body of yellowish hue and eyes and hair are brown, fat and elevated chest, big body, phlegmatic, intelligent and is after wealth. It has to do with knowledge, good qualities, teaching, prosperity, reverence to Gods, wisdom, and conquering of the senses. He is an astrologer, preceptor, minister, important personage and Brahmin. It is genius, wealth, physical development, sons and knowledge. The sense it rules is hearing.[17]

As the largest planet, Jupiter represents the areas of our lives through which we learn and grow. As the karaka of children, it represents anything we acquire which then becomes our possession or asset. Jupiter brings both material and spiritual expansion to whichever house of the horoscope it occupies and typifies the principles of learning, teaching, traveling, religion, the law, and sharing ideas with others. Jupiter represents sociability and affability, as well as the moral, ethical, and religious issues affecting life. There is mobility and a love of honesty and integrity. An emphasized Jupiter endows athletic ability, a love of outdoor sports, adventure and risk-taking.

If the planet is well-placed, there will be judiciousness, steadiness, concentration, and meditation. Knowledge and happiness are easily accessible and there will be benevolence, fruitfulness, and optimism. The disposition will be generous and candid. There is high reasoning ability and proper judgment along with geniality, generosity, joviality, prosperity, and good

---

[15] Mantreswara, *Phaladeepika*, p. 13.

[16] Varahamihira, *Brihat Jataka*, p. 20

[17] Mantreswara, *Phaladeepika*, p. 15.

health. If the planet is ill-placed there will be extremism, liberalism, extravagance, lavishness, overoptimism, carelessness, debts, disputes, speculative failure, religious fanaticism, misjudgment, and miscalculation. Diseases are liver ailments, hip injuries, gallstones, hernia, diabetes, and dermatological problems.

Although Jupiter (Guru) represents the principles of learning and teaching in the birth chart, the literal and more complex definition of the Sanskrit word *guru* is:

> [V]enerable, respectable, person (father, mother, or any relative older than one's self) . . . spiritual parent or preceptor (from whom a youth receives the initiatory Mantra or prayer).[18]

Very simply stated, a guru is one who transmits knowledge.

In the last two decades, many have flocked to India to study certain yogic and/or meditative techniques from skilled practitioners and religious adepts. Many of these yogis and swamis have grown long beards, draped themselves in either flowing robes or thin loincloths, and renounced the material world. Though this attire and attitude toward possessions is quite typical for a man of religion in India, it often creates an ominous and distrustful feeling for Westerners. Furthermore, because of the notoriety that a handful of swamis have received, *gurus* are sometimes associated with these few who cannot possibly convey the sanctity that a religious teacher represents in Indian society.

It is very difficult to convey the concept of *guru* to a Western audience since the idea of finding a teacher or master to whom to devote oneself in exchange for knowledge does not really exist in Western culture. It is more common to attend a university and, in some cases, acquire a special mentor with whom one has a unique one-on-one relationship. Though most often gurus are thought of as being religious masters, they may also be teachers of music, astrology, or any sacred art or science. What does distinguish them, however, from institutional

---

[18] Sir Monier Monier-Williams, *A Sanskrit-English Dictionary* (New Delhi: Motilal Banarsidass, 1974), p. 359.

teachers is the intense relationship cultivated with their disciples, and the way in which their expertise complements their spiritual practice. It is not unusual for the guru to meet students daily for an actual lesson. Instead of monetary payment for the tutelage, students are sometimes called upon to serve their teachers by performing duties ranging from administrative work to preparing tea. Some pupils live with the guru's family and help with the day-to-day running of the household. In addition to receiving traditional instruction, pupils spend as much time in the presence of their teachers in order to observe and, ultimately, absorb the gurus' knowledge. In essence, students are devoted to their teachers and are available to serve them at all times. Their arrangement is comparable to the master/apprentice relationship of feudal times, and is the most intensive and efficient way to become proficient in a chosen field.

It is probably safe to say that the majority of religious teachers, musicians, and astrologers have learned their craft from individual gurus. Both Indian classical music compositions and astrological techniques not included in ancient texts have been orally transmitted through generations and remain a testament to the importance of the guru/student relationship. Even Westerners who study in India regard their teachers as gurus, because they too have been instructed in this unique manner. I, myself, was taught by two gurus, whom I saw every day over a six-month period, and whom I addressed as "Guru-ji," which means "my teacher."

Venus (Sukra)

Sukra rules Taurus (Vrishaba) and Libra (Thula), the day of the week is Friday, the goddess is Lakshmi, the gemstone is diamond and zircon, and the color is "multi-colored." Parts of the body include eyes, reproductive system, skin, throat, chin, cheeks, and kidneys. Professions may include musician, filmmaker, actor, transport worker, jeweler, and tailor. Wealth is acquired through women's merchandise, animals, music and dance, silver, silk, and poetry. Venus represents desires and the sense that it rules is taste.[19]

---

[19] Mantreswara, *Phaladeepika*, p. 13.

Venus leads a comfortable life, has a beautiful body, fair eyes, a windy and phlegmatic nature, and black curling hairs . . .[20]

Venus wears multi-colors, black curled hair, limbs and body are huge, wind and phlegm, green and lovely and broad eyes, and he treasures his virility. It has to do with matters pertaining to clothes, song and dance and music, wife, happiness, flowers, poetry, charming speech and marriage. Venus is a musician, wealthy man, sensualist, merchant, dancer, weaver, peacock. It has to do with wives, vehicles, ornaments, love affairs, pleasure.[21]

Venus is the brightest and most visible star and, because it could clearly be seen rising and setting with the Sun, was commonly called the Morning and Evening Star. This planet represents the capacity for love, passion, enjoyment, and general contentment. It also signifies how many vehicles (cars, boats, etc.) are owned and how much money has been accrued. Kama, the God of Love, and equivalent to Cupid, is always depicted shooting arrows while sitting atop an elephant. The Kama Sutra, the ancient Hindu book illustrating love-making techniques, means "Song of Venus," as *Sutra* means "verse" or "song" and *Kama* is the God of Love.

If the planet is well-placed there will be kindness, amicability, a pleasing personality, good looks, attentiveness, good marriage, generosity, cheerfulness, artistic nature, general success, and popularity. If the planet is ill-placed, there will be sloth, amorousness, extravagance, excessive behavior patterns, and a general lack of emotional control. Diseases are eye infections, ovarian problems, skin eruptions, swellings, and anemia.

Saturn (Sani)

Sani rules Capricorn (Makara) and Aquarius (Kumbha), the day of the week is Saturday, the god is Yama, the gemstones are dark stones like sapphire, onyx, amethyst, lapis lazuli, and the

---

[20] Varahamihira, *Brihat Jataka,* p. 20.
[21] Mantreswara, *Phaladeepika,* p. 16.

color is black. Parts of the body include bones, hair, ears, and teeth. Professions are researchers, scientists, real estate agents, or construction workers. The career may involve working with metal, iron, wool, or leather products. Wealth is acquired through roots and fruits, servants, sculpture, and woods. Saturn represents sorrow and is associated with the sense of touch.[22]

> Saturn is lazy, has eyes of gold color, a thin and tall body, large teeth, stiff hair, and is of a windy nature.[23]

> Saturn is dark, lame, windy in composition, deep eyes with lean, tall body full of arteries and veins, idle and calumniating, governs muscle, cruel and has no pity, dull-headed, large nails, teeth, stiff hair and limbs, dirty and of a slow disposition, fierce and black. It has to do with longevity, death, fear, misery, sickness, misfortune, servitude, captivity and poverty. It defines the period of a person's life, livelihood, cause of death, adversity and servants. Saturn is an oil monger, servant, vile person, blacksmith.[24]

If the planet is well-placed, there will be prudence, frugality, self-control, loyalty and steadfastness, perseverance, industriousness, and remarkable patience. If the planet is ill-placed there will be laziness, lethargy, delays, consolidation, and depression. Illnesses associated with Saturn are arthritis, rheumatism, gallstones, growths, and anything related to weak knees, bones, and teeth.

North Node (Rahu)

Rahu does not rule a sign, but it is said to possess the qualities of Saturn. Its gemstones are agate and hessonite, while professions ruled by Rahu include aviators, physicists, pilots, flight attendants, computer programmers, engineers, and most highly technical fields. Rahu is associated with the nervous system.

---

[22] Mantreswara, *Phaladeepika*, p. 13.
[23] Varahamihira, *Brihat Jataka*, p. 20.
[24] Mantreswara, *Phaladeepika*, p. 16.

> The Dragon's Head is black, tall, has skin disease, is a heretic, speaks falsehoods, is cunning, and is devoid of intellect. Gemstone is agate. Rahu indicates paternal grandfather.[25]

Rahu bestows highly technical skills and talents. It represents materialism, compulsiveness, and intensifies anything with which it comes into contact. Rahu is relentless, highly disciplined, dissatisfied, and, at times, dishonest. If Rahu is well-placed, it will bring power and material success. If the Dragon's Head is poorly situated, there may be greed, ruthlessness and violent behavior. Although Rahu is said to have the same effect as Saturn, I feel that the Dragon's Head acts similarly to the astrological Pluto.

South Node (Kethu)

Just like Rahu, Kethu does not rule a sign but, according to the scriptures, possesses the qualities of Mars. Its gemstones are tiger's eye and turquoise, while professions ruled by Kethu include pharmacist, chemist, priest, researcher, and spiritual healer. Kethu is associated with depression and addictions.

> The Dragon's Tail is red, fierce in look, inhales smoke, has bruised limbs, is lean and malicious. Gemstone is turquoise. Kethu indicates maternal grandfather.[26]

Kethu provides a vivid imagination, spirituality, and escapist tendencies which, in the extreme, can lead to isolation, addiction, and withdrawal from reality. It represents confusion and lack of direction, and can create a conflict for the areas of life it affects. Kethu is dishonest and aimless. If Kethu is well-placed, there will be great sensitivity and compassion. A poorly situated Dragon's Tail, however, will result in an inability to believe in oneself and, at its most extreme, total chaos. Although Kethu is said to have the same effect as Mars, the Dragon's Tail, I believe, behaves similarly to the astrological Neptune.

---

[25] Mantreswara, *Phaladeepika*, p. 16.
[26] Mantreswara, *Phaladeepika*, p. 16.

Table 4.2. Signs of the Zodiac. *

SIGN	RULER	BODY PART	COLOR	DIRECTION	ELEMENT	GENDER	POSITIVE NEGATIVE	FRUITFUL BARREN
Aries	Mars	Head	Red	East	Fire	Masculine	+	Barren
Taurus	Venus	Face	White	South	Earth	Feminine	–	Semi-fruitful
Gemini	Mercury	Arms	Green	West	Air	Masculine	+	Barren
Cancer	Moon	Heart	Pink	North	Water	Feminine	–	Fruitful
Leo	Sun	Stomach	Brown	East	Fire	Masculine	+	Barren
Virgo	Mercury	Hips	Gray	South	Earth	Feminine	–	Barren
Libra	Venus	Abdomen	Multi-colored	West	Air	Masculine	+	Semi-fruitful
Scorpio	Mars	Genitals	Black	North	Water	Feminine	–	Fruitful
Sagittarius	Jupiter	Thighs	Gold	East	Fire	Masculine	+	Semi-fruitful
Capricorn	Saturn	Knees	Yellow	South	Earth	Feminine	–	Barren
Aquarius	Saturn	Ankles	Brown	West	Air	Masculine	+	Barren
Pisces	Jupiter	Feet	White	North	Water	Feminine	–	Fruitful

*Information compiled from *Brihat Jataka*, *Phaladeepika*, and *Saravali*.

The Moon's Nodes do not rule signs and, therefore, can never rule a house. However, they take on the qualities of the planets with which they are associated by aspect, as well as the dispositor, the ruler of the sign in which the Node is placed. Therefore, if Rahu or Kethu is placed in Capricorn, its dispositor will be Saturn.

Rasis (Signs of the Zodiac)

The zodiacal sign, or Rasi, that each planet occupies illustrates the energy which that planet may express. Most importantly, the meaning of each house of the Rasi Chakra is colored by the zodiacal sign occupying that particular house and its planetary ruler (see Table 4.2). The following are general descriptions of the twelve zodiacal signs and may be applied to people whose Ascendant matches that particular sign.[27] Because the signs are not described in the scriptures in great detail, these descriptions are greatly influenced by Western texts.

Aries (Mesha)

Aries (Mesha) is symbolized by a ram which is by nature rash, combative, lascivious, springy, and hardy. With Mars ruling this sign, people born under the sign of Aries are active, ambitious, bold, confident, courageous, and impulsive. Arians are always challenged and, once they have achieved their goals, they move on to the next project. They possess a childlike naiveté and Arians must learn to cultivate patience and to think before they act. They have an abundant amount of physical vitality which should never be suppressed. If it is not released, this energy is likely to emerge as aggression, anger, and hostility.

Taurus (Vrishaba)

Depicted by the fierce and determined bull, Taureans are productive, persevering, stubborn, and are always trying to con-

---

[27] It is customary in the West to identify ourselves by our Sun sign, whereas in India, one is identified by the Lagna, or Ascendant, of the chart.

vince others that their views are correct. Venus, the ruler of Taurus, endows these people with kindness, patience, charm, and a fondness and talent for the arts and the "finer" things in life. They are sensual, extremely passionate, possessive, and jealous. They are straightforward and direct and, as opposed to the previous sign of Aries, ponder for a long time before making a decision. Once they have a goal in mind, however, they are almost obsessive about attaining it. They are even-tempered and, while it takes some time before anger is ignited, their tempers can be vile and difficult to control. The accumulation of wealth is a major preoccupation and Taureans are either extremely well-off or notoriously wasteful. With difficult aspects, they may be inflexible, slow, lazy, and overly indulgent by overeating or spending too much money.

Gemini (Mithuna)

Signified by the symbol of the twins, the dual nature of Gemini appears in their versatility, restlessness, and need to be involved simultaneously in more than one project. As a Mercury-ruled air sign, Gemini rules communications and mental energy. Boredom is their worst enemy and they always seem to be searching for intellectual stimulation and other people to engage in conversation. They often play the devil's advocate for the sole purpose of stirring up a discourse and a debate. Gemini natives are adaptable, extremely intelligent, mechanical, and quick-witted. There is an inability to concentrate, and a constant need for instant gratification which may cause them to give up rather easily. With difficult aspects they can be too scattered, restless, and insensitive.

Cancer (Kataka)

This sign is symbolized by a crab. The ruling planet, the Moon, provides Cancerians with a fertile imagination, an emotional disposition, and a tendency toward moodiness and introversion. They are drawn to artistic media and they are extremely retentive. Due to extreme sensitivity, there may be nervous irritability and, at times, meaningless chatter which compensates for their general insecurity and shyness. They are sentimental, but their personalities are extremely changeable, ranging from extreme warmth to secrecy which is often mistaken for coldness. Cancerians need to feel safe and secure, and sometimes go through their entire lives searching for family and the comforts of home. With difficult aspects, they can be quick-tempered, irritable, and dishonest.

Leo (Simha)

Represented by the lion, king of the jungle, Leos must be in control of their lives at all times. They do not like working for others and everything they do must have their personal stamp. Because Leo represents one of the most generous and magnanimous signs of the zodiac, they make wonderful hosts and hostesses. In addition to being constructive and inventive, Leos are good organizers, directors, and "ideas persons" who leave the detailed and technical work to others. They enjoy being admired and praised for their accomplishments and desperately need the approval of others. Difficult aspects sometimes make them too demanding, too authoritative, and too egotistical to concern themselves with the needs and opinions of others.

Virgo (Kanya)

Signified by the virgin, Virgos search for purity through cleanliness, good health, proper diet, and exercise. They are sensitive, reserved, self-conscious, critical, and fastidious. Ruled by restless Mercury, Virgos are prone to change, whether it be through multiple residences, jobs, or points of view. They are conscientious and methodical workers, capable of functioning under any adversity and also make excellent secretaries, organizers, and editors. Virgos can be very insecure and reserved, qualities which may be interpreted as lack of warmth and good will. Because they are perfectionists, they are often dissatisfied and too critical of themselves as well as others. With difficult aspects, Virgos tend to have a pessimistic outlook on life, spending too much time analyzing and worrying, which may adversely affect their health.

Libra (Thula)

Libra is symbolized by the balancing scales of justice, indicating their love of fairness and harmony. With Venus ruling this sign, Librans are adverse to arguments and are always gentle, soft-spoken, modest, and courteous. They like beautiful objects and, like Venus-ruled Taureans, enjoy luxuries, having a good time, and patronizing the arts. Librans are not particularly self-motivated, do not like being alone, and can be much too preoccupied with finding a marriage partner. In fact, relationships usually direct the course of their lives. They have a difficult time making decisions and can be lazy, excessive with drugs and alcohol, and especially indulgent where affairs of the heart are concerned. With difficult aspects, too much emphasis is placed on appearances and very often Librans will adjust their personalities to suit their present partners.

Scorpio (Vrischika)

Scorpios are tireless workers, as well as incredible extremists. They work hard—sometimes too hard—trying to control their emotions. They know that admitting their true feelings means that, in addition to expressing love, they must also confront the accompanying jealousy, pain, and anger. Scorpios are amazing workaholics and the more challenges they accept, the more outlets they will have for all their energy. They are extremely determined, business-oriented, and possess a fertile imagination and sharp intelligence. Their need to communicate and form relationships is expressed not only through business dealings but through their sometimes insatiable sexuality. They have deep intuition, powerful emotions, and extremely high standards which they set for themselves and others. With difficult aspects, they can be ruthless and relentless in achieving their goals. To this end, there is a self-destructive tendency which can result in alcohol and drug abuse.

Sagittarius (Dhanus)

Sagittarius is symbolized by the centaur—half horse and half man—who is always pictured shooting his idealistic arrows into the air. Eternally optimistic and hopeful about the future, Sagittarians try to persuade others to develop this same attitude. They are always searching for the key to knowledge and happiness without working too hard to attain them, have very high principles, and are sometimes frank to the point of being painfully brutal. They have a joy and enthusiasm for life and a love of sports, traveling to foreign countries, learning, and teaching. These people enjoy meeting foreigners and very often live abroad or marry foreigners. There is interest in pursuing higher degrees in religion, philosophy, or the law. With difficult aspects they can be arrogant, bossy, and terribly indulgent with food and alcohol, especially when attending social functions (which they rarely miss).

Capricorn (Makara)

In accordance with their symbol, the mountain goat climbing up the peak of success, Capricorns have immense organizational skills and an overwhelming desire and ability to achieve goals at any cost. Whatever Capricorns set out to do will be followed through to completion, despite any obstacles encountered along the way. They are economical, frugal, cautious, and very rarely proceed without planning in advance. They are good and loyal friends, honest, upright, and persevering to a fault, without ever complaining. These people are faithful and extremely good providers, but need secure homes to which they can always return and reflect upon their busy lives. They are born leaders and possess great executive abilities. Capricorns can be extremely disciplined and calculating to the point of ruthlessness. They are very reserved and usually speak only when they have something important to say. Some people mistake the Capricornian reserve for coldness and insensitivity. For Capricorns, however, it is a way to pursue their goals without allowing extraneous emotions to deter them. Difficult aspects make them pessimistic, depressive, shy, uncommunicative, and ruthless.

Aquarius (Kumbha)

Aquarius, an air sign, is often mistaken for a water sign, since it is symbolized by the angel carrying the water of humanity and pouring it over the Earth. The element air represents the desire to communicate brotherhood and freedom to the rest of the world. Aquarians have inventive minds and are always seeking innovative projects in which they may become involved. They are very socially conscious and are identified with groups fighting social and political injustices. Interests range from technology to astrology to social work. They love meeting new people with whom they can exchange ideas and always enjoy surrounding themselves with others dedicated to the same causes. They have difficulty being intimate with one person because of their involvement with groups and causes. Other problems include a highly strung nature, day-to-day impatience, and an inflexibility to change habits and patterns which would put their lives on a more even keel.

Pisces (Meena)

Symbolized by two fish swimming in opposite directions, there is honesty, love of the arts, and an incredible empathy and compassion toward people. Pisceans lean toward cultivating a spiritual life or living abroad. They have vivid imaginations and relate to the world through their feelings and instincts. Pisceans are sometimes incapable of making a decision due to a lack of faith in their own judgment. They do not always express themselves clearly but are willing to help other people at a moment's notice. At times, Pisceans live in a world of their own creation and have difficulty facing reality. Because of this, they are sometimes withdrawn and moody. Their lack of clarity makes them difficult to understand but they are, nonetheless, extremely sensitive and incapable of hurting others. If they have hurt someone's feelings, they tend to feel guilt and remorse. With difficult aspects, there is a lack of confidence, dishonesty and self-destructive tendencies leading to either overeating or drug and alcohol abuse.

Houses (Bhavas)

One of the most important elements of the horoscope is the zodiacal house or *bhava*. In Sanskrit, the word *bhava* means
"state of being." The 1st, 5th, and 9th are Dharma (action)
houses; the 2nd, 6th, and 10th are Artha (wealth) houses; the
3rd, 7th, and 11th are Kama (desire) houses; and the 4th, 8th,
and 12th are Moksha (liberation) houses. In addition to representing twelve different areas of life, the houses are also categorized according to their auspicious or inauspicious natures. The
most beneficial houses in the zodiac are the 1st, 5th, and 9th,
or Trikona, houses. Any planet placed in, or ruling, the 1st, 5th
or 9th house, will be beneficially influenced. Also auspicious
are the angular 1st, 4th, 7th and 10th houses, known as
Kendra houses. The 1st house is classified as both a Kendra and
Trikona. The 6th, 8th, and 12th houses are inauspicious
Dusthana houses and the 3rd, 6th, 10th and 11th are Upachaya, or growth, houses. (Chapter 6 will describe how planets become either benefic or malefic, depending on the house
they rule and the house in which they are placed.)

In addition to the areas of life represented by each house, I
have included the karakas (planets whose meaning are shared
with particular houses) and the parts of the body each house
rules. Corresponding with the zodiacal signs, the Ascendant,
like the first sign, rules the head, with each sign/house sequentially ruling the anatomy from the head to the feet. It is interesting to note that Cancer and the 4th house rule the heart,
while Leo and the 5th house rule the stomach. Conversely, in
Western astrology, Cancer and the 4th house rule the stomach,
while Leo and the 5th house rule the heart.

1st House (Ascendant or Lagna)
(Body, Fame, Limbs, General Appearance, Head)[28]

The sign occupying the 1st house is also the sign of the Lagna
(or Ascendant) and defines the mood of the entire horoscope. It
describes the type of birth and entry into life. The 1st house de-

---

[28] Mantreswara, *Phaladeepika*, p. 6.

fines infancy, moral character, appearance, temperament, and confidence. The Lagna also describes how one is viewed by others and describes one's general outlook on life. Planets occupying the 1st house will be quite evident by one's personality and sense of destiny. Health and general constitution are evaluated through the parts of the anatomy ruled by the sign of the Ascendant. The body parts corresponding to the 1st house are the brain and the head. The karaka is the Sun, since they both represent ambition, confidence, and direction in life.

2nd House
(Family Wealth, Right Eye,
Speech, Truthfulness, Learning, Face)[29]

The 2nd house deals with how one earns and spends money, property, accumulation of assets, indulgences, appetites, and the food one likes. The 2nd house also describes learning abilities (and disabilities), the way in which one learns, early childhood experiences, primary education and the quality of one's speech. Since the 2nd house rules truth and imagination, benefic planets placed there provide originality and inventiveness. Malefic planets connected with the 2nd house might give an overactive imagination, or at its most extreme, a propensity for lying. Parts of the anatomy connected with the 2nd house are face, nose, mouth, neck, and right eye. Malefics in the 2nd house may cause extreme nearsightedness and an inability to concentrate. The karaka of the 2nd house is Jupiter, since that planet has to do with indulgence as well as accumulation of wealth.

The 2nd and 7th houses are considered to be *maraka*, or death-inflicting, houses. Planets ruling or occupying these houses represent death, or termination, of one stage of life. During the planetary periods of these planets, one may experience certain obstacles, the death of someone close, or a change from one way of life to another. It is, however, a mistake to try to time death as occurring during one of these maraka periods without observing other influences.

---

[29] Mantreswara, *Phaladeepika*, p. 6.

3rd House
(Brothers, Bravery, Meals, Right Ear, Courage, Breast)[30]

The 3rd house relates to one's travels, level of courage, desires, the creative arts, film, and photography.[31] Benefic planets situated here may make one a talented artist, but malefic planets will provide the ambition to nurture these talents. If the ruler of the 3rd house is well-placed in the horoscope, then one's inner desires will be fulfilled. Defined as the house of courage, it determines whether one may or may not embark on adventurous journeys in the course of one's life. Bill Clinton has Mars, the ruler of his 3rd house, placed in the 1st house—a good combination for publicly fulfilling one's greatest aims in life. This house indicates the nature of the general relationship with brothers and sisters. It also defines the nature of the younger siblings. Parts of the body ruled by this house include the hands, arms, right ear, lungs, and shoulders. The karaka of the 3rd house is Mars, since this planet also indicates courage, desires, and siblings.

4th House
(Relations, Education, Mother, House, Land, Comfort, Sister's Son, Maternal Uncle, Heart)[32]

It is the house of the mother, family, the domestic environment, property, real estate, inheritances, vehicles, the level of one's education, retirement, and the conditions of the latter part of one's life. The 4th house is generally the indicator of personal contentment and happiness. If this house is well-aspected, the individual may have had a loving, stable family, may be a home or land owner, and quite fortunate speculating in or acquiring real estate. If the 4th house is afflicted, there may be housing problems, an unstable family, and generally morose disposition. Parts of the body ruled by the 4th house are the heart, the

---

[30] Mantreswara, *Phaladeepika*, p. 7.

[31] Obviously, these were not mentioned in the scriptures. However, it is agreed by most astrologers that film and photography could be added to music, dance, and poetry, which all come under the auspices of the 3rd house.

[32] Mantreswara, *Phaladeepika*, p. 7.

chest, and the breasts. The karakas of the 4th house are Venus, since that planet is the indicator of vehicles and general happiness, and the Moon, which rules over the mother, home, and family.

5th House
(Offspring, Intelligence, Previous Karma, Vedic Knowledge, Entertainment, Education, Belly)[33]

The 5th house is concerned with the level of one's intelligence, children, creative and pleasurable pursuits, speculation, taxes, and, like the 4th house, the level of education. An examination of this house also reveals the good deeds which have been earned in previous lives. A well-aspected 5th house is indicative of someone with a great deal of religious, spiritual, and philosophical knowledge. Since the 5th house is associated with pleasure, it represents love affairs as opposed to marriage and committed relationships which are the domain of the 7th house. Parts of the body ruled by the 5th house are the stomach and the solar plexus. The karaka of the 5th house is Jupiter as the indicator of children, and speculation.

6th House
(Enemies, Kinsmen, Diseases, Humiliation, Debt, Anxiety, Servants, Hip)[34]

The condition of the 6th house will affect work habits, litigation, obstacles, health, and the propensity for serving and helping others. This house relates to cousins, nieces, nephews, aunts, and uncles, as well as employees and colleagues. The 6th house also describes "open enemies," which may encompass disagreements (usually on a professional level) with competitors, opposing parties in a lawsuit, and even a spouse or friend with whom one does not see eye to eye. Whereas the general constitution is indicated by the 1st house, the type of illness or vulnerable part of the anatomy is signified by the correspond-

---

[33] Mantreswara, *Phaladeepika*, p. 7.
[34] Mantreswara, *Phaladeepika*, p. 7.

ing body part or organ of the planet ruling or occupying the 6th house. Possible health crises may flare up during the planetary period ruled by the planets ruling or occupying the 6th house. Parts of the body ruled by the 6th house are lower back, navel, and hips. The karakas of the 6th house are Saturn, since it is associated with work and discipline, and Mars, as it rules arguments and adversaries.

7th House
(Wife or Husband, Generosity, Respect, Desire, Passion, Groin)[35]

Although the 7th house is primarily used to examine the type of partner for which one is most suited and the quality of the marriage itself, this area of the chart describes partnerships and relationships of any type, including business and legal. It is also used to demarcate the level of passion, desire, jealousy, and respect. The 7th house also indicates residence and travel abroad since it is the home (4th house) away from home (4th house). Like the 2nd house, the 7th house is also regarded as a maraka, or death-inflicting, house. Parts of the body ruled by the 7th house are intestines, abdomen, kidneys, and veins. The karaka of the 7th house is Venus, as it also indicates desires and marriage partner. Although Jupiter traditionally represents the husband in a female's chart, and Venus signifies the wife in a male's chart, Venus can be used for both sexes, since it is the general indicator of love.

8th House
(Duration of Life, Death, Mental Pain, Sorrow, Obstacles, Sexual Organs)[36]

The 8th house is the house of obstacles, accidents, and chronic illness, as opposed to the 6th house which indicates acute, or sudden onset of, illness. This area defines one's physical, sexual, and emotional well-being and a careful examination of this

---

[35] Mantreswara, *Phaladeepika*, p. 7.
[36] Mantreswara, *Phaladeepika*, p. 8.

house determines indications for longevity, sexual drive, depression, and general circumstances one experiences throughout life. As the 2nd (financial) house from the 7th (partnership) house, the 8th house is indicative of the marriage partner's financial capacity, as well as any money, windfalls, partnerships, insurance proceeds, inheritances, or lawsuit settlements. The 8th house represents the reproductive organs. The karaka of the 8th house is Saturn, since it rules longevity.

9th House
(Deeds of Virtue, Father, Medicine, Anything Auspicious, Luck, Worship, Duty, Fortune, Thighs)[37]

The 9th house indicates the nature of the father, higher education, and the way personal philosophy and/or religion affects our approach to life. It brings auspicious and "lucky" circumstances which occur due to the actions taken in a former lifetime. This house has to do with foreign travel, higher education, and whether or not an appropriate teacher or "guru" will be found. A well-aspected 9th house will provide the circumstances conducive for finding the right school, instructor, or mentor. If this house is not well-aspected or contains malefic planets, the individual may be self-educated, even arrogant, and less likely to listen to the opinions of, or accept the teachings of, others. Parts of the body ruled by the 9th house are the hips and thighs. The karaka of the 9th house are the Sun, since it is the indicator of the father, and Jupiter, which has to do with the quest for knowledge, religion, and good fortune.

10th House
(Vocation, Knowledge, Clothes, Honor, Occupation, Commerce, Knees)[38]

The 10th house points out the type of profession we gravitate toward and whether we will be successful at it or not. It also has to do with our status and the way in which we are viewed

---

[37] Mantreswara, *Phaladeepika*, p. 8.
[38] Mantreswara, *Phaladeepika*, p. 9.

by the public. Since it is the 7th (partnership) house from the 4th (mother) house, the 10th house is, in addition to the 9th, the indicator of father, especially his finances, since it is also the 2nd house (finances) from the 9th (father). To that end, it also represents the mother's second marriage. Whereas the 9th house stands for the character and individuality of the father, the 10th house signifies his status and earning capacity. Parts of the body ruled by the 10th house are the knees or skeletal system. The karakas of the 10th house are Mercury, since it rules one's reputation, and the Sun, as it represents ambition.

11th House
(Income, Fulfillment, Eldest Brother, Good News, Earnings, Left Ear, Calves, Result of Capabilities, Legs and Ankles)[39]

The 11th house shows us how we relate to groups of people, our friendships, community participation, and what we gain in life. Since it is the 2nd house from the 10th house (profession), it shows us our profits or that which we earn from our work. While this is mostly understood in monetary terms, it may also indicate popularity or other fringe benefits which we accrue from our position. It also represents our hopes, goals, and the ability to fulfill ambitions. Parts of the body ruled by the 11th house are the left ear, calves, legs, and ankles. The karaka of the 11th house is Jupiter, which is an indicator of financial gain.

12th House
(Loss, Bad Deeds, Travels, Misery, Left Eye, Feet)[40]

The 12th house is indicative of our expenditures and that which is beyond our personal control. On the positive side, it represents spirituality, lack of material needs, and residence in a foreign country, since it is the 9th house (foreign travels) from the 4th house (home). This house also refers to anything one

---

[39] Mantreswara, *Phaladeepika*, p. 9.
[40] Mantreswara, *Phaladeepika*, p. 9.

must do in solitude, such as research, practicing meditative techniques, praying, reading, or simply enjoying one's own space. On the negative side, it is a house traditionally related to isolation, imprisonment, limitations, and the inability to communicate with others. The 12th house has to do with financial loss and "secret enemies," i.e., people who may be a threat both personally and professionally. On the other hand, it may simply refer to self-destructive tendencies and addictions since we are our own worst enemies. Wherever the 12th-house ruler is placed is an area of struggle and, at times, loss. If the house is well-aspected it grants the ability to save and be generous with our earnings; if it is poorly aspected, we may be wasteful and spend money foolishly. Parts of the body ruled by the 12th house are the left eye and the feet. The karaka of the 12th house is Saturn, since it rules sorrow and isolation.

• • •

The categories and associations of the signs and planets listed in Tables 4.1 (page 66) and 4.2 (page 78) are utilized as interpretive aids. For instance, in India, medical astrology is a very specialized field used by astrologers, physicians, and healers. To learn about a person's health, we generally look to the zodiacal signs found on the Ascendant and the 6th house with their corresponding planetary rulers. The anatomical part or organ associated with that sign or planet is a vulnerable area of the body and may flare up during that planet's *dasa*, or period. The horoscope is also used by the Ayurvedic physician to assess which physical type an individual may be by viewing if the planets and signs influencing the Lagna are primarily pitta (bilious), vata (windy), or kapha (phlegmatic). In general, the Sun and Mars are pitta, Mercury, Venus and Saturn are vata, and the Moon and Jupiter are kapha.

If the planet signifying health is well-placed in the chart, then this will usually not present a serious problem. If that sign or planet, however, is exceptionally weak in the context of the birth chart, the astrologer may prescribe corresponding gemstones to be worn as an amulet or placed on an altar. A stone is said to have certain qualities which may improve the state of the afflicted planet and provide general protection before a crisis arises. The planet's color is compatible with the gemstone it rules and indicates the flower to be placed on the altar. The astrologer will also recommend certain *mantras* (Sanskrit for "sacred song") and prayers directed to the afflicted planet's corresponding god or goddess on a certain day of the week and hour of the day. Each planet is also affiliated with a different place or room in the house. This factor is utilized to establish the best place to live or to recover lost articles when doing Prashna, or Horary Astrology.

At first glance, these healing rituals may seem somewhat strange, but it is typical in many cultures or religions to pray to God at a time of crisis. Because Hinduism is a polytheistic culture, the prayers are simply directed to a particular deity, determined partially by one's region and partially by the contents of the horoscope. As for gemstones, there are many people throughout the world who will attest to the fact that stones contain physical properties which restore vitality, alleviate migraines, and even calm the nervous system. Wearing an amulet may give the person a feeling of being helped, thus restoring confidence and vitality. For this reason alone, the astrologer may recommend wearing one.

The direction associated with the sign of the Ascendant or Moon when a journey begins is important so the astrologer can ascertain whether a journey will be beneficial. For example, if the Moon is in the sign of Aries at the moment a journey commences, the trip will be forecast as successful because Aries is an auspicious sign for beginnings.[41] Direction is also an important consideration when advising about marriage; the sign which is contained in the 7th house signifies the direction (from the client's birthplace) from which the astrologer advises to seek a prospective marriage partner.

According to *Phaladeepika*, a woman's ability to conceive is determined by whether the signs occupying the 5th and 7th houses of the Rasi Chakra and the Chandra Lagna (Moon chart) are fruitful, semi-fruitful or barren (see Table 4.1, page 66). If there are fruitful or semi-fruitful signs occupying these houses, there is a greater likelihood of conception. If, however,

---

[41] Kalyana Varma, *Saravali* (New Delhi: Ranjan Publications, 1983), p. 35.

barren signs rule these houses, the astrologer may predict difficulty in conceiving or, in extreme cases, childlessness. Because of the availability of birth control and fertilization methods, it is very difficult to determine fertility. A woman whose chart may have originally indicated that she would have a certain number of children may have fewer children or none at all. Conversely, fertilization techniques may provide the birth of children when it was thought that none would be possible.

Using the aforementioned definitions of the planets, signs, and houses, the following chapters illustrate the actual steps involved in interpreting the Rasi Chakra according to the rules laid out in the scriptures. In the end, however, judgment is always left to the discretion, analytical skills, and intuitive ability of the individual astrologer.

ASCENDANT COMBINATIONS

SINCE JYOTISH EMPLOYS A whole-sign house system, each of the twelve Ascendants can only produce one combination of zodiacal signs which occupy the twelve houses of a chart. What follows, therefore, are 144 delineations of each sign when it occupies a particular house. It is important to note that descriptions are very general and will be modified by the planets which occupy and rule that house.

The characterization of the Libra Ascendant can be read with reference to Annemarie's chart, and the Taurus Ascendant can be examined in light of Barbara's horoscope. It is also important to remember that the classifications of individuals as "Arians," "Taureans," etc. refer to their Ascendants and not to their Sun signs.

Mesha (Aries) Lagna

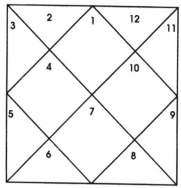 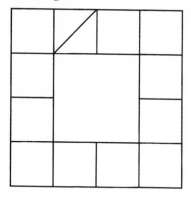

Figure 5.1. Mesha (Aries) Lagna.

Round eyes, weak knees, passionate, afraid of the water, eats sparingly, longs for women, uses his legs, fickle, speaks falsehoods . . .[1]

---

[1] Mantreswara, *Phaladeepika* (Bangalore: K. Subrahmanyam, 1981), p. 124.

People born under this sign are of middle stature. They possess a lean and muscular body and are neither stout nor thick. Their complexion will be ruddy and they will have a fairly long neck and face. Their head will be broad at the temples and narrow at the chin. They have bushy eyebrows, eyes gray to grayish brown with sharp sight. Their hair will be wiry, color varying from dark to sandy.[2]

Health is indicated by the 1st and 6th houses. The influence of Mars, the fighter, provides Arians with overall good health and resistance to infections. They are, however, prone to colds, fevers, and headaches, which may be due to overexertion and intense activities. Since their enthusiasm is boundless, the result could be either limitless energy or total exhaustion.

Their approach to life is usually impulsive with a tendency to act first and think later. Arians become restless and bored quite easily; to this end, they must learn to finish projects that they begin before they lose interest. Though they often view everything from the perspective of their own experiences, their egocentricity stems from childlike innocence rather than from any type of vindictiveness. Arians are considered by their friends to be good-natured and generous.

Taurus Occupying the 2nd House. With Venus-ruled Taurus occupying the 2nd house, Arians are obsessed with finances, possessions, and the attainment of financial security. They are usually economically well-established and enjoy accumulating works of art and other collectibles. Though they may be considered extravagant by some, their plans for the future almost always include wise investments and savings accounts. Rather than learn intellectually, Arians are usually gifted with creative talents.

Gemini Occupying the 3rd House. The ability to communicate and utilize one's mind in a clever, witty, yet analytical fashion is at a high premium with Mercury-ruled Gemini occupying the

---

[2] K.S. Krishnamurti, *Fundamental Principles of Astrology* (Madras: Mahabala, 1971), p. 73.

3rd house. The relationship with the younger sibling who may be extremely intellectual, adept in business, or high-strung, may have its ups and downs. Arians are usually excellent speakers and inventive storytellers. Their need to incessantly chatter shortens their attention span, making it difficult for them to listen to others. Since they love to be on the move, their residences and jobs may change frequently.

Cancer Occupying the 4th House. A description of the mother, attitudes toward home, and the level of contentment are all reflected by the 4th house. When Moon-ruled Cancer occupies this house, the mother may have been traditional and loving, but overbearing and domineering. Nonetheless, close-knit family ties are responsible for making Arians attentive but often controlling parents—similar to their own mothers. They may be moody and their search for happiness will have its ups and downs. In fact, the quest for domestic tranquility and compatible partners will oftentimes be all-consuming.

Leo Occupying the 5th House. Due to the barren quality of Aries and Leo, as well as their artistic, fiery temperaments, these individuals may postpone having children. If and when they do decide to parent, they may have difficulty extending quality time during their children's formative years. With the right balance of discipline and encouragement, their children will be creative, academically productive, and a continual source of pride. Arians are extremely passionate and sensual. They enjoy the theater, concerts, and movies. They are also extremely sports-minded and love to indulge in physical activities.

Virgo Occupying the 6th House. Since Mercury rules the 6th house, Arians are often high-strung and may have unstable job histories. They are happy being self-employed since working for others often creates conflicts and problems with authority figures. Unless anger is given a proper outlet, an inability to handle stress and pressure may predispose them to ulcers. In addition to stomach problems, the influence of Virgo may cause sensitive digestive systems and intestinal complaints. To increase resistance to illness, Arians require a great deal of physical activity, fresh air, and a diet consisting largely of fruit, vegetables, and water to cleanse their systems.

Libra Occupying the 7th House. As the ruler of the 7th house, Venus represents the type of partner Arians desire: beautiful, charming, sensual, sophisticated, and, above all, devoted. However, Arians are also extremely jealous since their partners are also attractive to others. Spouses are, for the most part, passionate and share the Arian's material outlook on life.

Scorpio Occupying the 8th House. Since Mars is the ruler of the 8th house, impulsiveness and hasty decision-making may cause Arians to spend and invest money rather foolishly. This placement may also be detrimental to the partners' finances. Arians are short-term thinkers rather than long-term planners. They can be emotional, argumentative, hot-tempered, and highly sexual.

Sagittarius Occupying the 9th House. As ruler of the 9th house, Jupiter describes the father as well-educated, religious, magnanimous, and fair-minded. He may also be fun-loving, social, and indulgent. Arians are ethical, spiritual, enjoy traveling and are interested in learning languages. A relentless pursuit of knowledge motivates their actions and they will usually be successful finding a teacher under the right set of circumstances. They love debating, often playing devil's advocate to argue the opposite point of view. They are prone to exaggeration and, due to their eloquence, are good performers and public speakers.

Capricorn Occupying the 10th House. Organizational skills and a drive to succeed are among Arians' most positive qualities. Despite obstacles and a slow start, Arians work hard and are committed to long-term objectives, thus attaining their goals. On a professional level, they may gravitate towards the sciences, research, academia, metallurgy, sculpture, or anything requiring form, structure, and discipline. Professions represented by Capricorn include managers, directors, administrators, and positions which require practical and leadership skills and the potential for advancement.

Aquarius Occupying the 11th House. Social and open-minded Arians are quite selective when choosing friends and colleagues. With Saturn ruling this house, friendships will be taken quite seriously with people who are responsible and loyal, and who uphold generally high standards. In fact, Arians tend to be too judgmental and hard on others. As ruler of the house of profits, Saturn breeds the ability to yield the financial rewards of hard work. The house which Saturn occupies and how it is aspected will indicate the source of income and whether it can be obtained effortlessly or with great difficulty.

Pisces Occupying the 12th House. There will be a tendency for Arians to spend time alone in order to explore their more religious and silent sides. They usually spend extravagantly (including contributions to worthwhile causes), and tend to be more indulgent than they should. With Taurus occupying the 2nd house, however, funds are usually replenished.

Vrishaba (Taurus) Lagna

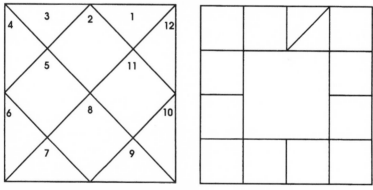

Figure 5.2. Vrishaba (Taurus) Lagna.

Broad thighs, big face, agriculture, happy in middle and end of life, fond of women, forgiving disposition, hardships, cattle, marks or moles on back, face and sides . . .[3]

---

[3] Mantreswara, *Phaladeepika*, p. 124.

The stature will be middle, body is plump, forehead is broad, neck is thick and stout. Eyes are bright, hair dark and complexion is clear. They are solidly built and are stocky with big shoulders and well-developed muscles.[4]

Since Venus rules the two houses associated with health—the 1st and the 6th—Taureans may feel the effects of self-indulgence, especially overeating and overspending. They may have difficulties with their thyroids, and are prone to sore throats, stiff necks, swollen glands, poor eyesight, and bad skin. When ill, they prefer to suffer in silence. Taureans are very good listeners who usually do not speak unless they have something important to say. They are patient, persevering, and extremely loyal to their families, friends, and colleagues. Taureans are sensual, passionate, and faithful, as well as jealous and possessive. Although Taureans are basically even-tempered, once the temper is ignited, they become bulls (after whom they are named) and "see red." Taureans are amazingly productive, relentless to the point of obsession, inflexible, and controlling. When things do not go according to plan, they find it difficult to readjust.

Gemini Occupying the 2nd House. Since restless Mercury rules the 2nd house, the state of Taureans' finances are perpetually fluctuating. Some of the "down" periods may stem from unwise investments, frivolous spending, and unexpected job changes. Frugality and a sensible attitude toward money, however, usually steer them back on track. Due to the rulership of the 2nd house over early education, Mercury brings intelligence, talkativeness, and an inability to concentrate due to nervous energy.

Cancer Occupying the 3rd House. The collective and associative quality of Moon-ruled Cancer, which rules the 3rd house of communications, contributes to the Taureans' retentive memory. They perceive the world in terms of images and colors and are, therefore, often accomplished musicians and painters.

---

[4] K.S. Krishnamurti, *Fundamental Principles of Astrology*, p. 78.

They are not lucid speakers, however, and prefer to listen and reflect rather than direct the conversation.

Leo Occupying the 4th House. Because Taureans may have spent so much time alone as children, they were able to develop artistic hobbies and talents. They are usually stern parents and their attitudes toward their children reflect how they were treated as youngsters. Taureans take great pride in their homes and their furnishings reflect the Leonine penchant for luxury, ornateness and extravagance. They act as though they are lords and ladies of the manor. Children are taught to respect their surroundings and regard their homes in the same manner.

Virgo Occupying the 5th House. Mercury, the ruler of the fifth house, causes changeability in relationships, often leading to insecurity and a cynical attitude toward love and partnerships. Since Virgo is considered to be a "barren" sign, many Taureans consciously choose not to have children. There may be difficulties conceiving or there may be children later in life. Impulsive spending, hasty investments and gambling should be avoided since Mercury rules both this house and the 2nd house of finances.

Libra Occupying the 6th House. Since Venus rules the 6th house, Taureans need absolute harmony in their work environment and good relationships with their colleagues. They enjoy work which involves dealing with the public, such as advertising, sales, distribution, representation, or the service professions. As far as health is concerned, a tendency toward overindulgence may cause problems with the eyes, skin, kidneys (ruled by Venus), or with their abdomens (ruled by Libra).

Scorpio Occupying the 7th House. In describing the partner, Mars-ruled Scorpio typifies people who are not only passionate, sensual, and emotional, but argumentative and jealous. Taureans are likely to marry more than once and their unions are always challenging and marked by crises. They can learn from their mistakes by cultivating more successful channels of communication with their spouses.

Sagittarius Occupying the 8th House. Jupiter rules the 8th house which pertains to legacies and the finances of others, especially those of the spouse. Because Jupiter is the "greater benefic," it is very likely that Taureans will inherit money at some time in their lives. Hindu astrological scriptures attribute this likelihood to the fact that "they command the good will and sincere affection of their relatives." Additionally, this is an excellent placement for business, but one must caution against extravagance and hasty decision making.

Capricorn Occupying the 9th House. Taureans have a conservative philosophy of life which is reflected in what is often perceived as inflexible behavior. The father may have been deeply religious, a strict disciplinarian, or someone who instilled the meaning of hard work and responsibility in his children. Because they are patient and have the need to communicate ethical values, Taureans are good teachers and counsellors.

Aquarius Occupying the 10th House. Saturn is a very beneficial planet in this chart since it rules both the 9th and 10th auspicious houses. As seen through the 10th house, the profession has its best expression through careers involving contact with others ranging from social work and community organizing to advertising. Their professions will reflect the Taurean need for financial stability accompanied by the Aquarian need for freedom of expression and service to others.

Pisces Occupying the 11th House. Jupiter-ruled Pisces should bring increased profits, gains through earnings, and pride in accomplishments. This may mean financial rewards or it may just indicate expanding circles of colleagues, friends, and acquaintances, who have entered the picture due to professional success.

Aries Occupying the 12th House. Since the Martian-ruled 12th house governs expenditures, and because Taureans enjoy basking in luxury, they tend to spend rather extravagantly. If Mars is poorly situated or aspected, these individuals may be extremely self-destructive. An overwhelming desire for economic stability, however, usually wins out to temper these indulgent habits.

Mithuna (Gemini) Lagna

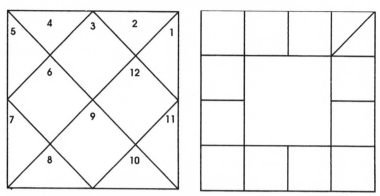

Figure 5.3. Mithuna (Gemini) Lagna.

> Black eyes, curled hairs, sporting with women, can interpret other people's thoughts, elevated nose, music and dance, home-keeping. . . .[5]

> Gemini gives a tall, upright, straight body and the hands will be long. The legs will be thin and the veins will be visible. The eyes will be hazel and the look quick, sharp and active. Nose will be long. Complexion will vary according to the ascendant.[6]

Worry and anxiety may weaken Geminis' already delicate nervous systems. Good health and physical well-being can be easily maintained with sufficient rest, fresh air, correct eating habits, and plenty of exercise. Gemini rules the lungs, making these people prone to colds, bronchitis, pneumonia and, at worst, emphysema. They should avoid smoking and try to pace their lives to allow time for relaxation.

Geminis may satisfy their need for constant mental stimulation through meaningful conversations and diversions such as lectures, museums, films, concerts, and the theater. They are intelligent, witty, wonderful conversationalists, but very poor lis-

---

[5] Mantreswara, *Phaladeepika*, p. 125.
[6] Krishnamurti, *Fundamental Principles of Astrology*, pp. 87–88.

teners. Their greatest challenge is to complete what they have started, since they are usually involved with two projects at once.

Cancer Occupying the 2nd House. With the Moon-ruled Cancer as the indicator of how Geminis earn money, these people may find themselves in the restaurant or music business. They may also be art collectors, architects, or historians. Like the phases of the Moon (ruler of Cancer), finances tend to fluctuate. Their early education may have been marked by restlessness and an inability to concentrate.

Leo Occupying the 3rd House. Geminis are talkative, outgoing, and, like the Sun, which rules the 3rd house of mentality and communications, self-assured and strong-minded. Though they are intelligent, mentally disciplined, willful, and highly creative, they may feel inferior to their siblings whom they perceive to be more successful. Geminis are extremely ambitious and will strive diligently to achieve their hopes and dreams.

Virgo Occupying the 4th House. As ruler of the 4th house, Mercury endows Geminis with restlessness and a need to change residences frequently stemming from their own unstable upbringing. Their parents may have been separated or one parent may have had a difficult relationship with his or her children. On the other hand, the upbringing and, especially the mother, may have encouraged communication and intellectual stimulation.

Libra Occupying the 5th House. Geminis adore flattery, appreciate admiration, and demand respect. They are passionate, charming, sensual, and artistic. They feel most productive when involved in a relationship or working in a creative partnership. Their children will be physically attractive and artistically gifted. Whether Venus is positively or negatively aspected will determine if they will benefit from wise investments, or be wasteful and extravagant.

Scorpio Occupying the 6th House. Scorpio-ruled illnesses affecting Geminis may include constipation, hemorrhoids and infections of the bladder, colon, or reproductive system. As ruler of the 6th house, Mars may cause arguments with co-workers and a tendency toward "workaholism." Geminis must learn to work cooperatively with others or opt for self-employment. In the latter situation, there is a need to be less rigid with their employees.

Sagittarius Occupying the 7th House. Geminis usually have attentive, loving partners who are also successful, good-natured, and considerate. With Jupiter-ruling Sagittarius occupying the 7th house, the partner may be an attorney, teacher, theosophist, journalist, or linguist. The position of Jupiter in the chart will determine whether the partner will be generous and well-educated, or extravagant and lazy. Geminis may meet their spouses while travelling and the partner may be foreign or live abroad. This is a good placement for successful marital partnerships.

Capricorn Occupying the 8th House. Since the 8th house is the 2nd house from the house of partnership, it describes the assets of the partner. Because Saturn-ruled Capricorn represents financial success and ambition, the partner may satisfy Gemini's need for material security. But with Saturn symbolizing frugality and limitations, important business decisions should be made only after ample research and with great foresight.

Aquarius Occupying the 9th House. With Saturn-ruled Aquarius occupying the 9th house, the father may have been serious, strict, a disciplinarian, or difficult to reach. On the other hand, the father may have been ambitious, responsible, a teacher, and a role model. These people take life extremely seriously and often have difficulty accepting advice or getting instruction from others. In fact, there may be a bit of arrogance and the need to be completely self-taught.

Pisces Occupying the 10th House. Geminis strive to be recognized for their sensitivity, generosity, and artistic talents. Often confused about which profession to choose, they may vacillate between several careers before finally deciding on one. Due to their varied interests, they often have more than one line of work and many hobbies. Jupiterian professions which may be pursued include teaching, the law, religion, or publishing. The way in which Jupiter, ruler of the 10th house, is aspected will indicate whether opportunities will be seized or overlooked.

Aries Occupying the 11th House. Because Mars-ruled Aries colors this house, there may be a tendency to spend money as quickly as it is earned. Because they often feel they are under-paid for the jobs they do, quarrels with colleagues are not un-common. With the 11th house symbolizing older siblings, brothers or sisters may have more aggressive personalities, re-sulting in a difficult relationship.

Taurus Occupying the 12th House. This placement concurs with other indications in the horoscope that Geminis are eco-nomical, even frugal. Despite this trait, if Venus is well-placed, Geminis may donate money to charity and even spend on aes-thetically pleasing objects, antiques, and other collectibles. If Venus is poorly placed, there is a tendency to indulge in overeating, overspending, or excessive sensuality.

Kataka (Cancer) Lagna

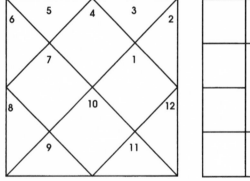 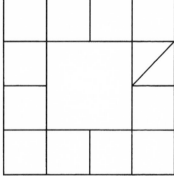

Figure 5.4. Kataka (Cancer) Lagna.

Henpecked, fleshy neck, surrounded by friends, possesses houses, elevated buttocks, rich, short, fast in walking, in-telligent, fond of water, possesses few sons . . .[7]

[7] Mantreswara, *Phaladeepika*, p. 125.

Physical features are clumsy body and slender limbs. Cancerians generally have a large upper body. As age advances, they acquire, by overeating, a prominent abdomen. Face is wide between the ears and the mouth will be large with chalky color. The hair will be brown and the complexion pale. As the limbs are extremely slender when compared to the large upper body, the whole body appears top-heavy and one will walk with a rolling gait.[8]

Like the phases of the Moon (which rules Cancer), health may fluctuate in conjunction with emotional states. Controlling their indulgent natures by adopting a reasonable diet and partaking in physical exercise allows them to lead healthy lives. The most vulnerable areas are the digestive and pulmonary systems, with a tendency toward gastric and asthmatic disturbances.

Cancerians are very sensitive, moody, introverted, and mysterious. They are motivated by a desire to nurture and be of service. In extreme situations, they may become "co-dependent" by developing relationships with weak, addictive personalities. Cancerians willingly give their time to others, but find it difficult to ask for assistance in times of crises. Although they are emotional, they are not communicative. Instead, they release their deepest feelings through art, poetry, or music.

Leo Occupying the 2nd House. Since Leo rules the 2nd house of finances, the Cancerians' self-image is inextricably tied to the acquisition of money and the accumulation of material possessions. In accordance with the security Cancerians so desperately need, this placement ensures sufficient earnings which should guarantee a lifetime of independence and financial security.

Virgo Occupying the 3rd House. Cancerians have extremely good memories, and are analytical, mentally alert, and retentive. Since Mercury-ruled Virgo occupies the 3rd house, there is an aptitude for mathematics, engineering, and computer pro-

---

[8] Krishnamurti, *Fundamental Principles of Astrology*, p. 97.

gramming—especially if Mercury, ruler of the 3rd house, is associated with disciplined Saturn or technical Rahu. They may also be prone to pessimism and self-doubt and are as critical of themselves as they are of others. Intellectual and changeable Mercury may also describe the personality and character of the siblings.

Libra Occupying the 4th House. As described by Venus-ruled Libra, the mother most likely enjoyed her traditional role in the family. Cancerian adults strive for the same strong family values as those instilled in childhood. They also need partners who share their vision of a harmonious family life and aesthetically pleasing, beautifully decorated homes. The influence of Libra will usually instill even-tempered personalities.

Scorpio Occupying the 5th House. Due to the impulsive character of Mars-ruled Scorpio, this placement reflects a tendency toward gambling or spending money foolishly. Because they can be secretive and do not articulate their feelings or thoughts, Cancerians may experience conflicts with their children. On the positive side, there is a love of sports, adventure, theater, music, and films. Boundless energy enables them to thoroughly enjoy what they are doing and be happy with whomever is sharing it.

Sagittarius Occupying the 6th House. If Cancerians are overindulgent, this placement may be accompanied by ailments involving the liver or pancreas, which is ruled by Jupiter, Lord of Sagittarius. Their work may involve the use of oratorical, theatrical, legal or teaching skills and there may be a need to travel a great deal. Although they enjoy frequenting exotic places, they soon become homesick.

Capricorn Occupying the 7th House. With Saturn-ruled Capricorn occupying the 7th house, the spouse may be older and more serious—someone who is looked upon as a teacher. Marriage may occur late in life due to the serious approach to relationships. Due to the Cancerians' taciturnity and need for solitude and secrecy, they seek partners with whom they can communicate nonverbally.

Aquarius Occupying the 8th House. Cancerians must be extremely cautious when starting business ventures. There is no room for speculation and financial risk-taking with Saturn ruling the business-oriented 8th house. If they invest wisely, they will reap long-term profits. It is advantageous for Cancerians to follow their intuition rather than depend on the advice of others where financial transactions are concerned.

Pisces Occupying the 9th House. As a description of the father, Jupiter-ruled Pisces points to a religious-minded or artistic figure whose honesty, fairness, and spirituality may have influenced the way Cancerians approach life. They love traveling and have a unique affinity for languages, mimicking accents and speech patterns.

Aries Occupying the 10th House. The influence of Mars-ruled Aries gives the propensity to join the military, pilot planes, or become professional athletes or executives. But whatever profession Arians choose, they are ambitious and strive to reach the top in their chosen fields. This is a perfect placement for doctors and surgeons who combine the caring qualities of the Cancer Ascendant with the ambition and passion inherent in the sign of Aries.

Taurus Occupying the 11th House. With Venus-ruled Taurus situated in the 11th house, Cancerians are able to profit considerably from all their hard work. They are quite able to fulfill many of their goals and will probably make lasting friends with those they meet on the job or through their travels. The older sibling may be quite artistic, or the relationship between the two may simply be vary harmonious.

Gemini Occupying the 12th House. There may be financial fluctuation due to the erratic manner in which Cancerians spend money. Depending on their moods, they may either be hoarders or totally extravagant. With Mercury ruling the 12th house, Cancerians have the ability to spend long hours doing research or work that involves detailed planning. Computer technology is a common metier among Cancerians and may be reaffirmed by the other placements in the chart.

Simha (Leo) Lagna

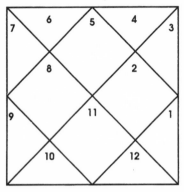
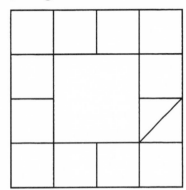

Figure 5.5. Simha (Leo) Lagna.

Reddish eyes, large cheeks, broad face, arrogant and powerful, angry at trifles, obedient to his mother. . . . [9]

One will have well-developed bones and broad shoulders and forehead. He will be tall, well built and muscular. Never will he be plump or ugly. His stature will be full and his appearance majestic, imposing, commanding and dignified, as Leo is fixed and fiery. Complexion will vary according to the exact position of the ascendant, and planets occupying or aspecting the ascendant.[10]

People with Leo Ascendants have strong constitutions. Due to self-induced stress and rigidity, however, they often develop chronic back trouble and are prone to high blood pressure which may result in heart attacks. If they catch a cold or the flu, which is not frequent, recovery is rapid. Leo represents the heart, the spinal column, spinal marrow, nerves, and nerve fibers.

Leos are very concerned with appearance and pride themselves on their independence and self-sufficiency. While they may exude extreme self-confidence, there is a need for constant

---

[9]Mantreswara, *Phaladeepika*, p. 125.
[10]Krishnamurti, *Fundamental Principles of Astrology*, p. 105.

reassurance that they are loved and needed. They are generous, creative, expressive, brutally honest, and thrive on admiration and flattery. Though they sometimes give the impression of being self-involved, they are generally magnanimous and loyal to those they love.

Virgo Occupying the 2nd House. Leo children have inquisitive minds, love school, and enjoy learning. Their financial situations are not as auspicious, however, and as ruler of the 2nd house, Mercury's influence will be one of economic fluctuation throughout their lives. They are able, however, to use their analytical minds and keen business sense to help increase their earning power.

Libra Occupying the 3rd House. Since Venus-ruled Libra occupies the 3rd house, Leos are usually eloquent speakers with a talent for journalism, poetry, acting, and public speaking. They have harmonious relationships with their siblings, who are usually equally talented and intelligent.

Scorpio Occupying the 4th House. Personified by Mars-ruled Scorpio, the mother may have a problematic relationship with her Leo children who very often leave home when relatively young. After they become responsible adults, Leos usually mend their differences (with their mothers) and close meaningful relationships may develop. These people often move frequently due to changes in domestic situations and difficulties with their landlords.

Sagittarius Occupying the 5th House. Beneficient, expansive Jupiter ruling this house may compel Leos toward fulfillment through creative self-expression. They may also be happy to work with children in addition to parenting, but must learn to balance both activities. They are optimistic, with an ability to remain hopeful and move forward even in the face of adversity. It is important for Leos to curtail some of their excessive and indulgent activities.

Capricorn Occupying the 6th House. This house is ruled by Capricorn which is associated with weak knees and bones and sensitive skin, teeth, and gums. Leos are ambitious, talented and can master practically any skill. While they are proficient at detailed work and/or organizational duties, success does not come easily and Capricorns must work hard to attain position and wealth.

Aquarius Occupying the 7th House. Since Saturn rules the 7th house of marriage, Leos' pragmatism is reflected in the desire for a partnership based on companionship rather than on romantic love. They crave intellectually stimulating partners from whom they can learn. This often results in relationships with older, well-educated, and more sophisticated people. They often find "true love" later in life.

Pisces Occupying the 8th House. Since the 8th house represents the finances of the partner, Jupiter-ruled Pisces indicates that the spouse has the ability to earn vast amounts of money and spend it just as quickly. Leos do not use sound judgment with regard to finances and should be cautious before they entrust money to those who profess to know more than they do. Leos are fortunate with inheritances and gifts because they are likeable and relationships usually remain amicable with families and friends.

Aries Occupying the 9th House. Due to the influence of Mars-ruled Aries in the 9th house of governing ideas and philosophies, Leos tend to be argumentative and insist that their opinions on politics, religion, and ethics are the right ones. They enjoy traveling and have a vital need to exercise their independence at all times. Ambitious, aggressive, and physically active Mars may describe the father's character or the quality of the paternal relationship.

Taurus Occupying the 10th House. Because Venus-ruled Taurus, a practical Earth sign, occupies this house, Leos usually choose a career which will enable them to earn enough money to support their extravagances and love of travel. Professions may be related to banking, entrepreneurial activities, or the stock market. Since the artistic planet, Venus, rules this house, the career may also be related to dancing, sculpture, jewelry making, designing, or music (especially singing, since Taurus rules the throat).

Gemini Occupying the 11th House. With Mercury-ruled Gemini occupying the 11th house, there may be strong communication with the older sibling who may be adept at business, clever, and highly intelligent. Profits may be acquired through financial wheeling and dealing, communication, or simply by using one's mind in an extremely clever and creative fashion.

Cancer Occupying the 12th House. Leos have a tendency to be withdrawn and spend long periods of time in self-imposed confinement, reflecting, writing, or retreating from the pressures of the world. They also tend to spend money indulgently and, more often than not, impulsively and irrationally.

Kanya (Virgo) Lagna

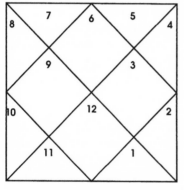 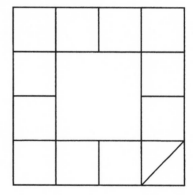

Figure 5.6. Kanya (Virgo) Lagna.

Shoulders and arms droop, enjoys wealth of others, truthful and speaks kindly, fond of enjoyment, limited children . . .[11]

---

[11]Mantreswara, *Phaladeepika*, p. 126.

Virgo is tall with a slender body, and he or she will have dark hair and eyes. Eyebrows will be curved with much of hair growth. Voice will be thin and even shrill. They will walk quickly and never have a pot belly. Due to their activity, they often appear younger than their actual age. Nose is straight, indicating that they are very clever and necessarily cunning. The forehead near the eyebrows will be pronounced. Expression of their eyes will be honest and frank. Among Westerners, most of the Virgoans will have beautiful blue eyes. That is because Venus-ruled Libra, representing beauty, is on the cusp of the second house which has to do with the eyes.[12]

Virgos are temperate people whose chances for good health and general well-being are increased because they strive toward moderation. Ailments include digestive and intestinal troubles, dysentery, and ulcers. Vulnerable parts of the body are the stomach and nervous system. However, with the inclusion of vitamin B supplements, a balanced diet, and regular exercise, these ailments can be avoided.

They are self-conscious and insecure when meeting new people. Virgos tend to be analytical and are very detail-oriented. At times, they are so finicky about minor details that nothing gets accomplished. They are good-natured, shy, and gentle, but their reserved manner is often mistaken for coldness.

Libra Occupying the 2nd House. Since Venus rules the 2nd house, Virgos are more successful doing business in conjunction with a partner than on their own. Under the influence of Libra, the sign personifying marriage, they may form business relationships with their spouses which can range from owning a boutique to collecting art or antique furniture.

Scorpio Occupying the 3rd House. Due to the competitive nature of Mars-ruled Scorpio, these people may experience conflicts or difficult relationships with siblings. Virgos are assertive speakers who, unfortunately, do not exhibit the same intensity

---

[12]Krishnamurti, *Fundamental Principles of Astrology,* p. 116.

and concentration when it comes to listening. They enjoy participating in debate and very often play the role of devil's advocate to stir up an argument. Above all, however, they are extremely intelligent, analytical, insightful, and possess probing and penetrating minds.

Sagittarius Occupying the 4th House. Virgos very often reside in countries other than the ones they hail from. This may be due to marriage to a foreigner or simply a desire to live in an exotic place. They will speak at least one other language fluently and will become involved with international affairs. Their parents may have been warm-hearted people or Jupiter's rulership could imply that the mother was foreign, religious, or academically inclined. Virgos are usually fortunate and find suitable homes in the neighborhoods they choose to live in and may even successfully dabble in real estate.

Capricorn Occupying the 5th House. Virgos are perfectionists with a somewhat authoritarian and rigid approach to raising a family. They may choose not to have children until later in life, or they may consciously choose to remain childless. They will have a very frugal approach to life, and may find it hard to simply let their hair down and have a good time.

Aquarius Occupying the 6th House. With Saturn-ruled Aquarius occupying the 6th house, there may be a great deal of rigidity, workaholism or a general tendency to work too hard. As a result, Virgos are prone to heart disease and related circulatory problems. Relaxation, proper diet, and exercise, however, can reduce the possibility of developing hypertension. As ruler of the 6th house, Saturn's influence may also lead to rheumatism and arthritis later in life.

Pisces Occupying the 7th House. Virgos thrive on being needed and, accordingly, choose partners who require assistance and sympathy. With Jupiter-ruled Pisces defining the spouse, the partner may be extremely creative and artistic as a dancer, writer, or artist. They may be attracted to exotic places, and there is a very strong possibility that the spouse is foreign or they will live abroad. (This influence is confirmed with Jupiter-ruled Sagittarius occupying the 4th house of home and family.)

Aries Occupying the 8th House. Since Mars rules the 8th house of business investments, there may be hasty decisions and faulty judgment resulting in unnecessary monetary losses. Many of those decisions will be made by a partner who is not very economical. These may result in lawsuits which will not be settled in the Virgo's favor. Due to insecurity, Virgos may be possessive and jealous. They have great physical strength and, in line with this, are very good athletes.

Taurus Occupying the 9th House. Virgos must work hard for their degrees but, with determination, they usually succeed. Because the 9th house of foreign travel is ruled by Venus, there is an indication that the partner may be from another country or may be involved with international business activities. (This theme has already been seen in the interpretation of the 4th and 7th houses.) There is a willingness to learn and these people will usually have a good relationship with their fathers and teachers.

Gemini Occupying the 10th House. Since Mercury-ruled Gemini occupies the 10th house of profession, Virgos will have careers involving journalism, writing, advertising, or any medium through which ideas and opinions are communicated. They are good business people, salespeople, and lawyers. Other possibilities include agents, distributors, bookkeepers, editors, and translators.

Cancer Occupying the 11th House. As ruler of the 11th house, the Moon indicates that the earning power fluctuates from being able to earn a great deal of money one minute and possibly experiencing devastating losses the next. Virgoans must be careful not to spend more than their earnings allow. The older sibling may have been extremely caring and protective.

Leo Occupying the 12th House. These people tend to squander money and their altruism often defeats their own best interest. On the positive side, however, Virgos are able to be alone for long periods of time and are excellent researchers who can master spiritual and physical disciplines.

Thula (Libra) Lagna

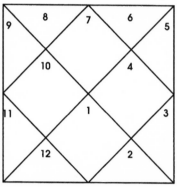
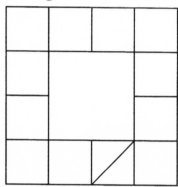

Figure 5.7. Thula (Libra) Lagna.

> Lean and frail body, wandering, God-worshipping, tall, clever, brave . . .[13]

> The person born with Libra as ascendant is tall with a well-proportioned body. His limbs are slender but strong. His appearance is graceful with a sweet smile and his countenance attractive. Eyebrows add to beauty.[14]

Librans can be excessive when it comes to drinking and eating and are often extremely lazy. They are prone to illnesses such as kidney ailments, bladder infections, bad skin, and digestive problems which directly relate to their indulgent natures. These problems are avoidable through temperate habits and decreased social activities, which tend to encourage alcohol and drug abuse. Because Librans are very concerned with acceptance by peers, difficulties can be averted by choosing friends wisely.

Since Venus rules the Ascendant, Librans are always impeccably clothed and are often obsessed with their appearances.

---

[13] Mantreswara, *Phaladeepika*, p. 126.
[14] Krishnamurti, *Fundamental Principles of Astrology*, p. 127.

They enjoy "dressing up" and use an abundance of make-up and jewelry for others to admire. Overly concerned with pleasing, their decisions often mirror the opinions of others, revealing an inability to make a decision. Librans are intent listeners and, because they relate well one-to-one, they make good therapists, counselors, and teachers. A desire to be of service to others extends to the point that they reserve too little time for themselves.

Scorpio Occupying the 2nd House. Because Mars-ruled Scorpio rules the 2nd house of early childhood, Librans may have been rebellious children who found it difficult to concentrate for long periods of time. Librans are comfortable working outdoors and make good physical education teachers and professional athletes. They find it difficult to focus on one profession and may seek ways to earn "easy money"—often leading to complex, or even underhanded, business dealings.

Sagittarius Occupying the 3rd House. Librans interact very well with their siblings and are popular with friends, neighbors, and colleagues. They enjoy traveling and are very concerned with religious, ethical, and philosophical issues. Since Jupiter-ruled Sagittarius occupies the 3rd house of communications, there is a tendency to exaggerate or be brutally honest. As a result, they may appear insensitive though "mental cruelty" is never their intention.

Capricorn Occupying the 4th House. The 4th house of Saturn-ruled Capricorn is usually interpreted by traditional astrologers as having "an unhappy mother and rigid childhood." There may have been an early separation or loss of one parent, but this influence can also mean that the parents were strict disciplinarians. They enjoy working at home and living in an organized and beautiful environment.

Aquarius Occupying the 5th House. Librans are politically and socially active and, with Saturn-ruled Aquarius occupying the 5th house, they may decide to have children either later in life or not at all. They enjoy activities which are creative and intellectually stimulating. Librans may, however, invest foolishly or suffer losses if they do not carefully budget their finances.

Pisces Occupying the 6th House. Illness, as represented by Pisces, may relate to water retention and swelling of the lymph nodes, signaling infection. They may also have weak feet, poor posture, and back problems. As far as work is concerned, they find it very difficult to follow orders and are, therefore, more comfortable in a partnership or self-employment. Librans are usually involved in professions which enable them to express and explore their creativity.

Aries Occupying the 7th House. Although Librans spend their entire lives searching for the "perfect" relationship, they often choose the "wrong" partner nonetheless. They are jealous and possessive and their partners are usually independent, short-tempered, and impulsive—qualities of the sign of Aries. It is not unusual for Librans to marry more than once and their partnerships are always challenging and difficult, though rewarding and worth the effort when all is said and done. Because they dislike being alone, they work very hard to make their unions successful.

Taurus Occupying the 8th House. They usually marry people with good earning potential and the ability to invest wisely. Librans and their partners enjoy collecting books, jewelry, antiques, etc. and they both take great pride in their possessions. Librans enjoy communicating with others and many opportunities present themselves through these connections.

Gemini Occupying the 9th House. Librans have a talent for advertising, writing, journalism, and teaching. These skills may take them abroad where they may reside for several years to satisfy their restlessness. The father was probably extremely intelligent and an excellent role model. Librans love to debate and become well versed in current affairs by reading voraciously and associating with all types of people.

Cancer Occupying the 10th House. Since Moon-ruled Cancer occupies the 10th house, professions suited to Librans relate to caring for others and may include therapy, nursing, or social work. They are excellent helpers, since they pay attention to the problems of others, a quality they incorporate into their work. Librans enjoy interior design and real estate. Other professions and interests may include owning a restaurant or shop, cooking, antique dealing, and studying history or architecture.

Leo Occupying the 11th House. With Sun-ruled Leo occupying this house, Librans love being admired and enjoy being the center of attention. There is great earning potential and the ability to gain public recognition. Once they target their goals, they are self-directed, ambitious, and know how to make their desires a reality. The older sibling may be someone who is extremely self-assured and assertive but the relationship may be far from perfect.

Virgo Occupying the 12th House. The Mercury-ruled sign of Virgo occupying the 12th house provides the ability to spend hours in solitude doing research, exploring their creativity, or simply meditating and reflecting. While this placement gives Librans a talent for working independently, there is also a tendency to become depressed and overly analytical about themselves and the world at large.

Vrischika (Scorpio) Lagna

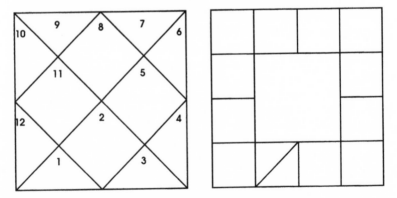

Figure 5.8. Vrischika (Scorpio) Lagna.

Broad eyes, broad chest, round loins and knees, diseases at an early age, will separate from parents, cruel acts, honored by sovereign . . .[15]

The body will be well-proportioned. Hands are generally long. The stature is above average. They will have a broad face, commanding appearance, short, curly hair and muscular body. Good personality.[16]

Scorpios are prone to bladder infections and problems related to the reproductive systems. Due to their high-strung nature and the stressful circumstances they themselves create, Scorpios may also have back and heart problems and should be more aware that their eating and drinking habits may cause digestive malfunction. When they become depressed, there may be a tendency toward alcohol and drug abuse.

Immense ambition and single-minded determination enables them to carry almost anything through to its logical conclusion. Their relentless drive may turn into ruthlessness which can ultimately destroy what they've created. They do not always know how to handle their successes. Scorpios are often authoritarian, inflexible, and find it difficult to change direction under adverse circumstances.

Sagittarius Occupying the 2nd House. Innovative Scorpios always seem to have financial opportunities lying at their doorsteps. Due to Jupiter-ruled Sagittarius occupying the 2nd house of material assets, however, money often slips away as soon as it is earned. Optimism and an uncanny ability to replenish assets sees them through seemingly hopeless situations. Because Jupiter rules both the 2nd and 5th houses, they are interested in speculation. If Jupiter is well-placed, Scorpios will make wise and profitable investments. If ill-placed, they tend to be foolhardy and incur heavy losses.

Capricorn Occupying the 3rd House. Scorpios have difficulty communicating their feelings, which affects their rapport with

---

[15] Mantreswara, *Phaladeepika*, p. 126.
[16] Krishnamurti, *Fundamental Principles of Astrology*, p. 135.

siblings, friends, colleagues, and neighbors. They have the ability to concentrate and are almost obsessive about their interests. They are very serious, extremely depressive, and sometimes even reclusive.

Aquarius Occupying the 4th House. With Saturn-ruled Aquarius occupying the 4th house, Scorpios may have a difficult relationship with the mother or may have simply been lonely and asocial growing up. As adults, they may still be loners who would rather spend time alone than among large groups of people. Their higher education may have been interrupted and they may experience obstacles when it comes to real estate.

Pisces Occupying the 5th House. Scorpios will have joyful experiences with their children, who will be instrumental in their lives and from whom they will learn a great deal. These people are attracted to the arts and will either participate in or patronize sporting events, concerts, theater, and dance performances. Although Scorpios will have sound financial opportunities, they may be attracted to more high-risk speculative investments. It is important to weigh each situation carefully before making a decision.

Aries Occupying the 6th House. The effect of Mars-ruled Aries occupying the 6th house predisposes these people to chills, colds, fevers, and headaches. Due to the impulsive nature of both Aries in the 6th house and Scorpio ascendant, there may have been an uncommon number of cuts, bruises, and burns due to minor accidents incurred during childhood. These people may conflict with colleagues and, though they are ambitious, may find it more advantageous to work for themselves.

Taurus Occupying the 7th House. Since the conservative sign of Taurus inhabits the 7th house, Scorpios generally bring old-fashioned values to their marriages. Because of an ultimate commitment to this sacred rite they are cautious when choosing partners. Once they are in love and finally decide to marry, they are passionate, jealous, and demand loyalty and fidelity. Because the 7th house is ruled by Venus, Scorpios seek partners who are comforting, loving, and patient. In return, they will be reliable, generous, and faithful.

Gemini Occupying the 8th House. With Gemini occupying the 8th house, these people have an instinct for financial dealings. This quality enables Scorpios to initiate innovative projects, to raise financial backing, and to be successful managing their own businesses and those of others. They may, however, be manipulative and not always above-board.

Cancer Occupying the 9th House. Many people with a Scorpio Ascendant live abroad, since Moon-ruled Cancer, symbol of home and family, occupies the 9th house of foreign travel. They have an uncanny ability for languages and their interest in anthropology, history, or architecture could lead to academic careers. Their fathers may have been home-loving, artistic, or musically inclined, but found it difficult to express their feelings.

Leo Occupying the 10th House. The 10th house of Sun-ruled Leo makes these people enterprising and ambitious, with a need to control their own destinies. They prefer to work independently or take charge of all situations of a professional nature. Career options associated with Leo are actors/actresses, directors, entrepreneurs, and executives. Their preference, however, is self-employment.

Virgo Occupying the 11th House. Mercury-ruled Virgo occupying the 11th house indicates that their fulfillment lies in intellectual activities and communicating with their peers. Their earnings will probably stem from writing, business activities, teaching, or even astrology. They may have an intellectually stimulating relationship with the older sibling, who may also be involved in the communication fields.

Libra Occupying the 12th House. With Venus-ruled Libra in the 12th house, these people may incur losses due to indulgences and extravagances. It is quite possible that their marriage partner will be foreign or that they will live abroad due to a relationship or through creative work. They often find it difficult living up to the image they are attempting to project.

Dhanus (Sagittarius) Lagna

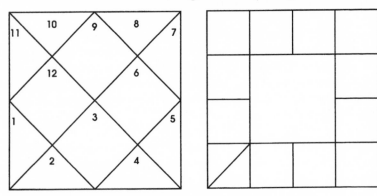

Figure 5.9. Dhanus (Sagittarius) Lagna.

> Long face and neck, ears and nose are big, intent on business, short, favorite of king, eloquent, liberal in gift, destroying his enemies . . .[17]

> Sagittarians are well-proportioned with a well-developed body. They will have a tall large forehead, high and bushy eyebrows, long nose, bright eyes, charming appearance, graceful look and fair complexion.[18]

Because these fun-loving people are constantly attending social functions, the opportunity to indulge in food, drugs, and alcohol is heightened. Their health is affected by a tendency toward excessive behavior and they must work hard at practicing self-control and discipline. Problem areas include the hips, pancreas, and liver, which are affected by too much alcohol.

Sagittarians are outgoing, honest, friendly, and extremely fair-minded. They are social animals who appear optimistic but hide their problems and difficulties. Because of the need to keep up appearances, they are never able to be completely honest

---

[17] Mantreswara, *Phaladeepika*, p. 127.
[18] Krishnamurti, *Fundamental Principles of Astrology*, p. 143.

about their feelings and emotions. They love traveling, socializing, learning, and teaching.

Capricorn Occupying the 2nd House. The Saturnian influence on the 2nd house indicates that Sagittarians must work hard for whatever they earn. As children they may have been slow learners or had an inability to concentrate due to restlessness. A desire to maintain high standards of living will encourage frugality and wise investing.

Aquarius Occupying the 3rd House. With Saturn ruling this house, they may have had tense relationships with their siblings. Sagittarians often feel superior to others, which discourages mutual understanding or open lines of communication. They are serious students and are probably very talented writers.

Pisces Occupying the 4th House. Sagittarians may have experienced happy childhoods which have a direct bearing on their optimistic personalities. There may have been close ties with both parents, especially the mother, who may have been artistic, spiritual, or foreign. They search for perfection in their relationships and may even reside abroad for a portion of their adult lives.

Aries Occupying the 5th House. Since Mars-ruled Aries occupies the house of entertainment, there will be a great deal of talent and interest in competitive sports, dancing, acting, and directing. Due to their need to be constantly preoccupied, Sagittarians may opt to have children later in life. Their kids may also be individualistic and often rebellious. There may be impulsive spending and rash investing.

Taurus Occupying the 6th House. The placement of Venus-ruled Taurus in the 6th house describes resistance to illness but it may also indicate ailments due to excessive habits. If overindulgence pertaining to food, drinking, and spending are tempered, it can lead to a balanced and healthy life. Sensitive areas include the throat, neck, tonsils, facial muscles, and eyes. Gum disease is also very common.

Gemini Occupying the 7th House. Mercury-ruled Gemini occupying the 7th house of marriage indicates that their choice of partners should fulfill intellectual and economic as well as emotional needs. They may marry when they are young and inexperienced, and, for this reason, are likely to have more than one marriage.

Cancer Occupying the 8th House. Moon-ruled Cancer indicates that the finances of the spouse may fluctuate. Business decisions may be emotionally based rather than carefully thought out. Difficulties with the mother or general restlessness may prove to be one of the greatest obstacles to overcome.

Leo Occupying the 9th House. The father may have been highly ambitious and successful and, most probably, the authority figure at home. Although a role model, work schedules may have prevented the father from spending quality time with the child. There is a tendency to be self-taught and the quest for knowledge will propel you through life.

Virgo Occupying the 10th House. With Mercury-ruled Virgo occupying the 10th house, the profession will involve anything having to do with written or oral communication. Sagittarians will succeed in business ventures, mathematics, research, or highly detailed work. They wish to be known and respected for their intellectual abilities as well as their originality and inventiveness.

Libra Occupying the 11th House. The 11th house of Venus-ruled Libra indicates that the source of fulfillment stems from friendships and being surrounded by loved ones. There should be success at artistic professions and the capacity to profit greatly from hard work. They should enjoy a good relationship with older siblings who also may be good-natured and artistic.

Scorpio Occupying the 12th House. Scorpio's influence on the 12th house indicates excessive spending in order to support expensive habits and lifestyles. Many conflicts arise due to unsolicited advice, opinions, and suggestions offered by friends which Sagittarians do not appreciate and which most times go unheeded.

Makara (Capricorn) Lagna

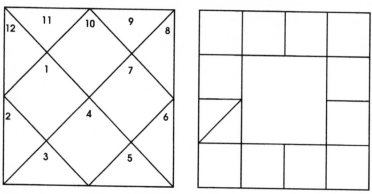

Figure 5.10. Makara (Capricorn) Lagna.

Weak in lower limbs, strength, will understand and follow when advised, indolent, religious, fortunate, wind disease . . .[19]

Saturn shows that one will be emaciated, weak and will grow slowly. Tall and slender. The face will be thin and oval and the nose will be long and the eyes deep set. Hair will be coarse.[20]

Health problems incurred by people with a Capricorn ascendant may be related to skin, bones, teeth, weak knees and, later in life, rheumatism and arthritis.

Capricorns are reserved and, like Taureans (also an earth sign), very rarely speak unless they have something significant to say. They are ambitious, serious, and reliable. The attainment of success is important, sometimes overpowering everything else in life. They can be ruthless and are capable of unscrupulous behavior in order to succeed.

---

[19] Mantreswara, *Phaladeepika*, p. 127.
[20] Krishnamurti, *Fundamental Principles of Astrology*, p. 150.

Aquarius Occupying the 2nd House. Since the 2nd house is ruled by the planet Saturn, there may be an inability to concentrate and an impatience with early education. The occupancy of Aquarius indicates earning money through participation in social causes and group activities. Capricorns acquire income through hard work and tend to be frugal. They are often referred to as "stingy" or "penny-pinching."

Pisces Occupying the 3rd House. Interests in theosophy, law, philosophy, languages, and political science are all related to the planet Jupiter as ruler of the 3rd house. Capricorns also enjoy traveling and usually maintain a good relationship with their brothers and sisters.

Aries Occupying the 4th House. The family background, represented by Mars-ruled Aries, was most likely problematic. The parents may have argued a great deal and there may even have been the loss or separation of one parent early in life. The mother was most likely dynamic and opinionated and may have provoked much discord. Capricorns may find it difficult to discover the key to personal contentment.

Taurus Occupying the 5th House. Venus-ruled Taurus occupying the 5th house indicates a love of the arts and a true desire to have a good time. Of course, that means there may, at times, be too much indulgence and excess. With the 5th house ruling speculation, there will be a great temptation to invest too much. They will usually have a harmonious relationship with their children, but tend to spoil them, while still maintaining their status as strict disciplinarians. Since this is no easy task, they find the parenting role very challenging.

Gemini Occupying the 6th House. Mercury-ruled Gemini occupying the 6th house may indicate weakness in the arms and lungs. Their tendency to overwork may activate bronchial infection, tonsillitis or, at worst, pneumonia. They may also have fragile nervous systems. Capricorns should have an easy time communicating with co-workers.

Cancer Occupying the 7th House. Since the Moon-ruled Cancer occupies the 7th house of partnership, the spouse is certain to be someone who will provide emotional security and domestic tranquility. There will probably be more than one marriage or major relationship, as the Moon personifies phases and/or changes.

Leo Occupying the 8th House. Sun-ruled Leo gives these people the capacity to be initiating and to make things happen despite adversity. Due to their ambition and self-confidence, these people have a knack for achieving success in whatever areas their energies are directed. Because of their relentless pursuit of prosperity, they tend to marry equally ambitious and successful partners. If they follow their own instincts rather than the recommendations of outside advisers, their businesses will flourish.

Virgo Occupying the 9th House. Not only were their fathers extremely intellectual, but their own capacity for accumulating knowledge is boundless. Capricorns love learning new languages and may even be multi-lingual. They also lean toward degrees in psychology, chemistry, journalism, or the law.

Libra Occupying the 10th House. Because of their aptitude for speaking and listening to others, Capricorns may utilize the influence of Venus-ruled Libra in careers as lawyers, salesmen, consultants, or therapists. Their professions may also be connected to arts such as dancing, film-making, and dress or jewelry making. It may also just imply owning a boutique, since Libra symbolizes clothes and jewelry, or working in a cooperative partnership.

Scorpio Occupying the 11th House. With Mars-ruled Scorpio occupying the 11th house, they derive much of their fulfillment from physical activities, as well as any competitive activities ranging from sports to business affairs. There may be conflicts with the older sibling, who is aggressive and difficult to get along with. Capricorns work hard, and are incredibly ambitious, but should watch that they do not spend their profits as quickly as they are earned.

Sagittarius Occupying the 12th House. Jupiter-ruled Sagittarius occupying the 12th house is defined as expansion in the area this house represents—inner space, solitude, and expenditures. Capricorns are deeply religious and may devote much of their time to humanitarian causes, leaving little time for their families. Jupiter tends to hoard and these people may, in fact, be quite stingy and overly frugal. If Jupiter is ill placed, however, there is a great deal of indulgence, waste, and money may be spent quite foolishly.

Kumbha (Aquarius) Lagna

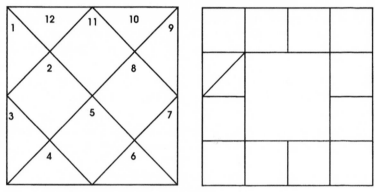

Figure 5.11. Kumbha (Aquarius) Lagna.

Commits sinful deeds secretly, does hindrance to others, means are limited, covetous and utilizes others' wealth, fond of perfumes and flowers . . .[21]

Aquarians are tall with full stature. They are strong, face is oval and complexion is fair. The signs of Venus, Taurus and Libra, and Aquarius produce beautiful children. Teeth may be defective and the hair has a brown shade.[22]

---

[21] Mantreswara, *Phaladeepika*, p. 127.
[22] Krishnamurti, *Fundamental Principles of Astrology*, p. 160.

Aquarians are extremely high strung and must temper their mood swings. Due to these personality traits, their health concerns are heart ailments, circulatory weakness, water retention (especially around the ankles), and hypertension.

Aquarians are irritable, generous, serious, inflexible and active in social causes. They tend to be workaholics and must learn to relax. Although they are extremely humanitarian and concerned with the world at large, they are frequently inconsiderate to the people they love. Their eccentricities and extremes of mood make them difficult to understand and their impatience does not always make them sympathetic friends.

Pisces Occupying the 2nd House. Despite frequent mismanagement of finances, there will always be steady income and constant replenishment of one's resources. With Jupiter-ruled Pisces ruling the 2nd house, there may be the acquisition of land or even money earned through business done abroad. Aquarians can be extravagant and are often guilty of being "penny wise and pound foolish."

Aries Occupying the 3rd House. Aquarians are inventive, open-minded, and inquisitive but equally argumentative and aggressive. By playing devil's advocate, they often invite an interesting exchange of opinions. They are good writers, journalists, broadcaster, researchers—professions where ideas must be conveyed to the public. Aquarians are known for their oratorical ability, but have little capacity for listening. There may also be conflicts with siblings who very possibly have aggressive natures themselves.

Taurus Occupying the 4th House. Venus-ruled Taurus occupying the 4th house describes an upbringing that may have been financially comfortable, or a mother who was loving, attentive, and the backbone of the family. Aquarians try to be cooperative and their general disposition is usually optimistic. Because Aquarians are social-minded, they frequently entertain and their homes may serve as meeting places for friends or social groups.

Gemini Occupying the 5th House. Classified as a "barren" sign, Mercury-ruled Gemini occupying the 5th house indicates that there will be a great deal of indecision as to whether to have children. If they do, their children may be very precocious and highly intelligent. Aquarians are involved with many extracurricular activities, and do not always devote as much time to their families as they would like. The gap closes when their children mature and they can relate as equals rather than as parent to child.

Cancer Occupying the 6th House. Since Moon-ruled Cancer governs the chest and abdomen, there may be digestive problems and possible stomach ailments. They may also be prone to bronchitis, gallstones, and asthma. Cancer signifies a tendency to retain water which, coupled with the swollen ankles symbolized by Aquarius, may lead to heart disease. With regular eating habits and proper exercise, these physical conditions may be remedied. Working with people will be most satisfying to Aquarians.

Leo Occupying the 7th House. Sun-ruled Leo occupying the 7th house indicates that these people are extremely passionate and romantic. Aquarians are faithful and attentive to their independent, career-minded partners. Despite the mutual respect, Aquarians are possessive and demanding and often feel that their own work is more important than that of their partners.

Virgo Occupying the 8th House. Due to their sharp, analytical minds, Aquarians are extremely shrewd business people and are especially adept at sales, public relations, finances, and advertising. They will make profitable investments, but Mercury's rulership tends to cause income to fluctuate.

Libra Occupying the 9th House. The 9th house, represented by Venus-ruled Libra, indicates that there was a good relationship with the father, who was good-natured and loving. Aquarians are likely to fall in love with well-educated people, as well as with someone from a different nationality. Because of their eloquence, they make very good lawyers and teachers.

Scorpio Occupying the 10th House. In an effort to work for political and social ideals, Aquarians are passionate, relentless, and often intolerant of those who do not share their beliefs. Work may include chemistry, research psychology, medicine, dentistry, law, or investigative journalism. They will most probably be active in at least one political or social organization.

Sagittarius Occupying the 11th House. The 11th house, occupied by Jupiter-ruled Sagittarius, provides Aquarians with lively, high-spirited, cheerful personalities enabling them to work well with those who share their goals of social and political reform. Their fulfillment ultimately lies in the wide circle of friends who they usually keep for many years. Since Jupiter rules both the 2nd and 11th houses, Aquarians will be financially successful, generous, but somewhat indulgent with their earnings. There may be an extremely productive relationship with the older sibling.

Capricorn Occupying the 12th House. Aquarians can overwork themselves to the point where they desperately need solitude and time to meditate. Although they spend money foolishly from time to time, they are always conscious of a need for material security and will eventually buckle down and save.

Meena (Pisces) Lagna

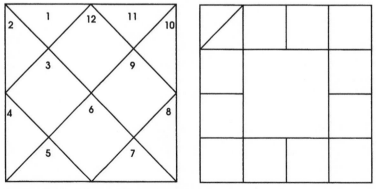

Figure 5.12. Meena (Pisces) Lagna.

Drinks excess water, symmetrical and shining body, fond of his wife, learned, feels grateful for favors done to him, overcomes enemies, good eyes and is fortunate . . .[23]

Pisceans generally produce short people and will weigh as much as a tall person as they will be plump and the hands and feet will appear to be short and stout. The shoulders are muscular and spherical. The eyes will be big and protruding and the hair will be soft and silky.[24]

Due to Pisces rulership over the lymphatic system, the body's defense against disease, these individuals must consciously strive toward maintaining good health despite their tendency toward overindulgence. This includes drinking plenty of water to cleanse their systems, curtailing late night activities, and avoiding alcohol, fatty foods, and drugs. Pursuing creative interests should be a major part of Piscean activities. They may have a tendency to put on weight, and Pisceans often suffer from weak feet, poor posture, and back problems.

Pisceans are imaginative, romantic, spiritual, good-natured, generous, and childlike. They can live in a world of their own creation, enabling them to work well with children or be involved with acting, dancing, painting, or music. At times insecurity and lack of conviction may prevent assertiveness and often result in manipulation by others.

Aries Occupying the 2nd House. The influence of Mars-ruled Aries on the 2nd house brings an enterprising spirit and a challenge to embark on new business ventures. If a project should fail, they quickly move to the next endeavor without a backward glance. However, they must be cautious since there is a tendency toward impulsiveness and poor judgment. They should heed the advice of financial advisers and/or friends more knowledgeable in the area of finance.

Taurus Occupying the 3rd House. Pisceans are slow learners and are not particularly interested in memorizing facts and fig-

[23] Mantreswara, *Phaladeepika*, p. 128.
[24] Krishnamurti, *Fundamental Principles of Astrology*, p. 170.

ures. They are visual thinkers and use intuition, images, and colors the way others use logic and reasoning. Since Venus rules the 3rd house, they are soft-spoken, tactful, diplomatic, and have the ability to "sweet talk" others. Pisceans usually have good relationships with their friends, neighbors, and siblings.

Gemini Occupying the 4th House. Pisceans may have moved around a bit as children, changing residences due to the job fluctuations of one parent. Their homes were stimulating centers of activity where their parents entertained an interesting and diverse circle of friends and acquaintances. As adults, Pisceans attract creative people in an effort to recreate happy childhood experiences. They enjoy the unusual and will travel at the "drop of a hat."

Cancer Occupying the 5th House. When the 5th house is occupied by the Moon-ruled Cancer, a fruitful sign, there is a strong desire to either have children at an early age or work with youngsters as a pasttime. Pisceans are extremely attentive parents, devoted to the emotional needs of their children. They are able to combine intellect and intuition when it comes to important decision making.

Leo Occupying the 6th House. Since the 6th house is ruled by Leo, associated with the heart and spine, Pisceans must watch their blood pressure, control hypertension, and eat correctly to avert a tendency toward heart disease and stomach problems. They are extremely hard workers but may have difficulties working with others. Self-employment may not come easy, but it is usually the preferable path.

Virgo Occupying the 7th House. Pisceans' selection of spouses is dependent on a mutual ability to nurture the other both intellectually and romantically. As represented by Virgo, the spouse may be highly critical but will definitely fulfill the Pisceans' needs to learn "temperance." Since Mercury, a changeable planet, rules the 7th house, Pisceans often marry at a young age and more than once.

Libra Occupying the 8th House. This placement indicates that the partners are not very adept at handling finances and that both Pisceans and their spouses spend money extravagantly. There will be many opportunities for business partnerships and the probability of some type of patronage at some point in their lives.

Scorpio Occupying the 9th House. Pisceans are argumentative and do not willingly accept criticism. They dislike analyzing situations and sometimes lack the ability to confront anger, hate, and greed. There will be unresolved conflicts with the father who may not have communicated well with his children though he cared deeply.

Sagittarius Occupying the 10th House. Jupiter-ruled Sagittarius occupying the 10th house of profession is quite a fortunate placement. Pisceans have many work opportunities and must be cautious not to waste or overlook them. They usually need discipline to achieve their goals. Professional aspirations could include becoming a lawyer, banker, journalist, teacher, or physician.

Capricorn Occupying the 11th House. With Saturn-ruled Capricorn ruling this house, they will never earn as much money as they would like to. Because they are cautious yet frugal, their investments will probably reap slow but steady gains. There may be difficulty with older siblings, or a brother or sister may be extremely serious and withdrawn. They are loyal and their friendships are lasting. Because they expect too much from others, they are often disappointed.

Aquarius Occupying the 12th House. With Saturn the ruler of the 12th house, these people are often dedicated to a spiritual ideal and may have a very rich inner life. They will probably spend hours alone due to artistic activities or merely because they feel themselves to be loners. There may sometimes be a tendency to deny themselves pleasurable and sensual experiences.

• • •

It is important to remember that this system of classifying and analyzing each Rasi Chakra according to its Ascendant is quite general and must always be modified according to the position of the house ruler and how it is aspected. Using these general descriptions for each Ascendant is very helpful for rectification, the term applied to the astrologer's adjustment of an estimated or unknown birth time usually based on (a) the sequence of events in a person's life, and (b) whether the signs occupying each house actually describe the corresponding personality traits. It is by analyzing the horoscope in this latter context that I have been able to use Ascendant combinations for purposes of rectification in my own practice.

One example is a close friend who knew he was born sometime in the morning. I calculated the Ascendant for the earliest and latest possible times he could have been born, which produced three different Ascendants—Virgo, Libra, and Scorpio. Reviewing the house descriptions for each of the three Ascendants, I realized that a description of the house lords and signs occupying each house of a Virgo Ascendant was an almost accurate representation. He finally obtained the exact time of birth from his birth certificate and, sure enough, he had a Virgo Ascendant. Though this is certainly not a foolproof system, it has worked for me enough times over the years to merit consideration. It is important to realize that this system can only be used to determine the sign on the Ascendant and not the exact time of birth, which must be derived from a review of major events. It is also easier to rectify a chart when the approximate time of day is known so that the choices are narrowed down.

CHAPTER 6

PLANETS AND HOUSES:
STRENGTHS AND WEAKNESSES

THE FIRST STEP IN INTERPRETING an individual Rasi Chakra is to ascertain the strength or weakness of each planet according to its placement in the horoscope. It is important to keep in mind while assessing planetary power that each planet not only embodies the house it rules, it also expresses that identity through the sign and house it occupies in the Rasi Chakra. The following illustrates how the positions of the planets are used to evaluate strength and weakness.

Determine Signs of Rulership, Exaltation, Debilitation (Fall), or Moolatrikona

Table 6.1 (page 140) lists the planets, the zodiacal signs they rule, and the exact degrees where they are exalted, fallen, or in their moolatrikona. With the exception of the moolatrikona, the relationships between a planet and its zodiacal sign—rulership, exaltation, and fall—are also utilized in Occidental astrology.

1. *Rulership:* Each planet, except for the Sun and the Moon, rules two signs. The rulership sign may be viewed as the place where the planet operates most comfortably and whose attributes are shared by both the zodiacal sign and its ruling planet. For example, both Cancer and its planetary ruler, the Moon, are concerned with maternal instincts, home, and the family.

2. *Exaltation and Fall:* In addition to the zodiacal sign it rules, each planet is exalted, or at its strongest, when it occupies a particular sign. Although it "shines" most brightly at its exact degree of exaltation, the planet is exalted throughout the entire sign, gradually growing stronger as it moves toward its exaltation degree and losing strength as it moves away. The same can be said about the fallen, or debilitated, degree and sign, where the planet is exceptionally weak and can never "be itself." The

Table 6.1. Determining Planetary Strength.

PLANETS (GRAHAS)	SIGN OF RULERSHIP (SWAKSHETRA)	EXALTATION DEGREE (UCHCHA)	FALL DEGREE (NEECHA)	MOOLATRIKONA DEGREES
Sun	Leo	10° Aries	10° Libra	1–20° Leo
Moon	Cancer	3° Taurus	3° Scorpio	3–30° Taurus
Mars	Aries, Scorpio	28° Capricorn	28° Cancer	1–12° Aries
Mercury	Gemini, Virgo	15° Virgo	15° Pisces	16–20° Virgo
Jupiter	Sagittarius, Pisces	5° Cancer	5° Capricorn	1–10° Sagittarius
Venus	Taurus, Libra	27° Pisces	27° Virgo	1–5° Libra
Saturn	Capricorn Aquarius	20° Libra	20° Aries	1–20° Aquarius

planet becomes progressively weaker as it moves toward debilitation, and recovers its power as it moves away. As seen from Table 6.1, a planet's exaltation and fall are always opposing signs of the zodiac.

3. *Moolatrikona:* One of the most favorable positions a planet can occupy, the moolatrikona, a concept unique to Jyotish, is either the sign of the planet's exaltation or rulership. Like exaltation and fall, this position is strongest when the planet occupies specific degrees even though it is still powerful merely occupying that sign.

Determine Malefic, Benefic, or Neutral Influence

As seen in Table 6.2, the planets are categorized as either naturally benefic (beneficial), malefic (difficult), or neutral. Although it may seem that there are many more malefics than benefics, this is not as clear cut as the list may imply. The Sun, for instance, is a mild malefic, while the Moon is generally considered to be benefic. The waning Moon, however, is less effective than the waxing Moon, and is sometimes considered to be mildly malefic. While Mercury is neutral, it is generally regarded as having more of a benefic than malefic influence. Like the other planets, its effect will be altered if aspected by benefic or malefic planets. Some of these classifications are explained below.

Table 6.2. Benefic, Malefic, and Neutral Influences.

BENEFIC	MALEFIC	NEUTRAL
Waxing Moon Venus Jupiter	Sun Waning Moon Mars Saturn Rahu Kethu	Mercury

In India, the Sun is considered to be malefic, as its heat parches the land, ruins crops, and leaves behind a general feeling of lethargy and fatigue. As is the case in most tropical countries, shops and businesses close between the hours of noon and four o'clock when the Sun is in its strongest position—directly overhead. Most people take this opportunity to eat and rest before resuming work. The Sun is also malefic due to its rulership of the individuality and the ego. While these qualities are encouraged here in the West, self-involvement is frowned upon in India, as it lessens the ability to be devoted to the family.

The Moon is waxing when it is 0°–180° ahead of the Sun or until the moment the Moon is full. It is waning when it is 180°–360° ahead of the Sun, the time elapsed between Full and New Moon. Because the intensity of illumination increases as it proceeds toward fullness each month, the waxing Moon has a benefic and abundant influence. Conversely, during the half of the month when this luminary changes its position from full to new, the Moon's decreasing light does not encourage fecundation, a positive lunar principle. The waning Moon is, therefore, considered to be mildly malefic.

Since Jupiter is the largest planet and Venus is the brightest and most beautiful, they are both considered benefic influences. Jupiter is known as the "greater benefic" and Venus is called the "lesser benefic."

Mercury's character is changeable and, depending on its position in the horoscope, can be benefic or malefic. If, for instance, Mercury shares the occupancy of a house with a benefic planet in the birth chart, its character will be beneficial. If Mercury is conjoined with a malefic, it will bring adversity.

Saturn, the greater malefic, and Mars, the lesser malefic, cause depression and aggression respectively, which, when taken to extremes can be extremely debilitating. Saturn, which has a ring around its circumference, projects a sense of restriction, one of its symbolic characteristics.

In addition to being either a "natural" benefic, malefic, or neutral planet (see Table 6.2, page 141), a planet's categorization can change in accordance with the house it rules in an individual chart. The general principles are as follows:

1. A planet ruling the 1st, 5th, or 9th Trikona house will become individually benefic.

2. A natural malefic ruling the 4th, 7th, or 10th Kendra house will become individually benefic, while a natural benefic ruling the same house will become individually malefic, unless the planet also owns the 1st house. (An example of this is a Sagittarius ascendant where Jupiter, as ruler of the Ascendant, also rules the 4th house of Pisces. In this case, Jupiter is considered neutral, although it rules the 4th Kendra house.)

3. A planet ruling the 3rd, 6th, or 11th Upachaya house will become individually malefic.

4. Rulership of the 2nd, 8th, or 12th house will have a neutral effect.

Table 6.3 (pages 144–145) lists the planets the astrologer Satyacharya considered to be benefic, malefic, and neutral for each of the twelve Ascendants, according to the aforementioned principles.[1] (Throughout the book, I refer to planets as both *naturally* benefic, malefic, or neutral (Table 6.2, page 141) or *individually* benefic, malefic, or neutral (Table 6.3, pages 144–145).

When a planet other than the Sun or Moon (each of which rules one sign) rules two houses of which one is neutral, the planet will usually adopt the auspicious or inauspicious character of the other house it governs. My client Jane's chart (figure 6.1, page 146), has a Leo Ascendant. Jupiter rules both the 5th Trikona house and the 8th neutral Dusthana house, causing Jupiter to become neutral. Because of its rulership of the 8th house, however, it is weaker than a planet such as Mars, which rules the 4th Kendra house and 9th Trikona house. Any planet which becomes individually benefic by virtue of each of the houses it rules is called *Yogakaraka* (meaning "union indica-

---

[1] Some of Satyacharya's classifications do not quite fit the aforementioned formulas due, in part, to the 2nd and 7th house ruler's classification as a maraka planet. Rather than try to calculate how the sage arrived at his figures, it is recommended to take these definitions from this list. It should also be noted that these classifications vary somewhat according to the sage.

Table 6.3. Satyacharya's List of Individual Benefics, Malefics and Neutrals.*

ASCENDANT	BENEFIC	MALEFIC	NEUTRAL
Aries	Jupiter (9 and 12) Sun (5) Mars (1 and 8)	Saturn (10 and 11) Mercury (3 and 6) Venus (2 and 7) Moon (4)	
Taurus	Saturn (9 and 10) Mercury (2 and 5) Mars (7 and 12) Sun (4)	Jupiter (8 and 11) Venus (1 and 6) Moon (3)	Venus† (1 and 6)
Gemini	Venus (5 and 12) Saturn (8 and 9)	Mars (6 and 11) Jupiter (7 and 10) Sun (3)	Moon (2) Mercury (1 and 4)
Cancer	Jupiter (6 and 9) Mars (5 and 10)	Venus (4 and 11) Mercury (3 and 12)	Saturn (7 and 8) Moon (1) Sun (2)
Leo	Mars (4 and 9) Sun (1)	Mercury (2 and 11) Venus (3 and 10)	Jupiter (5 and 8) Moon (12) Saturn (6 and 7)
Virgo	Venus (2 and 9)	Moon (11) Mars (3 and 8) Jupiter (4 and 7)	Saturn (5 and 6) Sun (12) Mercury (1 and 10)

*The house each planet rules within each Ascendant is listed next to that planet.
†Venus is both neutral and malefic with a Taurus Ascendant.

Table 6.3. Satyacharya's List of Individual Benefics, Malefics and Neutrals (continued).

ASCENDANT	BENEFIC	MALEFIC	NEUTRAL
Libra	Saturn [4 and 5] Mercury [9 and 12] Venus [1 and 8] Mars [2 and 7]	Sun [11] Jupiter [3 and 6] Moon [10]	
Scorpio	Moon [9] Jupiter [2 and 5] Sun [10]	Mercury [8 and 11] Venus [7 and 12]	Mars [1 and 6] Saturn [3 and 4]
Sagittarius	Mars [5 and 12] Sun [9]	Venus [6 and 11] Saturn [2 and 3] Mercury [7 and 10]	Jupiter [1 and 4] Moon [8]
Capricorn	Venus [5 and 10] Mercury [6 and 9] Saturn [1 and 2]	Mars [4 and 11] Jupiter [3 and 12] Moon [7]	Sun [8]
Aquarius	Venus [4 and 9] Sun [7] Mars [3 and 10] Saturn [1 and 12]	Jupiter [2 and 11] Moon [6]	Mercury [5 and 8]
Pisces	Moon [5] Mars [2 and 9]	Saturn [11 and 12] Sun [6] Venus [3 and 8] Mercury [4 and 7]	Jupiter [1 and 10]

146 ⟩ VEDIC ASTROLOGY

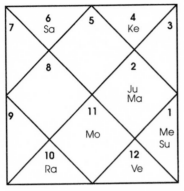 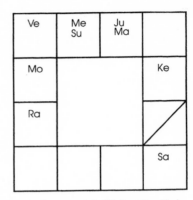

Figure 6.1. Jane's chart. Left: North Indian model; Right: South Indian model. Birth data withheld for confidentiality. Source: Birth certificate.

tor"). The strongest planet for a particular Lagna, the Yogakaraka for each Ascendant is as follows:

Aries:	Sun (5th house)
Taurus:	Saturn (9th & 10th)
Gemini:	Mercury (1st & 4th)
Cancer:	Mars (5th & 10th)
Leo:	Mars (4th & 9th)
Virgo:	Mercury (1st & 10th)
Libra:	Saturn (4th & 5th)
Scorpio:	Moon (9th)
Sagittarius:	Sun (9th)
Capricorn:	Venus (5th & 10th)
Aquarius:	Venus (4th & 9th)
Pisces:	Moon (5th)

Let's return to Barbara's chart. She has a Taurus Ascendant. Saturn rules Capricorn in the 9th house (a Trikona house) and Aquarius in the 10th house (a Kendra house). Since the 9th and 10th houses are both auspicious houses, Saturn, a natural malefic, becomes not only individually benefic, but the Yogakaraka—the most beneficial planet within the context of that chart.

Determine Planetary Friendship, Enmity, and Neutrality

Natural[2] friendship, enmity, and neutrality between planets, another means of judging planetary strength, is an interesting concept with no equivalent in Western astrology. Table 6.4 (page 148) lists these definitive planetary relationships according to the astrologer Satyacharya.[3] They are used to define the affinity of a particular planet with its dispositor (the ruler of the sign it occupies) and a planet with which it is conjoined (sharing the same sign/house).

To illustrate the concept of friendship and enmity between planet and house ruler, I like using the analogy of tenant and landlord. Every planet in the chart can be seen as the occupant, or guest, of the house in which it is placed. The planetary ruler of that house is viewed as the landlord. When there is friendship between tenant (planet) and landlord (planetary ruler), there will be excellent conditions surrounding the affairs of that house. A planet occupying a friendly house is empowered and the house will experience extreme good fortune. During its planetary period,[4] there will be success and a general sense of well-being. Neutrality between occupant and ruler brings relative harmony. While there will be problems from time to time, they will not be without resolution. However, when the house lord is inimical to the house occupant, the difficulties the planet experiences are comparable to a landlord harassing a tenant. In addition, the affairs of the house suffer, since it is similar to having an unwanted guest (or planet) in one's home. For example, if the planet ruling the 2nd house of finances is an enemy of the occupant, there may be some degree of financial difficulties especially during that planet's period.

> Effect of a planet occupying a friend's house in a nativity
> will be to make the owner thereof gain success. Through

---

[2] The concept of temporary friendship will not be discussed in this particular volume.

[3] Some Indian astrologers have also added Rahu and Kethu to this list but we will not use them here.

[4] Planetary periods will be discussed at length in chapters 9 and 10.

Table 6.4. Satyacharya's List of Natural Friendship, Enmity and Neutrality between the Planets.

PLANETS	FRIEND	ENEMY	NEUTRAL
Sun	Moon Jupiter Mars	Saturn Venus	Mercury
Moon	Sun Mercury		Venus Jupiter Mars Saturn
Mars	Sun Moon Jupiter	Mercury	Venus Saturn
Mercury	Sun Venus	Moon	Mars Jupiter Saturn
Jupiter	Sun Moon Mars	Mercury Venus	Saturn
Venus	Mercury Saturn	Sun Moon	Mars Jupiter
Saturn	Venus Mercury	Sun Moon Mars	Jupiter

*Varahamihira, *Brihat Jataka*, p.23.

his friends in all his attempts, cultivate new friendships, possess good sons, wife, wealth, corn and other fortunes and receive help from all people . . . If a planet should occupy an inimical sign the person concerned will have a base disposition of mind. He will live in others' houses eating their food. He will be utterly destitute and will always be teased by enemies. Even a person who was originally his friend will prove inimical to him in its planetary period.[5]

It is interesting to note that the relationship between two planets is not always reciprocal. As the most important heavenly body in Indian mythology, the Moon has no enemies. But whereas Mercury may be friendly towards the Moon, the Moon is Mercury's enemy. In viewing friendship and enmity, it is important to remember that the occupying planet is the subject of the inquiry. Therefore, if the Moon is posited in Mercury-ruled Virgo, it is situated in a friendly house since Mercury is its friend. By the same token, if Mercury is placed in Moon-ruled Cancer, it is in an inimical house since the Moon is Mercury's enemy. Satyacharya also states that if two planets are friendly one way and inimical another way, their relationship is neutral. Mercury and the Moon would, therefore, be considered to be neutral toward each other. Another example is Venus and Saturn, which are both neutral to the Moon while the Moon is an enemy to both. In this case, the Moon's enmity toward Venus and Saturn overpowers their neutrality. Because of the neutral influence, however, their inimical relationship is not as deadly as it would have been had they been enemies from both directions. It is also important to see that, while the Moon has no enemies, Jupiter can never be inimical to another planet since it is, after all, the "greater benefic."

Determine Aspects (Drishtis)

One of the most important means through which a planet is strengthened or weakened is an assessment of the aspect, or relationship, it receives from a *natural* benefic or malefic planet. For example, the natural malevolence of Saturn will be greatly re-

---

[5] Mantreswara, *Phaladeepika*, p. 121.

duced if it receives an aspect from Venus, a natural benefic. This means that the house which Saturn both rules and occupies will benefit by its relationship with Venus. By the same token, if Venus, a natural benefic, is aspected by Saturn, a natural malefic, the house Venus rules and occupies will be greatly weakened.

In Jyotish, aspects are calculated according to the number of houses separating the two planets rather than by the number of degrees, as in Occidental astrology. A planet is said to be *mutually* aspecting another planet when it is either situated in the same sign/house or seven signs/houses apart. In addition to aspecting a planet seven houses away, Mars, Jupiter, and Saturn each have special aspects. Mars always aspects the 4th and 8th houses from it, Jupiter aspects the 5th and 9th, and Saturn aspects the 3rd and 10th. When calculating aspects, it is important to remember that the planet is counted as the 1st house.

In addition to one planet aspecting another, a planet always aspects a house even if it is unoccupied. This principle is especially significant when applied to planets in the 7th house which aspect the Lagna (1st house). Since the Ascendant is the primary house of the zodiac from which everything emanates, any planet in the 7th house will influence health, appearance, and outlook on life—all that the Lagna represents. To this end, a benefic planet in the 7th house enhances one's constitution, appearance, and general well-being, while a malefic planet in the 7th house adversely affects those same concerns. In Jane's horoscope (see figure 6.1, page 146), the Lagna is aspected by the Moon in the 7th house so that the appearance and personality are influenced more by the Moon than the Sun, the Ascendant ruler. To this end, there is a highly emotional temperament, moodiness, and a round face and full figure like the Moon (see the Moon's description on page 142).

Utilizing figure 6.1 (page 146), let's see which planets and houses each graha aspects. The Sun aspects Mercury, which is in the same house, as well as the 3rd house, which is 7th from the Sun. The Moon aspects the Ascendant, Mercury aspects the Sun and the 3rd house, and Venus aspects Saturn, which is in the 2nd house, seven houses away. Mars aspects Jupiter (same house), the Ascendant by 4th house aspect, the 4th house by 7th house aspect, and the 5th house by 8th house aspect. Jupiter aspects Mars (same house), Saturn by 5th house aspect, the 4th house by 7th house aspect, and Rahu by 9th house aspect. Finally, Saturn aspects the 4th house by 3rd house aspect, Venus by 7th house aspect and the 11th house by 10th house aspect. Rahu and Kethu always aspect each other and in this particular chart there are no planets which share their houses. Although some sages believe that Rahu and Kethu provide a 5th and 9th house aspect, we will not be utilizing these aspects in this book.

It is important to remember that while aspects are considered most exact when they share the same numerical degrees, they are formed according to the houses which the planets occupy and not according to the degrees which lie between them. This is probably a difficult concept to understand for those whose background is Western astrology. In my client Steven's chart (figure 6.2), Saturn and Venus aspect one another, although Saturn is situated at 1° Leo in the 6th house and Venus is situated at 27° Aquarius in the 12th house. The relationship between Venus and Saturn constitutes a mutual aspect since they occupy opposing houses and signs. (In Western astrology they are 154° apart, and would not comprise an aspect.)

Other aspects used in Jyotish include three-quarter aspects (two planets which are 4 and 8 houses apart with three-quarter strength), half aspects (two planets which are 5 and 9 houses apart with half strength), and quarter aspects (two planets which are 3 and 10 houses apart with quarter strength).

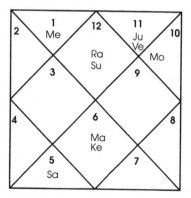 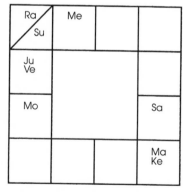

Figure 6.2. Steven's chart. Left: North Indian model; Right: South Indian model. Birth data withheld for confidentiality. Source: Birth certificate.

Evaluate the House a Planet Occupies

A planet is said to be powerful when placed in an auspicious Trikona (1st, 5th, or 9th) or Kendra (1st, 4th, 7th, or 10th) house, and loses its strength when positioned in an inauspicious Dusthana (6th, 8th, and 12th) house. When a planet is placed in an Upachaya, or growth, house (3rd, 6th, or 11th), it will gradually gain strength throughout one's life.[6] Whereas benefic planets are somewhat neutrally placed in these houses, malefic planets fare exceptionally well as they have reserves of strength with which to overcome obstacles. It is important to understand that, while malefics function optimally in these houses, difficulties and challenges still remain to be dealt with—usually successfully. The remaining 2nd house is somewhat neutral to its occupying planets.

Determine if a Planet is Vargottama

If a planet's zodiacal sign is identical to its corresponding Navamsa position, that planet is said to be placed in its Vargottama. In its Vargottama position, the qualities of the particular planet will become more emphatic. That means that Mars will become more assertive and perhaps aggressive, while Venus will become loving and sensual, yet more indulgent. It is important to remember that Jyotish practitioners believe that, above all else, the horoscope should provide moderation and balance. If there are too many benefic influences, there may be too much ease, indulgence, and a wasting of one's energies. By the same token, strongly malefic influences can often provide the discipline and courage to meet life's challenges. Table 6.5 (abbreviated from Table 3.5 on pages 50–52) lists the degrees of each sign that share the same navamsa sign and, therefore, comprise its Vargottama position.

Other means by which Jyotishis evaluate planetary strength has to do with retrogradation. Retrograde planets, which appear to be moving backward due to the slowing up of

---

[6] Since the 6th house is both an Upachaya and Dusthana house, it is usually considered to be the least malefic of the Dusthana houses and most difficult of the Upachaya houses.

Table 6.5. Vargottama Positions.

DEGREES	SIGN	NAVAMSA
0.00– 3.20	Aries	Aries
13.20–16.40	Taurus	Taurus
26.40–30.00	Gemini	Gemini
0.00– 3.20	Cancer	Cancer
13.20–16.40	Leo	Leo
26.40–30.00	Virgo	Virgo
0.00– 3.20	Libra	Libra
13.20–16.40	Scorpio	Scorpio
26.40–30.00	Sagittarius	Sagittarius
0.00– 3.20	Capricorn	Capricorn
13.20–16.40	Aquarius	Aquarius
26.40–30.00	Pisces	Pisces

planetary motion, are also employed to evaluate the condition of a planet. Although Hindu astrologers disagree as to whether retrograde planets are strengthened or weakened, I have come to the conclusion that the latter is more appropriate.[7] When the planets are retrograde, they seem to have the following effects:

> *Mercury:* An inability to think and communicate clearly and effectively;
> *Venus:* An inability to form relationships and be contented;
> *Mars:* Fear to move forward and take risks; lacking vitality;
> *Jupiter:* A tendency to waste opportunities; things do not always go according to plan;
> *Saturn:* A lack of discipline and an inability to concentrate.

If Venus or Jupiter is retrograde, for example, their beneficence is weakened. By the same token, if Mars or Saturn is retrograde, their malevolence is softened. Evaluation of a retrograde

---

[7] The ancients thought that retrograde planets were strengthened, since they are closest to the Earth during that part of the orbit. Modern western astrologers think of them as more inner-directed.

Mercury would obviously depend on whether that planet is in-dividually benefic or malefic.

Shad Bala

In Jyotish, the term *Shad Bala* (Sanskrit for "six strengths") refers to the six sources from which a planet draws its strength: position, aspect, natural strength, motion, direction, and time.

1. *Position (Sthanabala)*: According to their position in the horoscope, the planets are listed in their descending order as follows:

A.	Planet in its exaltation	} most
B.	Planet in its moolatrikona	} powerful
C.	Planet in its rulership	3/4 power
D.	Situated in a friend's house	5/8 power
E.	Situated in a Trikona or Kendra house	1/2 power

A planet is also in a position of power when it is placed in its rulership or exalted sign throughout the Varga charts.

A planet is stripped of its strength when placed in its fallen sign in the Rasi Chakra, in its fallen sign in some of the Varga charts, in the house of its enemy, and/or in a Dusthana house.

2. *Aspect (Drigbala)*: A planet becomes powerful when it is as-pected by a benefic, but loses its power when aspected by a malefic. (*Note*: Only Sthanabala and Drigbala comprise the steps that will be used in this book to judge planetary strength and weakness).

3. *Natural Strength (Naisargika Bala)*: The natural strengths of the planets are: (1) Rahu and Kethu, (2) The Sun, (3) The Moon, (4) Venus, (5) Jupiter, (6) Mercury, (7) Mars, and (8) Saturn.

4. *Strength of Motion (Chestabala)*: The Sun and the Moon are strong when placed in northern latitudes, i.e., those of Capricorn, Aquarius, Pisces, Aries, Taurus, and Gemini.

5. *Directional Strength (Dikbala)*: Mercury and Jupiter are strongest in the 1st house. The Moon and Venus are most powerful in the 4th house. Saturn displays the most strength in the 7th house. The Sun and Mars are at their best in the 10th house.

6. *Strength of Time (Kalabala)*: The Sun, Venus, and Jupiter are strongest in diurnal horoscopes while the Moon, Mars, and Saturn are strongest in nocturnal horoscopes.[8] Mercury, however, is equally powerful at all times. Benefics have stronger results when placed in a horoscope where there is a waxing Moon, whereas malefics have more strength in a chart with a waning moon.[9]

Shad Bala is a complicated system involving the assignation of numerical ratings to each planet. Planets are "rewarded" for each of the above positions of strength and "penalized" for each position of weakness. Whichever planet receives the highest rating according to Shad Bala will be the horoscope's strongest planet, thus enhancing the house that planet rules and that which it symbolizes. During that planet's period, everything it represents is likely to be realized. Although most Jyotish software includes planetary strengths and weaknesses according to Shad Bala, the programs will often disagree slightly. I recommend utilizing the methods set forth in this book alongside the figures supplied by the programmer.

Strengths and Weaknesses in Annemarie's Chart

The aforementioned steps used to determine planetary strength and weakness are exemplified in Annemarie's chart.

Step 1: Referring to Table 6.1 (page 140), there are no planets in their rulership, debilitation, exaltation, or moolatrikona in Annemarie's chart.

---

[8] Diurnal charts are those born during the daytime, i.e., after sunrise, while nocturnal charts are those born during the nighttime, i.e., after sunset.
[9] Krishnamurti, *Fundamental Principles of Astrology*, p. 24.

Table 6.6. Natural and Individual Temperaments of Annemarie's Planets.

PLANET	QUALITIES	HOUSE RULED	HOUSE OCCUPIED
Sun	Naturally Malefic Individually Malefic	11th	3rd
Moon	Naturally Benefic Individually Malefic	10th	7th
Mars	Naturally Malefic Individually Benefic	2nd, 7th	5th
Mercury	Naturally Neutral Individually Benefic	9th, 12th	2nd
Jupiter	Naturally Benefic Individually Malefic	3rd, 6th	7th
Venus	Naturally Benefic Individually Benefic	1st, 8th	4th
Saturn	Naturally Malefic Individually Benefic	4th, 5th	1st

Step 2: From Tables 6.2 (page 141) and 6.3 (pages 144–145), we can list the natural and individual temperaments of the planets according to a Libra Ascendant, along with the houses they rule and occupy. Mars, Mercury, Venus, and Saturn are benefic influences while the Sun, Moon, and Jupiter, on the other hand, are malefic due to the houses they rule.

Step 3: Annemarie's planets are listed according to the relationship the house occupant has to its house lord:

OCCUPYING PLANET	SIGN	HOUSE	RULER	RELATIONSHIP
Sun	Sagittarius	3rd	Jupiter	Friend
The Moon	Aries	7th	Mars	Neutral
Mars	Aquarius	5th	Saturn	Neutral
Mercury	Scorpio	2nd	Mars	Neutral
Jupiter	Aries	7th	Mars	Friend
Venus	Capricorn	4th	Saturn	Friend
Saturn	Libra	1st	Venus	Friend

Annemarie is fortunate that, from this perspective, none of her planets fall into inimical houses. Her planetary periods will be relatively beneficial due to the friendly houses each of her planets occupy.

Step 4: The planets are listed, accompanied by the planets and houses they aspect, as follows:

Sun:	9th house;
Moon:	Jupiter, Saturn;
Mars:	8th house, 11th house, 12th house;
Mercury:	8th house;
Jupiter:	Moon, 11th house, Saturn, Sun;
Venus:	Rahu and Kethu;
Saturn:	Sun, Moon, Jupiter, Kethu;
Rahu and Kethu:	Venus, 10th house.

It is interesting to note that, while Saturn is a natural malefic, it is (a) exalted, (b) in the 1st house, (c) an individual benefic, (d) yogakaraka, and (e) is aspected by two natural benefics—Jupiter and the Waxing Moon. This means that the affairs of the Saturn-occupied 1st house and the Saturn-ruled 3rd and 4th houses will be especially auspicious. In fact, Annemarie has a strong sense of destiny, works extremely hard to make her dreams realities, and has always been able to find a comfortable place to live.

Because the 1st house is the domain of the appearance, the aspect from Jupiter and the Moon should indicate a full figure. But since Saturn, "a thin and tall body,"[10] is by far the strongest and most beneficial planet in this chart, its placement on the Ascendant is conducive to Annemarie's slender figure. Jupiter and the Moon, excessive grahas aspecting the 1st house, nonetheless contribute to Annemarie's indulgent personality and poor habits which affect her health and general well-being. Saturn's protection of the Ascendant, however, will prevent the consequences of excess which the Moon and Jupiter would oth-

---

[10] Varahamihira, *Brihat Jataka*, p. 20.

erwise bestow. In addition, Venus, as Ascendant ruler adds its qualities of beauty to her physical appearance.

The influence of Venus, as the ruler of both the 1st and 8th houses, placed in the 4th house indicates that her parents and three sisters were extremely stable due to benefic Venus being placed in that house. On the other hand, the fact that Venus is the 8th house ruler, and the 4th house is aspected by Rahu and Kethu, explains not only the difficult relationship Annemarie has with her mother, but her unstable early years.

Step 5: Mars is in the auspicious 5th Trikona house while Saturn, Venus, Rahu, the Moon, Jupiter, and Kethu are placed in the 1st, 4th, 7th, and 10th Kendra houses, respectively—all auspicious Kendra houses. Mercury is in the neutral 2nd house. As both a natural and individual malefic, the Sun works well in the 3rd Upachaya house. There are no planets in the 6th, 8th, or 12th Dusthana houses.

Step 6: Table 6.8 (page 160) lists Annemarie's planets and their corresponding navamsa signs. Note that Saturn is in its Vargottama position which, along with its exalted placement in Libra, makes it one of the strongest planets in Annemarie's chart.

To facilitate the judgment of strong and weak planets, I have devised Tables 6.7 (page 159) and 6.10 (page 162), which is the "first layer" of rating planetary strength/weakness and encompasses Steps 1 and 2 above. As we delve further into other interpretive tools, these factors may be altered. By viewing this table, however, planetary strengths and weaknesses can be seen at first glance.

According to Table 6.7, the Moon, Jupiter, Sun, and Kethu have both weak and strong points. Based solely on house occupancy of planets, the 3rd, 7th, and 10th house will have both positive and negative associations. When students ask if this is contradictory, I simply respond that the horoscope reflects life which is composed of both positive and negative experiences. For those schooled in Western astrology, it is quite easy to understand how a planet can be both beneficially and detrimentally aspected.

Table 6.7. Determining Planetary Strength in Annemarie's Chart.

STRENGTH	SUN	MOON	MARS	MERCURY	JUPITER	VENUS	SATURN	RAHU	KETHU
Exaltation							X		
Moolatrikona									
Rulership									
In a friendly house	X				X	X	X		
In a Trikona or Kendra house		X	X		X	X	X	X	X
Aspected by a natural benefic	X	X			X		X		
In its Vargottama							X		

WEAKNESS	SUN	MOON	MARS	MERCURY	JUPITER	VENUS	SATURN	RAHU	KETHU
Debilitation									
In enemy's house									
In Dusthana					X				
Aspected by malefic	X	X			X				
Retrograde									X

Table 6.8. Annemarie's Planets and Navamsa Signs.

PLANETS	PLACEMENT	NAVAMSA
Ascendant	28 Libra 34	Gemini
Sun	11 Sagittarius 19	Cancer
Moon	12 Aries 00	Cancer
Mars	3 Aquarius 18	Libra
Mercury	21 Scorpio 00	Capricorn
Jupiter	18 Aries 02	Virgo
Venus	25 Capricorn 08	Leo
Saturn	**2 Libra 45**	**Libra**
North Node	20 Capricorn 01	Cancer
South Node	20 Cancer 01	Capricorn

Strengths and Weaknesses in Barbara's Chart

Barbara's chart will be analyzed in the same manner, according to the six steps for judging planetary strengths and weaknesses.

Step 1: There are no exalted or fallen planets in Barbara's chart. However, Jupiter is located at 1° Sagittarius 40', its moolatrikona and rulership sign, and is conjoined with Venus. Since these are among the most powerful placements for a planet, Jupiter will receive "high marks" for this position, as it will for its beneficial placement throughout the Varga charts (Tables 3.5, 3.9, and 3.10 on pages 50–52, 58, 59). However, there are other positions which diminish Jupiter's power, namely individual malevolence, aspects by Saturn and Mars, and its placement in the 8th house. According to Shad Bala (which can be computed with any software program), Jupiter is the strongest planet in Barbara's chart. However, these calculations will vary, depending on the particular program.

Step 2. With a Taurus Ascendant, Saturn (Yogakaraka), Mercury, Mars, and the Sun are individually benefic planets and enhance the houses they occupy (see Table 6.9). Ironically, the naturally benefic Moon, Venus and Jupiter are individually malefic in this chart. Because Jupiter is in Sagittarius, the sign

Table 6.9. Natural and Individual Temperaments of Barbara's Planets.

PLANET	QUALITIES	HOUSE RULED	HOUSE OCCUPIED
Sun	Naturally Malefic Individually Benefic	4th	9th
Moon	Naturally Benefic Individually Malefic	3rd	10th
Mars	Naturally Malefic Individually Benefic	7th, 12th	8th
Mercury	Naturally Neutral Individually Benefic	2nd, 5th	9th
Jupiter	Naturally Benefic Individually Malefic	8th, 11th	8th
Venus	Naturally Benefic Individually Neutral	1st, 6th	8th
Saturn	Naturally Malefic Individually Benefic	9th, 10th	8th

of its rulership and moolatrikona, its role as a malefic will be somewhat reduced.

Step 3: Let us now repeat the process with Barbara's chart to see if there is friendship, enmity, and neutrality between each planet and its house lord.

OCCUPYING PLANET	SIGN	HOUSE	RULER	RELATIONSHIP
Sun	Capricorn	9th	Saturn	Enemy
The Moon	Aquarius	10th	Saturn	Neutral
Mars	Sagittarius	8th	Jupiter	Friend
Mercury	Capricorn	9th	Saturn	Neutral
Jupiter	Sagittarius	8th	Jupiter	Own House
Venus	Sagittarius	8th	Jupiter	Neutral
Saturn	Sagittarius	8th	Jupiter	Neutral

The Sun, occupying the Saturn-ruled 9th house, is the only planet placed in an enemy's house. Because the Sun is uncom-

Table 6.10. Determining Planetary Strength in Barbara's Chart.

STRENGTH	SUN	MOON	MARS	MERCURY	JUPITER	VENUS	SATURN	RAHU	KETHU
Exaltation									
Moolatrikona					X				
Rulership					X				
In a friendly house			X						
In a Trikona or Kendra house	X	X		X				X	
Aspected by a natural benefic			X		X	X	X		
In its Vargottama									

WEAKNESS	SUN	MOON	MARS	MERCURY	JUPITER	VENUS	SATURN	RAHU	KETHU
Debilitation	X								
In enemy's house									
In Dusthana			X		X	X	X		
Aspected by malefic		X	X	X	X	X	X	X	
Retrograde								X	X

fortable there, a certain degree of conflict will arise pertaining to her father and higher education. The Sun's individual benefi-cence and conjunction with Mercury will help to resolve these problems which Barbara had with her father at one time. As far as education is concerned, while Barbara did indeed attend sev-eral different colleges, Barbara not only received her B.A., but eventually went on to receive a graduate degree.

Step 4: The planets are listed, accompanied by the planets and houses they aspect, as follows:

Sun:	Mercury, 3rd house;
Moon:	4th house;
Mars:	Venus, Jupiter, Saturn, Kethu, 2nd house, 3rd house;
Mercury:	Sun, 3rd house;
Jupiter:	Venus, Mars, Saturn, 12th house, 2nd house, 4th house;
Venus:	Mars, Jupiter, Saturn, 2nd house;
Saturn:	Venus, Mars, Jupiter, Moon, 2nd house, Rahu;
Rahu and Kethu:	5th and 11th house.

Since Barbara's planets (other than Rahu and Kethu) are placed within the 8th, 9th, and 10th houses, she does not have two planets which *mutually* aspect each other by 7th house aspect. The 2nd house of finances and appetite, however, receives a 7th-house aspect from Venus, Mars, Saturn, and Jupiter in the 8th house. The fact that these planets are both benefic *and* malefic affects her erratic eating habits as well as her finances. Despite the fact that Barbara and her husband have a better than average earning capacity, extravagance is constantly de-pleting their assets.

Saturn aspecting so many planets in the chart has a pro-found effect on her melancholic disposition. Its aspect to the Moon, which rules the 3rd house of mentality and courage, makes it difficult for her to dispel negativity and face life head on. The aspect which the 3rd house receives from the Sun and Mercury, however, enables Barbara to call upon her reasoning abilities. Together with the self-esteem she extracts from professional achievements, Barbara is able to overcome her initial self-doubt and strive for success.

Step 5: The Sun and Mercury are placed in the 9th Trikona house and the Moon is in the 10th Kendra house. Saturn, Jupiter, Venus, and Mars lose their power by virtue of their placement in the 8th Dusthana house. Rahu and Kethu are well-situated in the 5th Trikona house and 11th Upachaya house where a malefic placement brings good results.

It is clear from this first layer that Mercury is Barbara's strongest planet, since it is the one placed unequivocally in positive categories. As stated earlier, Jupiter is exceptionally powerful placed in Sagittarius—its moolatrikona and rulership sign; but it also has other elements which present it with some difficulty. On the other hand, Venus may be the Ascendant ruler conjoined with Jupiter, but it also governs the 6th house, is placed in the 8th house, and is aspected by Mars and Saturn—detrimental influences. Because the planets personify the houses they rule, Barbara's health (6th house) may be fragile and she must pay attention to the body parts ruled by Venus (eyes, kidneys) and by the sign of the 6th house, Libra (abdomen). These health problems may surface during the planetary periods ruled by Venus or during times of emotional stress. Because Jupiter, Saturn, and Mars all occupy the same house, Venus is somewhat protected but not completely immune.

Step 6: Barbara does not have any planets in their Vargottama position.

Determining House Strength

The strength or weakness of a house may be evaluated by determining the following:

1. Whether its occupant and house lord have a friendly or inimical relationship (as seen from Table 6.4, page 148);

2. Whether the house is aspected by a benefic or malefic planet;

3. Whether a benefic, neutral, or malefic occupies that house.

Although there are many categories of houses in Jyotish, the ones we will be working with are once again as follows:

Trikona Houses (1st, 5th, 9th)—the most auspicious houses;

Kendra Houses (1st, 4th, 7th, 10th)—auspicious houses;

Upachaya Houses (3rd, 6th, 10th, 11th)—growth, or difficult, houses;

Dusthana Houses (6th, 8th, 12th)—inauspicious houses.

The qualities of each house change depending on the nature of the planet situated there. Generally speaking, the following principles are used to determine house strength when a naturally *and* individually benefic or malefic planet occupies that house:

1. A benefic planet enhances the house it occupies or aspects;

2. A malefic planet weakens the house it occupies or aspects;

3. The exception to Rule 2 states that a malefic planet occupying the 3rd, 6th, 10th, or 11th[11] Upachaya houses will cause struggle, effort and eventual success.

If a house is occupied by a planet that is naturally benefic and individually malefic or vice versa, the effect on that house is both positive and negative. In figure 6.1 (page 146), Venus, a natural benefic and individual malefic, adds generosity to the 12th house, as well as a tendency toward extravagance.

---

[11] The 6th house (classified as Dusthana and Upachaya) and the 10th house (classified as Kendra and Upachaya) are considered Upachaya houses when this principle is applied.

A difficult concept to grasp in Jyotish is how a planet may enhance a house it occupies at the same time the house weakens the planet. In other words, a malefic planet can be empowered by occupying a benefic house, yet the benefic house is ruined by that malefic planet, and vice versa. Due to the exalted position of Venus in the 8th house in Jane's horoscope (figure 6.1, page 146), longevity, business transactions, and the partner's finances are enhanced. The 8th house influence on Venus, however, not only affects Jane's relationships adversely, but hurts the affairs of the 3rd and 10th house which Venus rules. Her professional status (10th house) has, in fact, gone through a series of ups and downs.

With so many planets in Barbara's 8th house, her chart is a perfect example of the contradictions between house strength and planetary strength. Each planet—Venus, Mars, Jupiter, and Saturn—is weakened by its placement in the 8th Dusthana house. On the other hand, a benefic planet placed in the 8th house will bring good fortune to that house. Although the affairs of the 8th house will, therefore, be less devastating, the house still weakens its occupying planets and the houses they rule.

There are different ways to judge the strength of both a planet and a house and the use of one method alone is never sufficient. Although this seems contradictory and unworkable, the two systems can actually work as checks and balances so there is never any pronouncement until all facets of the chart are considered. In the end, it is important to weigh every factor carefully before making a definitive pronouncement.

PLANETARY YOGAS

YOGAS (SANSKRIT FOR "UNION") refer to any type of planetary combination or signature in the horoscope which yields specific results and can include conjunctions (two or more planets in the same sign/house), mutual receptivity, aspects, or certain spatial relationships (e.g., Moon in the 2nd house from Venus). Although there are hundreds of yogas mentioned throughout the scriptures, what follows are descriptions of the ones which are most commonly utilized and which, according to my experience, have proven effective in chart analysis. It is important to remember that, while yogas call attention to certain subtleties in the personality, they only yield the maximum results when the Lagna, the Moon, and the yoga-forming planets are not connected with malefic planets. These combinations usually have the most profound effect during the *dasa* (planetary period) and *bhukti* (sub-period) of the planets involved.

Pancha Mahapurusha Yogas[1]

Mahapurusha yogas occur when Mars, Mercury, Jupiter, Venus, or Saturn occupy their exaltation or rulership signs in the 1st, 4th, 7th, or 10th house (Kendra houses) from the Lagna or Moon. It is important to note that these combinations will give especially positive results if the Lagna, Moon, or yoga-forming planets are not conjoining malefic planets.

Ruchaka Yoga: Mars occupying Capricorn (Exaltation), Aries (Rulership) or Scorpio (Rulership), in the 1st, 4th, 7th, or 10th house (Kendra houses) from the Lagna or Moon. This yoga will endow the individual with assertiveness, aggression, commanding presence, strong physicality, sense of adventure, and the ability to initiate projects and follow them through. There may also be the pursuit of fame, which is likely to be realized during the dasa or bhukti of Mars.

---

[1] Mantreswara, *Phaladeepika* (Bangalore: K. Subrahmanyam, 1981), p. 61.

Ted Bundy, the serial killer, has a Leo Ascendant with Kethu (19°), Mars (20°), and Moon (24°) in Scorpio in the 4th house. Mars is in its rulership sign in both the Rasi Chakra and Chandra Lagna, thereby causing Ruchaka yoga. Since Mars is "hemmed in" by Kethu[2] and a fallen Moon in Scorpio, the positive side of this yoga is eclipsed, and the darker side of Mars has emerged. While Ruchaka yoga provided Ted Bundy with an assertive, driven personality, it emphasized its cunning, aggressive, and murderous side. In her book *The Stranger Beside Me*, Ann Rule, a personal acquaintance of Bundy, states clearly that Bundy, like many serial killers, was obsessed with being famous. In Bundy's case, infamous is more like it.

Bhadra Yoga: Mercury positioned in Virgo (Exaltation and Rulership), or Gemini (Rulership) in the 1st, 4th, 7th, or 10th house from the Lagna or the Moon. There is a great deal of intelligence, curiosity, sensuality, and the individual is blessed with friends, physical comfort, and generosity. There will be opportunities for professional advancement and financial success which may be realized during the planetary period or subperiod of Mercury.

Hamsa Yoga: Jupiter occupying Cancer (Exaltation), Sagittarius (Rulership), or Pisces (Rulership) in the 1st, 4th, 7th, or 10th house from the Lagna or the Moon. These people are benevolent, generous, stately, graceful, and often domineering both physically and socially. They are noted for being philosophical, religious, righteous, and well-liked.

Malavya Yoga: Venus positioned in Pisces (Exaltation), Taurus (Rulership), or Libra (Rulership) in the 1st, 4th, 7th, or 10th house from the Lagna or the Moon. This is the mark of someone who is extremely attractive, creative, sensual, and extravagant. Although one particular Malavya yoga, Venus in the 7th house, is profitable and creative, it also places too much emphasis on sexual desires, especially in the horoscope of a male. A prime ex-

---

[2] When a house or planet is surrounded by malefics in the houses on either side, it is considered to be "hemmed in" or receiving a malefic influence. By the same token, if a house or planet is boxed in by two benefic planets, that house or planet will be enhanced.

ample is Hugh Hefner, whose penchants for beautiful women and hedonistic parties are legendary. He is, however, extremely successful, wealthy, and, of course, made his fortune through sexual associations. With Venus in the 7th house, creative and successful Charlie Chaplin, obsessed with younger women, was forced to leave Hollywood due to numerous scandals involving sexual liaisons with women young enough to be his daughters.

Sasa Yoga: Saturn occupying Libra (Exaltation), Capricorn (Rulership), or Aquarius (Rulership) in the 1st, 4th, 7th, or 10th house from the Lagna or the Moon. This person is extremely bright, single-minded, ambitious, and ruthless in a quest for financial success. There will be a display of leadership abilities, fearlessness, and fierce independence. One client with Saturn in Capricorn in the 4th house, a very affluent entrepreneur, admitted to engaging in business practices which could be viewed as ruthless and unethical but which he considered necessary to assure success. With Saturn in Aquarius in the 7th house from the Moon in Leo, Shirley MacLaine (figure 7.1) has

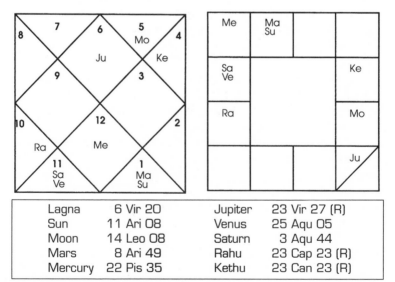

Lagna	6 Vir 20	Jupiter	23 Vir 27 (R)
Sun	11 Ari 08	Venus	25 Aqu 05
Moon	14 Leo 08	Saturn	3 Aqu 44
Mars	8 Ari 49	Rahu	23 Cap 23 (R)
Mercury	22 Pis 35	Kethu	23 Can 23 (R)

Figure 7.1. Shirley MacLaine's chart. Krishnamurti Ayanamsa 22°50'. True Nodes. Left: North Indian model; Right: South Indian model. Birth data: April 24, 1934, 3:57 P.M. EST (GMT-5), Richmond, VA (37N33, 77W27). Source: Birth certificate.

not only succeeded as an actress but has managed to remain at the top of her profession. The fact that she was the only female member of the "Hollywood Rat Pack" may be attributed to her toughness.

Chandra, or Lunar, Yogas

There are quite a few significant yogas which are defined by the position of the Moon in relation to other planets. It is important to note that in discussing the following yogas, reference is made to the general, and not individual, states of benefics and malefics. Therefore, benefic planets include Venus, Jupiter, Moon, and Mercury[3] and malefic planets include Sun, Mars, Saturn, Rahu, and Kethu.

Kesari Yoga: This occurs when the Moon and Jupiter are angular from one another, that is, either in the same house or 4, 7 or 10 houses apart. For example, if the Moon is in the 2nd house and Jupiter is in the 5th house, the yoga is formed because they are 4 houses apart. This yoga will bestow prosperity, good health, honesty, and a reputation for high moral and ethical standards. The person will possess intelligence, passion, emotional intensity, and "will destroy his enemies like a lion."[4]

This yoga occurs quite frequently, since it takes the Moon 2 to 2½ days to traverse a zodiacal sign. Therefore, the luminary will be angular to Jupiter, which stays in one sign for approximately one year, for 8-10 days out of every month.

The following yogas describe the effect of planets which are situated in the 2nd and 12th houses from the Moon. Because the Moon represents how we think and feel about life, planets surrounding this heavenly body directly affect whether we will be content and optimistic, or sorrowful and lonely.

---

[3] Although Mercury is usually classified as neutral, in much the same way the waning Moon is considered a mild malefic, Mercury and the Moon are usually considered benefic when thrown into the context of yogas.

[4] Mantreswara, *Phaladeepika* (New Delhi: Ranjan Publications, 1991), p. 70.

Sunapha Yoga: If a planet other than the Sun and the Nodes occupies the 2nd house from the Moon, the individual will be wealthy, respected, intellectual, spiritual, and virtuous. If the planet is malefic, there may be difficulty earning and saving money—the same interpretation as a malefic situated in the 2nd house from Lagna.

Anapha Yoga: When a planet other than the Sun and the Nodes occupies the 12th house from the Moon, the person will be robust, influential, well known, content, and virtuous. If the planet is malefic, the individual may be indulgent, wasteful, and lack physical vitality—the same interpretation as a malefic in the 12th house from Lagna.

According to K. S. Charak, author of *Elements of Vedic Astrology*, Sunapha yoga is concerned with the 2nd house qualities of accumulation and possession, whereas Anapha yoga is concerned with the 12th house qualities of spending and enjoyment.[5]

Durudhara Yoga: This occurs when planets occupy both the 2nd and 12th houses from the Moon. If the planets are benefics, the yoga endows the individual with wealth, possessions, generosity, loyal colleagues, and friends. If the planets are malefic, there may be emotional instability or insensitivity. It is important to see which house the Moon occupies and rules before making a final judgment.

The effects of Sunapha, Anapha and Durudhara yogas are modified by whether the surrounding planet is a natural benefic, which strengthens the emotions, or a natural malefic, which causes emotional instability and mood swings. If both a malefic and benefic surround the Moon, they should be judged according to which falls in the 2nd or 12th house from the Moon.

---

[5] K. S. Charak, *Elements of Vedic Astrology* (New Delhi: Vision Wordtronic, 1994), p. 143.

Kemadruma Yoga: The Kemadruma Moon occurs when there are no planets other than the Sun and the Nodes situated in the 1st, 2nd, and 12th houses from the Moon. The individual may feel cut off or out of touch with emotions which are, as represented by the Moon, isolated from the rest of the horoscope. As a result, this position usually brings with it a certain degree of loneliness, sorrow, and/or an inability to express feeling. Depending on the remainder of the horoscope, there may also be an absence of empathy, sensitivity, and the ability to enjoy life.

According to most sages, the effects of Kemadruma Moon may be mitigated if the 1st, 4th, 7th, or 10th house from the Lagna or Moon are occupied. Although O. J. Simpson's Moon is placed in the 8th house and is not surrounded or aspected by any other planets, Mars in the 10th house would lessen its effect, according to this rule.

Solar Yogas[6]

The following yogas are based on the same principles as the Sunapha, Anapha, and Durudhara yogas and describe the effect of planets which are situated in the 2nd and 12th houses from the Sun. Because the Sun represents our ambition and strength of character, planets on either side of the Sun directly affect our ability to define and ultimately fulfill our goals.

Subhavesi Yoga: If a benefic planet other than the Moon and the Nodes occupies the 2nd house from the Sun, the individual will be wealthy, respected, intellectual, spiritual and virtuous. If the planet is malefic, the yoga is called Papavasi, and there may be difficulty earning and saving money—the same interpretation as a malefic situated in the 2nd house from Lagna.

Subhavasi Yoga: When a planet other than the Moon and the Nodes occupies the 12th house from the Sun, the person will

---

[6] See Mantreswara, *Phaladeepika*, p. 66.

be robust, influential, well-known, contented and virtuous. If the planet is malefic, the yoga is called Papavasi, and the individual may be indulgent, wasteful, and lacking physical vitality—the same interpretation as a malefic in the 12th house from Lagna.

Subhobhayachari Yoga: This occurs when planets occupy both the 2nd and 12th houses from the Sun. If the planets are benefics, the yoga endows the individual with wealth, possessions, generosity, loyal colleagues and friends. If the planets are malefic, the yoga is called Papobhayachari, and there may be emotional instability or insensitivity.

The effects of these solar yogas are always modified by whether the surrounding planet is a natural benefic, which strengthens the confidence, or a natural malefic, which causes lack of ambition and self-doubt. If both a malefic and benefic surround the Sun, the effects should be judged according to which falls in the 2nd or 12th house from the Sun.

Yogas Affecting the Lagna

The following two yogas affect the appearance and health when the Lagna is hemmed in by benefics and malefics:

Subhakartari Yoga: This yoga is formulated when a natural benefic occupies the 2nd and 12th house from Lagna. The combination endows the individual with courage, good health, beauty, social skills, popularity, and happiness.

Papakartari Yoga: This yoga, which occurs when a natural malefic occupies the 2nd and 12th house from Lagna, will provide low vitality, possible health problems, a degree of loneliness, and, at times, an inability to get along with others.

Because the Lagna represents general constitution, both Subhakartari and Papakartari yogas affect the health, especially in the planetary periods corresponding to the yoga-forming planets and/or Lagna lord. Malefic planets occupying both the 12th and 2nd houses from Lagna often indicate severe nearsightedness, since these houses represent the right and left eye

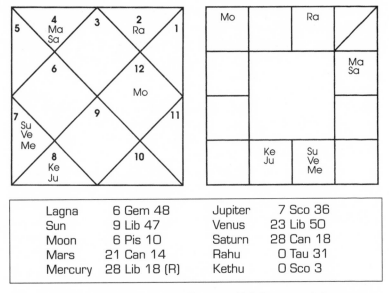

Mo		Ra	
			Ma Sa
	Ke Ju	Su Ve Me	

Lagna	6 Gem 48	Jupiter	7 Sco 36
Sun	9 Lib 47	Venus	23 Lib 50
Moon	6 Pis 10	Saturn	28 Can 18
Mars	21 Can 14	Rahu	0 Tau 31
Mercury	28 Lib 18 (R)	Kethu	0 Sco 3

Figure 7.2. Hillary Rodham Clinton. Krishnamurti Ayanamsa 23°02′03″. True Nodes. Left: North Indian model; Right: South Indian model. Birth data: October 26, 1947, 8:00:00 P.M. CST(GMT-6), Chicago, IL, 41N52′00″ 87W39′00″. Source: Given to astrologer Celeste Longacre, but there are other birthtimes for her.

respectively. A very myopic Hillary Rodham Clinton (figure 7.2) has Rahu in the 12th house, with Mars and Saturn in the 2nd house. I have Kethu in the 12th house and Saturn in the 2nd house, and have been afflicted with severe nearsightedness from the time I was a child.

As is the case with most yogas, the effects of benefics will be somewhat lessened if they are aspected by malefics or are situated in their fallen positions. Conversely, the effects of malefics may be tempered if they are aspected by benefics or occupy their exaltation or rulership positions. If the Sun is in Aries (Exaltation) in the 12th house, its effects on the Ascendant will be somewhat favorable. On the other hand, if Venus is in Virgo (Fall) in the 2nd house, it will not have a positive effect on one's constitution.

The principle of being surrounded by benefics or malefics can apply to any house of the Rasi Chakra. If malefics, for example, occupy the 6th and 8th houses of the horoscope, the 7th house of marriage will be adversely affected especially during the Dasa periods corresponding to those malefics or the 7th house lord. If benefics, however, are situated in the 6th and 8th houses, there will be excellent results for marriage and partnership during those particular dasas.

Parivartana Yoga

Parivartana yoga, known in Occidental astrology as mutual reception, occurs when two planets occupy the signs/houses that the other rules (e.g., Sun in Libra and Venus in Leo). This placement strengthens the relationship between the two planets, causing them to function as though they were actually aspecting one another. In addition, this yoga will forge a bond between the two houses which the planets rule and occupy. If one of the planets constituting this yoga is lord of the 6th, 8th, or 12th house, the affairs of the house that planet occupies will be problematic. Mantreswara divides Parivartana yogas into three categories:

Maha Yogas: This yoga involves a mutual reception between two house lords with the exception of the rulers of the 3rd, 6th, 8th, and 12th houses. The yoga will bestow professional success, personal happiness, and favorable circumstances for the two houses involved, and success will come to fruition during the dasa and bhukti period of the two planets.

In addition to her Sasa yoga, Shirley MacLaine has a Parivartana (Maha) yoga with Jupiter in Virgo and Mercury in Pisces. Mercury ruling the 1st–10th houses and Jupiter ruling the 4th–7th houses constitutes a Maha yoga, which accounts for her remarkable successes. MacLaine's Parivartana yoga, which consists of Jupiter in Virgo and Mercury in Pisces, also results in a Neecha Bhanga yoga, or cancellation of Mercury's debilitation by virtue of the 7th house exchange with the Lagna.

Dainya Yogas: This yoga occurs when one of the planets involved is the ruler of the 6th, 8th, or 12th house. This combination will be beneficial for the Dusthana house whose ruler will be placed in an auspicious house. It will, however, be detrimental to the affairs of the auspicious house whose ruler will be posited in a Dusthana house. A Parivartana yoga between the 8th and 10th houses, for example, will elevate the affairs of the 8th house by placing its ruler in a positive Kendra house and, at the same time, it will present obstacles to the 10th career house which lessens the ability to achieve and maintain professional recognition.

Kahala Yogas: This yoga involves the exchange of the 3rd house lord with any other house ruler except for the lord of the 6th, 8th, or 12th. The individual with this yoga will experience ups and downs throughout life, alternating between periods of success and disappointments.

Raj Yogas

Raj yogas, meaning "royal combinations," are specific planetary combinations which promise prosperity, success, and generally fortuitous circumstances. Of the hundreds of Raj yogas mentioned throughout the scriptures, the following are the ones I recommend that beginning students utilize.

It is important to note that, if the yoga-forming planets are benefic and are situated in a Trikona or Kendra house, the combination will be stronger and more beneficial than if the yoga-forming planets are malefic and situated in an Upachaya or Dusthana house. Raj yogas generally enhance the affairs of the house which the planets occupy or rule, and the effects will be felt especially during the planetary period and sub-period of the planets involved.

The simplest Raj yogas are formed when several planets occupy their exaltation and/or rulership signs and are as follows:

1. A person with three planets occupying their rulership or exaltation signs will be extremely powerful, successful, and will

either own land or a business if raised in an affluent family. Conversely, if not born into a wealthy family, that person will be financially successful, but not likely to own a company or employ others. Achievements will be the result of persistence and hard work.

With Sun in Aries (Exaltation), Moon in Cancer (Rulership), and Mars in Capricorn (Exaltation), three planets in their rulership and exaltation signs, Queen Elizabeth II is a perfect example of one who was literally, rather than figuratively, destined to be Queen. Born into a royal family, she ascended the throne after the death of her father, who only became King when the true heir, his brother, the Duke of Windsor, abdicated.

2. If four or five planets occupy their exaltation or rulership signs, a person will be powerful, successful, own land, head a company, or be in the public eye—regardless of family background. The horoscope of a client whom I will call "Rama" perfectly exemplifies this particular yoga. Born into a poor-to-middle-class family in India, he has the Sun in Aries (exalted), Venus in Pisces (exalted), Jupiter in Cancer (exalted) and Saturn in Libra (exalted). Under normal circumstances, he would have gone into the same line of work as his father. Due to a twist of fate, he went to live with a relative as a teenager, studied hard, and was encouraged to attend medical school. Currently a successful doctor, Rama is in the midst of his Mercury dasa. Even though he is quite respected and affluent, Mercury conjoins Mars natally and is in its fallen position in the navamsa chart. As a result, Rama suffers from mental depression and constantly doubts his own worth. It is important to note that, while Raj yogas promote professional accomplishments, they are not an indication of personal happiness or peace of mind.

These horoscopes indicate that when the scriptural language is transposed into modern terminology, ancient teachings which at first glance often seem irrelevant can suddenly apply to contemporary horoscope interpretation. Belonging to a "king's family" implies that one comes from a family of means who can provide countless opportunities, while a "lowly family" implies that one has come from modest circumstances.

The ancient concept of "Kingship" is tantamount to asserting complete autonomy over one's domain, which may include owning a thriving business or holding a powerful corporate or political position. Instead of maintaining servants and dwelling in palatial luxury, however, the person may simply employ a large work force and/or be a homeowner—the scope of the "domain" will depend on other chart factors and the individual's background. And if one is "equal to a king or wealthy," he or she will have good earning power, but will probably always work for someone else. Additionally, natural benefics occupying rulership or exaltation signs will produce a "good king" or, in modern terms, a fair employer, while naturally malefic planets placed in those same positions will produce a "dictator" or what we consider to be a tyrannical boss.

One of the most potent yet simplest Raj yogas to compute is the association of the 5th and 9th house rulers by conjunction, mutual aspect,[7] or mutual reception. Because this particular combination also constitutes a Dhana, or wealth-producing yoga (see below), it will produce financial as well as professional success. The planets which can form this Raj yoga for each Ascendant are as follows:

Ascendants	*Yoga-forming planets*
Aries	Sun and Jupiter
Taurus	Mercury and Saturn
Gemini	Venus and Saturn
Cancer	Mars and Jupiter
Leo	Jupiter and Mars
Virgo	Saturn and Venus
Libra	Saturn and Mercury
Scorpio	Jupiter and Moon
Sagittarius	Mars and Sun
Capricorn	Venus and Mercury
Aquarius	Mercury and Venus
Pisces	Moon and Mars[8]

---

[7] A mutual aspect only occurs with a 7th house aspect since both planets influence one another. This is not the case with the special aspects of Mars, Jupiter, and Saturn which are not reciprocated.

[8] Parasara, *Hora Sastra* (New Delhi: Ranjan Publications, 1991), p. 395.

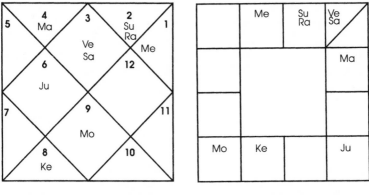

		Me	Su Ra	Ve Sa

Lagna	15 Gem 35	Jupiter	25 Vir 22 (R)
Sun	5 Tau 59	Venus	2 Gem 46
Moon	25 Sag 17	Saturn	28 Gem 06
Mars	20 Can 21	Rahu	27 Tau 47 (R)
Mercury	23 Ari 30	Kethu	27 Sco 47 (R)

Figure 7.3. Cher. Krishnamurti Ayanamsa: 23°00′51″. True Nodes. Left: North Indian model; Right: South Indian model. Birth data: May 20, 1946, 7:25:00 A.M. PST(GMT-8), El Centro, CA; 32N47′00″ 115W34′00″. Source: Birth certificate.

The affairs of the houses these planets occupy or rule will greatly benefit from this fortuitous placement and may hold the key to the individual's accomplishments. In Cher's horoscope (figure 7.3), Venus (ruler of 5th) conjoins Saturn (ruler of 9th) in the 1st house of destiny. This panned out for Cher, whose career was decided for her when, as a teenager, she met and married Sonny Bono.

In Hillary Rodham Clinton's chart (figure 7.2, page 174), Mercury (ruler of 1st) conjoins Venus (ruler of 5th) to form a Raj yoga in the 5th house of children and intelligence. Although she only has one child, Rodham Clinton has a passionate, long-term involvement with the Children's Defense Fund and serves on its Board of Directors. Additionally, the 5th house represents intelligence and originality—qualities which have catapulted Rodham Clinton to the top of her profession.

Another very common Raj yoga is formed when the lord of a Trikona house (1st, 5th, or 9th) and lord of a Kendra house (4th, 7th, and 10th) are related either by conjunction, mutual aspect, or mutual reception. In fact, the planetary ruler of any of these houses placed in one of these houses is the simplest form of this yoga. Since Lakshmi and Vishnu are associated with Trinal houses and Kendra houses respectively, this yoga is said to endow the individual with blessings of the deities. This yoga also occurs when the lord of a Trikona is placed in a Kendra or when the ruler of a Kendra is placed in a Trikona.[9] The affairs of the houses these lords occupy will be greatly enhanced, especially during the planetary periods and sub-periods of the yoga-forming planets.

Shirley MacLaine's chart contains a Raj yoga formed by two planets which are in mutual reception, as well as aspecting one another. Because Mercury as Trikona lord (1st house) and Jupiter as Kendra Lord (4th and 7th houses aspect each other), this combination constitutes a Trikona Kendra Raj yoga. Since the Sun is in Aries (Exaltation), Mars is in Aries (Rulership), and Saturn is in Aquarius (Rulership), she also has the Raj yoga which states that one will become a king if one is born into a royal family. Although MacLaine's background was middle class, her mother encouraged her to take dancing lessons throughout her youth, and to go to New York as a budding performer.

Dhana Yogas

Dhana, or wealth-producing, yogas provide the potential to amass income which is usually connected to the areas of life represented by the houses occupied or ruled by the yoga-forming planets. Like Raj yogas, these yogas do not always fulfill the promise of prosperity until the planetary period and sub-period of the two planets involved. The simplest Dhana yogas are formed when the rulers of the 1st, 2nd, 5th, 9th, and 11th houses are conjoined, mutually aspected, or in mutual recep-

---

[9] It is important to note that this yoga will not occur if only the 4th, 7th, and 10th rulers are involved.

tion with one another. On a much simpler level, it occurs when the ruler of one of these houses is placed in another one of these houses. These houses are associated with this yoga because the 2nd (money) and 11th (profit) are financial houses, while the 1st, 5th, and 9th generally provide favorable circumstances throughout one's lifetime. Like Raj yogas, the houses occupied by these planets define the areas of life which will supply the sources of income.

In addition to the Sasa yoga, Parivartana yogas, and Raj yogas already discussed, Shirley MacLaine possesses Dhana yogas which have surely been instrumental in her continued success. In fact, MacLaine's chart is a perfect example of one whose plethora of yogas is responsible for her multi-talented achievements which have propelled her in many different directions throughout the world. Venus, ruler of the 2nd and 9th house, conjoins Saturn, ruler of the 5th and 6th house, in the 6th house, making it both a Raj yoga (ruler of 5th conjunct ruler of the 9th) and Dhana yoga (ruler of 5th conjunct ruler of the 2nd and 9th). This yoga provides the ability to acquire wealth through hard work and the ability to "conquer her competitors." As in Cher's chart, the 5th and 9th house rulers are not only the most auspicious houses in the horoscope but individually benefic planets and friends of the Ascendant ruler. Both Cher and MacLaine's Raj yogas are conjunctions between Venus and Saturn with a Mercury-ruled Lagna (Cher's is Gemini, while MacLaine's is Virgo). This yoga, coupled with the Raj yogas, definitely had a hand in MacLaine's overnight success when, as an understudy, she replaced the ailing star of a Broadway show. As luck (or the Dhana/Raj yoga) would have it, a Hollywood producer happened to be in the audience that night, and the rest is history.

Chandra Mangala Yoga: This yoga, which is classified as a Dhana yoga, is formulated when the Moon and Mars are either conjoined, mutually aspected, or in mutual reception.

In addition to providing financial resources, this yoga quite often presents a problematic relationship with the mother who is more often than not perceived as overbearing, domineering, and smothering. A friend who has this yoga with the Moon in Scorpio (Fall) and Mars in Cancer (Fall) has practically described his mother as being demonic. However, since it is both a wealth-producing Dhana yoga, as well as a Neecha Bhanga yoga, wherein the debilitation of the Moon and Mars are reversed by virtue of their mutual reception, he inherited a great deal of money from her.

Aristha Yogas

Aristha yogas are formed when the rulers of the 6th, 8th, and 12th houses are conjoined, mutually aspected, or are in mutual reception. The antithesis to Raj and Dhana yogas, Aristha yogas present obstacles to the affairs of the house which the yoga-forming planets occupy or rule. This does not, however, mean that the areas of life affected by this yoga will be afflicted beyond resolution. In fact, an aspect by a benefic planet or trinal lord can often mitigate or lessen the effects of this combination. It is of utmost importance to assess the strength of the entire horoscope in addition to analyzing the particular dasa in which this combination may or may not be active.

Oftentimes, a planetary combination may simultaneously be a Raj or Dhana yoga as well as an Aristha yoga, which means that it is possible for one to enjoy a successful career, yet be unhappy on a personal level. The Venus/Saturn conjunction in Gemini in the 1st house of Cher's chart is a perfect example of a Dhana, Raj, and Aristha yoga all rolled into one. As the rulers of the 5th (Libra) and 9th (Aquarius) houses, Venus and Saturn, conjoined in the 1st house, form both a Raj and Dhana Yoga. At the same time, as the rulers of the 12th (Taurus) and 8th (Capricorn) houses, Venus and Saturn form an Aristha yoga. The conjunction posited in the 1st house of destiny gives Cher an incredibly strong personality and a chance of attaining success in any undertaking. As we know, she chose to become a creative artist with the help of an older partner, as exemplified by a Venus-Saturn conjunction and its aspect to the 7th house. However, this conjunction, in its role as an Aristha yoga implies that, while success will be achieved, fame may come at the price of personal unhappiness and lack of vitality (1st house), which Cher has indeed experienced.

Hillary Rodham Clinton's horoscope displays a Mars-Saturn conjunction in Cancer in the 2nd house. Since Mars and Saturn rule the 11th (Aries) and 9th (Aquarius) houses, the combination constitutes a Dhana Yoga. However, Mars and Saturn also rule the 6th (Scorpio) and 8th (Capricorn) houses, making it an Aristha yoga as well. With the 2nd house ruling earning power and speaking ability, this combination gave Rodham Clinton the capacity to earn money, even though the profits have also been the cause of public humiliation. And while these planets make her a convincing, often brilliant orator, her speech patterns are often harsh and intimidating.

• • •

Vipareeta Raja Yoga: According to *Phaladeepika*, this yoga, formed when the 6th, 8th, and/or 12th house rulers are situated in the 6th, 8th, or 12th house, brings prosperity and leadership rather than adversity. It must be noted that while Mantreswara endorses this yoga in *Phaladeepika*, there is no mention of it by Parasara in *Hora Sastra* other than as an obstacle-ridden Aristha yoga.[10]

Kala Sarpa Yoga: With Sarpa meaning "serpent," Kala Sarpa yoga occurs when all planets are contained within the Nodal Axis. This situation, whereby the planets cannot exceed an arc of 180°, can be seen in Barbara's chart, since all the planets lie between Rahu (2° Virgo 14′) and Kethu (2° Pisces 14′). This placement, which is labeled in the scriptures as malevolent and unhappy, provides inflexibility, stubborness, and a high-strung personality.

---

[10] Parasara, *Hora Sastra*, p. 395.

INTERPRETING THE PLANETS IN THE SIGNS AND HOUSES

AS SEEN IN PREVIOUS CHAPTERS, each planet functions in two ways: as a general indicator or karaka, and as a personification of the house it rules in the Rasi Chakra. This means that the planet ruling the Ascendant is the indicator of health, personality, appearance, and general approach to life; the planet ruling the sign occupying the 2nd house represents finances and early childhood; the planetary ruler of the sign of the 3rd house indicates the nature of the siblings and describes if one is likely to fulfill one's innermost desires; the planet ruling the sign of the 4th house represents the mother, home life, and level of contentment, etc. If the Moon rules the 7th house in a particular horoscope, for example, it will be the karaka of mother, home, and emotional responses, as well as marriage and partnership, which the 7th house signifies.

Going one step further, the zodiacal sign where a planet is placed describes how the planet expresses itself, while the house a planet occupies reveals the area of life in which that planet is expressed. Rather than use elaborate explanations, I have used key words and phrases—more commonly called "cookbook definitions"—to describe these planetary actions. As usual, its positive or negative manifestation depends on the evaluation of each planet according to some of the principles discussed in chapter 6.

With the exception of planetary rulership, exaltation, fall, and moolatrikona, the zodiacal signs the planets occupy are usually considered less significant than their house positions. The signs the planets occupy *are* vital for determining friendship between planets and their dispositors. It is important to remember that in Jyotish, each and every factor must be carefully weighed before arriving at a definitive conclusion, since a planet can be positive in one way and negative in another. Ultimately, the accuracy of the chart also depends on the ability of the astrologer to synthesize each element in the horoscope.

Planets in the Signs

The following definitions are taken in part from *Brihat Jataka* and *Saravali*, and have been reworked into Western terminology. The planets are often defined similarly when placed in two signs which share the same planetary ruler. There is no mention of the nodes in relation to the signs in which they are placed.

Sun

Aries (Exalted): Respected in one's field, well-off financially (if on exaltation degree, wealthy), aggressive, good worker, ambitious, may become a physician or surgeon, self-confident, will have successful father.

Taurus: Financially secure, work may involve clothing, perfume, or other sensual and aesthetically pleasing items, skilled in the arts.

Gemini: Communication skills, financially comfortable, interest in astrology.

Cancer: Independent, not financially well-off, will work for others.

Leo (Rulership and Moolatrikona): Powerful, self-confident, aggressive, ambitious.

Virgo: Skilled in writing and art, mathematically oriented, well-traveled.

Libra (Fall): Tendency toward indulgence, instability, lack of self-confidence.

Scorpio: Aggressive, mechanical, impulsive.

Sagittarius: Religious, rich, independent, interested in medicine and sculpture.

Capricorn: Engages in business, possible ruthlessness, financially comfortable but frugal, does not always live up to potential.

Aquarius: May not work up to potential, may spend money foolishly, serious, ambitious yet frugal.

Pisces: Will earn money through water products, gets along very well with women, insecure.

Moon

Aries: Round eyes, forgiving, fond of travel, sensuous, financial instability, haughty and fickle.

Taurus (Exaltation and Moolatrikona): Beautiful appearance, loyal friend, especially close to women, good appetite, interest in the arts.

Gemini: Sensual, gets along well with women, writing and speaking ability, sharp intellect, interested in classical texts, witty, beautiful features and sweet speech, skilled and fond of the arts, well-traveled.

Cancer (Rulership): Influenced by women, loyal friend, interest in astrology, financial ups and downs, fortunate with real estate, domestic happiness, close to mother.

Leo: Temperamental, large cheeks, broad face, difficulty with women, holds grudges, mentally anxious, generous, principled, attached to mother, arrogant.

Virgo: Lovely eyes, modest, financially comfortable, soft-spoken, intelligent, may live abroad, skilled in the arts.

Libra: Religious, intelligent, philosophical, tall and thin, fond of traveling, wealthy, may be involved with commercial ventures.

Scorpio (Fall): Broad eyes, mental instability, may be estranged from or disagree with family, weak health as child, law-abiding, does not express ideas clearly, tendency towards dishonesty.

Sagittarius: Long face and neck, generous, well-read, good oral and written communication skills, may inherit money or receive support from family, skilled in the arts, intelligent, creative.

Capricorn: Family-minded, seeks appreciation and respect, works at a slow pace, likes to travel, powerful, can be ruthless, well-liked by friends and colleagues.

Aquarius: Tall and large-boned, professional ups and downs, may be involved in commercial business, loyal friend, likes beautiful articles such as flowers, perfumes, and fine materials.

Pisces: Beautiful appearance, good salespeople, fair-minded, financially comfortable, well educated, money may come from unexpected sources.

Mars

Aries (Rulership and Moolatrikona) and Scorpio (Rulership): Respected position of authority, active in government affairs, fond of travel, sensual and sometimes indulgent, immense vitality, business-minded, financially comfortable.

Taurus and Libra: Influenced by women, single-minded, sensual, enjoys aesthetically pleasing items, shy, lazy.

Gemini and Virgo: Physically attractive, well-dressed, helpful to others, skilled in music and writing, fearless.

Cancer (Fall): May travel or live abroad, financially well-off, intelligent, can be self-centered, stomach troubles, unkempt appearance.

Leo: Financial ups and downs, patient, aggressive, courageous, self-centered, may have children later in life.

Sagittarius and Pisces: Well-known and respected in chosen field, work for the government, will have adversaries, fearless.

Capricorn (Exaltation): Wealthy, active in politics and social causes (perhaps government worker), leadership, good family background, strong relationship with children.

Aquarius: Unhappy, poverty-stricken, well-traveled, independent, dishonest.

Mercury

Aries and Scorpio: Indulgent habits, argumentative, intellectual, opinionated, deceitful and dishonest.

Taurus and Libra: Persuasiveness, oratorial skills, family-minded, capable of earning money, generous, enjoys learning.

Gemini (Rulership): Proud, scientific-minded, skilled in the arts, persuasive, strong speaking quality, financially comfortable.

Cancer: Strong-minded, good memory, easily antagonizes people, earns money through water connected fields.

Leo: Opinionated, strong personality, financial ups and downs .

Virgo (Rulership, Exaltation and Moolatrikona): Generous, well educated, strong values, comfortable, patient, brilliant mind.

Sagittarius: Respected by people in authority, scientific-minded, interested in the law.

Capricorn and Aquarius: Prefers to work for others, financial ups and downs, may incur debts, difficulties with money, talent for sculpture, does volunteer work.

Pisces (Fall): Makes friends easily, open to others' views, lacks confidence, skillful in crafts, nervous, irritable.

Jupiter

Aries and Scorpio: Financially well-off, leadership qualities, generous nature, patient, bright appearance, well-known in chosen field, happy domestic situation.

Taurus and Libra: Strong constitution, lives comfortably, wealthy, many friends and acquaintances, generous and well-liked.

Gemini and Virgo: Well-dressed, may own more than one home, wide circle of friends, financially comfortable, professionally successful, may own business, counselling skills.

Cancer (Exaltation): Likes beautiful things, blessed with good marriage and children, materially comfortable, intelligent, influential, and well-known in chosen field.

Leo: Executive abilities, likes taking charge, enjoys flattery and admiration, flair for the dramatic.

Sagittarius (Rulership and Moolatrikona) and Pisces (Rulership): Enjoys positions of authority, religious-minded, financial stability, comfortable, politically active.

Capricorn (Fall): Allergies and other chronic ailments, unhappiness, inflexibility.

Aquarius: Loyal friend, interested in astrology and other occult studies, financial stability, domestic happiness.

Venus

Aries and Scorpio: May have conflicts with family, willful, sometimes unreliable, extremely sensual, possessive.

Taurus (Rulership) and Libra (Rulership and Moolatrikona): Financially successful, entrepreneurial, powers of discrimination, intelligence, artistic sensibilities, well-liked.

Gemini: Position of responsibility and authority, financially well established, fond of music.

Cancer: More than one marriage, timid, financial ups and downs, arrogant, loner.

Leo: Professional associations with women, devoted spouse, may have children late in life.

Virgo (Fall): Insecurity in relationships, accepts difficult tasks, unhappy in chosen profession.

Sagittarius: Integrity, honesty, financially well-off.

Capricorn and Aquarius: Well-liked, influenced by the opinions of women and a need to be appreciated by them.

Pisces (Exaltation): Extravagant, artistic, likeable, well educated, sensuous, respected in one's field, wealthy.

Saturn

Aries (Fall): Foolish, restless, lonely.

Taurus: Sensual and indulgent nature, usually marries more than once, difficulty accumulating money.

Gemini or Virgo: Unhappy, difficulty saving money, will have a position of authority.

Cancer: Difficult family life, may be estranged from mother, foolish.

Leo: Must work hard for what is achieved, sadness.

Libra (Exaltation): Financially well-off, commands respect and recognition in chosen field.

Scorpio: Often feels isolated and depressed, difficulty making friends, self-conscious.

Sagittarius or Pisces: Loyal worker, saves money, domestic happiness.

Capricorn (Rulership) or Aquarius (Rulership and Moola-trikona): Earns a good living, high status, intelligence, position of authority, fortunate with homes and real estate.

Planets in the Houses

The following delineations, taken in part from *Phaladeepika*, illustrate the way the planets are likely to manifest in the houses of the Rasi Chakra. The definitions have been reworked into Western terminology.

Sun

1st House: Aggressive, impetuous, ambitious, proud, vital, good health, impatient.

2nd House: Modest, learning problems, must work hard for money, many financial ups and downs, difficulty expressing oneself.

3rd House: Intelligent, generous, financially well-off, position of authority, liberal, quarrels with siblings.

4th House: May work for the government or in an "official" capacity, unhappy, moody, pessimistic, difficult relationship with mother.

5th House: Intelligent, wealthy, difficulty with one's children, high-strung, risky for investments, indulgence in love affairs.

6th House: Wealthy, vital, concerned with health, enjoys helping others, service profession, good worker, successful career (possibly in a position of authority), will "defeat one's enemies."

7th House: Restlessness, difficulties with marriage which may take place later in life, strong sexuality.

8th House: Difficulty making friends, financial ups and downs, poor eyesight.[1]

9th House: Difficulty with father, interested in the law, religion, philosophy, fair-minded, financially comfortable, respected in chosen field.

10th House: Intelligence, wealth, fame, self-confident, leadership and success in chosen field, may be the head of a company or own land.

11th House: Ambitious, reaches goals, able to make money from wise investments, powerful position.

12th House: Difficult relationship with the father, financial ups and downs, lack of wealth, may live abroad, lack of confidence, must work hard for achievements, poor eyesight.

Moon

1st House: Strong constitution, enthusiasm, vacillating, nice-looking, works with the public, emotional, passionate.

2nd House: Financially well-off (even wealthy), educated, sensual, good family background, well-spoken with good speaking voice.

3rd House: Relationship with siblings goes through phases, younger sibling may be unstable, strong communication skills, artistic abilities, frugal, strong-minded, sensual.

4th House: Happy, sensually indulgent, many friendships, good relationship with mother, generous, open-minded.

---

[1] It is said that there may be poor eyesight because the Sun will aspect the 2nd house which rules the eyes (especially the right).

5th House: Happiness through one's children, intelligent, love of sports and the arts, passionate, romantic, high position in government or corporation.

6th House: Difficult relationship with the mother and possibly with co-workers, stomach troubles, service profession.

7th House: Beautiful, highly romantic and passionate, money through partner, may be married more than once but generally the marriages are successful unions, round-faced.

8th House: Little willpower, weak health especially as a child, intelligence, difficulty with the mother, lack of confidence.

9th House: Prosperous, successful career, good relationship with father and children, generous, interested in religion.

10th House: Conquers adversaries and competitors, ethical, well-liked, career involves helping others, good relationship with the mother.

11th House: Integrity, successful with children, wealthy, ambitious, capable of reaching goals through hard work, head of own business.

12th House: Reflective, lack of physical activity, emotional problems, difficulty making friends.

Mars

1st House: Adventurous, temperamental, aggressive, independent, assertive, accident prone, physical prowess.

2nd House: Poor judge of character, difficulty learning, must work hard for success, short-tempered.

3rd House: Difficult relationships with siblings, adventurous, good communication skills, contented, powerful, strong-minded.

4th House: Loner, difficult relationship with mother, comfortable home, successful career.

5th House: Impetuous, intelligent, high-strung, aggressive, work involves physical expression, may incur debts, difficulty with children.

6th House: Passionate, desire fulfilled through ambition and hard work, good earning power, wealthy, sensual, will topple the competition and overcome adversaries and obstacles.

7th House: Strong sexuality, argumentative, restless, difficulty with or separation from partner.

8th House: Weak health, must work hard for money, strong sexuality, may be accident prone.

9th House: Difficulty with father, not many friends, great drive and ambition to get ahead, achieves recognition.

10th House: Self-centered, highly ambitious, achieves career goals through sheer persistence, charitable.

11th House: Wealthy, many ambitions will be realized, influential in the community, many friends who will help with career goals, influential.

12th House: Lonely, strong sexuality, difficulties with siblings, may incur debts.

Mercury

1st House: Soft-spoken, sweet-speaking, sharp-witted, intelligent, generous, friendly, well-educated, charming, knowledgeable about religion and philosophy.

2nd House: Wealth through intelligence, writer or poet, good communicator, well-educated.

3rd House: Risk-taker, business skills, written communication skills, good relationship with siblings, low physical energy.

4th House: Good conversationalist, witty, well-educated, contented, has many friends, financially comfortable, unstable upbringing, intellectual mother.

5th House: Educated, loves learning, energetic, contented, good investments, generous, happiness through children.

6th House: Interested in health matters, argumentative, restless, lethargic.

7th House: Intelligent, well-dressed, wealth through marriage partner, competitive, will succeed through hard work.

8th House: Gains fame and recognition, good health, benefits through finances of others, has difficulty learning because mind is restless.

9th House: Well-educated, good earner, eloquent speaker, charming, interested in philosophy and religion.

10th House: Successful career, well-respected in chosen field, learning ability, strength, intelligent, good speaker, ethical.

11th House: Successful with finances, friendships cultivated with intelligent and artistic people, honesty, happiness, wealthy.

12th House: Sorrowful, learning problems, lacks physical energy, weak nervous system, insecure, frugal.

Jupiter

1st House: Attractive, fortunate, strong constitution, luck through children, religious-minded, intelligent, contented.

2nd House: Talkative, lover of good food, educated, earns a good living, eloquent speech, beautiful face.

3rd House: Frugal, siblings are successful, good communication skills, artistic.

4th House: Enjoys extravagant lifestyle, happy, close relationship with family, successful career.

5th House: Highly optimistic, good investments, dramatic talent, position in politics or government, unhappiness through children, educated.

6th House: Success by overcoming adversaries and obstacles, lethargic, clever, can be excessive, good worker, charming.

7th House: Friendly, popular, respected, generous and well-liked, good marriage.

8th House: Works well within partnership, dependent on employees and colleagues for success, professional ups and downs, good health.

9th House: Philosophical, religious, fair-minded, good teacher, well-educated, prosperous, happiness through children, generous, well-known.

10th House: Very ambitious, professionally successful, good reputation and well-respected, fair-minded, position of leadership, interested in education, law, or government.

11th House: Wealthy, initiates projects and works diligently to fulfill goals, opportunities, support of friends, good health.

12th House: Lethargic, may antagonize others, difficulty communicating, loner, problematic relationships, will work for others.

Venus

1st House: Healthy, beautiful, happiness, strong constitution, passionate, extravagant.

2nd House: Likes material possessions and luxurious lifestyle, money earned through artistic endeavors, extravagant, creative writing.

3rd House: Loner, good relationship with siblings, talented in the arts.

4th House: Comfortable home, likes clothes, art and luxuries, good relationship with mother, family-minded.

5th House: Intelligent, artistic, romantic and sensual, financially stable, blessed with children.

6th House: Many friends, work may involve the arts, gets along well with co-workers, good health.

7th House: Many friends, fortunate in marriage and other relationships, romantic, money through marriage partner, overly sensual.

8th House: Strong constitution and good health, wealthy, happiness and money through partner, sensual.

9th House: Prosperous, spouse may be foreign, blessed with spouse, children, and friends.

10th House: Many fulfilling friendships, recognition through lucrative career most likely in the arts, respected and well-known, will do volunteer work or help others.

11th House: Material comforts, financial stability, surrounds oneself with many friends, especially women.

12th House: Sensual enjoyment, wealthy, extravagant.

Saturn

1st House: Emaciated, sorrowful, solemn, difficulties in childhood, health problems, success later in life, works hard, disciplined. (If Saturn is in Libra, Capricorn, or Aquarius, they will be head of a corporation, own a business, or own land.)

2nd House: Financial instability, but comfortable later in life, success.

3rd House: Generous, good marriage, lack of physical activity, success through hard work but possibly later in life, intelligent.

4th House: Unhappy, ill-health in childhood, disciplined and serious, spends much time alone, may be alienated from family.

5th House: Expresses oneself seriously, problematic relationships, difficulty with children, depressed, financial instability, restless.

6th House: Financially comfortable, highly ambitious and proficient in whatever one sets out to do, arrogant.

7th House: Difficult relationships with friends and marriage partner, disciplined, may marry late in life to someone older.

8th House: Must overcome many obstacles in life, difficulty in communicating with others, argumentative personality.

9th House: Solemn and religious, works hard for rewards, difficult relationship with family especially the father, arrogant, self-educated.

10th House: Accepts challenges, recognition, fulfills ambition through perseverance and discipline, well-known.

11th House: Strong constitution, good income, intelligent, leadership abilities, powerful figure within the community, influential friends.

12th House: Spends money rather foolishly, may have difficulty concentrating, loner, spiritual.

Rahu

1st House: Prone to headaches, wealthy, strong constitution, weak health, difficulties in marriage.

2nd House: Inability to express oneself clearly, often misunderstood, is known to tell white lies, good-natured, contented, money through hard work, short-tempered.

3rd House: Proud, difficulty with siblings, strong-willed, good health, adventurous, financially well-off.

4th House: Difficult relationship with the mother, lonely, but happy most of the time nonetheless.

5th House: Difficult relationships with children, intelligent but lacks confidence in abilities, problematic love affairs, stomach ailments.

6th House: Difficulties with co-workers, prefers to be self-employed, misunderstood by others, ability to earn money through hard work, good health.

7th House: Spends too much money on relationships, separation from loved ones, strong-willed and independent.

8th House: Difficulty with children, lack of domestic tranquility, inability to handle finances, weak health.

9th House: Argumentative, authoritative, active in community, philosophical, religious-minded.

10th House: Recognized for professional achievements, leadership skills, works with others, earns money through hard work.

11th House: Prosperous, lucky with children, strong constitution, many powerful friends, influential within the community.

12th House: Spends money foolishly, spends much time alone.

Kethu

1st House: Poor health, unhappy, difficulty in marriage, lack of confidence in abilities, professional ups and downs.

2nd House: Difficulties in learning, financial instability, harsh speech quality.

3rd House: Strong constitution, financial know-how, fame, problematic relationship with brothers and sisters.

4th House: Loss of property, may live and travel abroad, problematic relationship with mother.

5th House: Difficulty with children, stomach ailments, self-centered.

6th House: Generous, fame, authority figure, can be excessive and jealous, will achieve success through persevering.

7th House: Intestinal problems, difficulty in marriage and other relationships.

8th House: Separations from friends and family, argumentative.

9th House: Difficulty with father, must work hard to get past many obstacles.

10th House: Energetic, takes risks, successful career.

11th House: Quite frugal, maternal nature, generous, successful in fulfilling goals.

12th House: Spendthrift, religious pursuits, loner, poor eyesight.

● ● ●

Before presenting a closer examination of the horoscopes of Annemarie and Barbara, let's review the techniques that have been set out thus far for interpreting the Rasi Chakra. It must

be emphasized that these techniques only represent an introduction to the variety of methodologies that may be used. Each
astrologer will choose a personal style and method developed
by years of experience to evaluate and synthesize each available
factor in order to understand the entire Rasi Chakra. As stated
in this section, the principles are as follows:

1. Examining the basic definitions of the planets, signs,
and houses (chapter 4);

2. Reviewing the descriptions of the 12 possible Ascendant
combinations to see exactly how the zodiacal signs and
planetary rulers associated with each house manifest in a
particular Rasi Chakra (chapter 5);

3. Evaluating the strengths and weaknesses of each planet
according to its placement in the horoscope (chapter 6);

4. Defining how each planet—modified by its role as house
ruler—is expressed through the sign and house placement
(chapter 8).

What follows are more extensive interpretations of Annemarie's and Barbara's charts. By applying the aforementioned
principles, we will ascertain information concerning character
traits, personality development, family background, as well as
attitudes toward marriage, children, and career. The conclusions are by no means exhaustive or finite and, in the end, it is
the free will of both Annemarie and Barbara which determines
how these traits ultimately manifest.

Annemarie's Life

Let's begin by providing some background information on Annemarie's life. Annemarie, a free-lance photographer, was
raised throughout Central and South America where her father,
a diplomat in the Dutch Diplomatic Corps, met and married
her Peruvian mother. Annemarie and her three sisters attended
international and American schools where their education was
conducted in English. Their classmates were children of ambas-

sadors, foreign businessmen, journalists, international corre-
spondents, and visiting officials from other countries. Annemarie spoke three languages fluently—Spanish (with her
mother, sisters, maternal relatives, and the community), English
(at school and with her friends), and Dutch (with her father).
When she was a teenager, her family returned to the Netherlands, where they still reside.

The descriptions which follow are listed in the order of the
houses. Because many planets rule more than one house, some
of the delineations overlap and will be described only once. To
get a thorough interpretation of the affairs of a particular
house, it is important to analyze that house from three angles:
the condition of the house itself (i.e., planets occupying and aspecting the house); the condition of the house ruler (i.e., what
house it is placed in and how it is aspected); and the condition
of the karaka of the house.

Annemarie's Lagna

Since Venus-ruled Libra occupies the 1st house of appearance,
Annemarie is very attractive to the opposite sex and is, for personal and professional reasons, very conscious of her public
image. She is artistic and sensual, but also has excessive habits
and extravagant tastes due to the aspect the 1st house and its
occupant Saturn receive from the Moon and Jupiter in the 7th
house.

In addition to being examined in light of the Libra Ascendant, the 1st house must also be viewed through the eyes of its
occupant, Saturn. Saturn is: a) auspiciously placed in the 1st
Kendra house; b) exalted in the sign of Libra; c) in its vargottama position; and d) categorized as one of the most beneficial
planets in a chart with a Libra Ascendant. Annemarie is thin,
bony, and sometimes depressive, but in this particular horoscope, Saturn's positive traits enhance rather than limit her personality and general approach to life. These traits include discipline, integrity, seriousness, and goal-orientation—all of which
assist Annemarie in the expression of her creativity. There will
still be the expected self-consciousness, frugality, and lack of
physical vitality, but they will not overpower the more positive
aspects of Saturn. Because Saturn rules the 4th house it is safe

204 Ⓓ VEDIC ASTROLOGY

to say that Annemarie's mother was a very strong influence, and that Annemarie's combined home/work space (4th house) reflects her individuality (1st house).

As ruler of the Lagna, Venus, the indicator of Annemarie's personality, is the key to her self-identification. Venus' occupancy of the 4th house indicates that her home environment is of utmost importance and many of her personality traits are revealed by the way her house is decorated. Through family connections and benefits attained from her varied background, she will be presented with artistic job opportunities that, when taken advantage of, will allow her to succeed in most of her endeavors. She will also be quite fortunate in finding suitable living and studio space. Since Venus is conjoined with Kethu in the 4th house and is aspected by Rahu in the 10th house—both malefic influences—there will be a conflict between enjoying the comforts of home (4th house) and the need to be recognized professionally by the public and her peers (10th house). This clash is also illustrated by the differences both her mother (4th house) and her father (10th house) have concerning Annemarie's lifestyle.

As ruler of the 8th house of business and finances, Venus (an aesthetic planet) appropriately describes Annemarie's career as a photographer. It also signifies the creative partnership she maintained with her lover, which successfully produced a series of greeting cards. Since the 8th house is not the best house for a planet to rule, Venus' placement in the 4th house creates tension with the mother and, in times of crisis, a tendency to withdraw from the world. In keeping with the full aspect Venus receives from malefic Rahu in the 10th house of society, the way in which Annemarie handles her business affairs, as well as her bisexuality, will also be problematic for her parents, since it is unconventional. Because Venus is a fairly well-rated planet in the chart, however, these family disagreements will ultimately be resolved, and she will, in fact, be noted for her uniqueness.

Annemarie also has a plethora of interesting yogas with which to work. She has a Parivartana yoga (mutual reception) due to the fact that the ruler of the 1st house (Venus) is situated in the 4th house, while the ruler of the 4th house (Saturn) is in the 1st house. Since this is also an exchange between two beneficial houses (Maha Yoga), this will mean that she has achieved her success due to the support of her family. Furthermore, the interaction of these two houses has been a pronounced theme in Annemarie's life. She also has Kesari yoga, which makes her honest and admired, and Sasa yoga, which makes her single-minded and ambitious.

Annemarie's 2nd House

The 2nd house, a neutral house, does not alter the nature of its occupant, Mercury, whose status in this horoscope is benefic. Since Mercury rules both the 9th and 12th houses, it is possible that the father, travel (9th house), higher education (12th house), research (12th house) and/or creativity (12th house) will help her to earn money.

The 2nd house of Scorpio is ruled by Mars and, therefore, the nature of her finances and general productivity depends on this impetuous planet's position in the 5th house, an auspicious Trikona House, but one which rules speculation and investments. Since Annemarie is self-employed, she may depend on projects before they actually materialize, and may spend money recklessly, especially with two excessive planets, the Moon and Jupiter, conjoined and aspecting her Lagna. She may also invest money in creative ventures which were idealistically conceived rather than realistically evaluated. Ultimately she will once again be able to earn money through creative projects in conjunction with a romantic partner due to Mars' position as a benefic in this chart.

Annemarie's 3rd House

In accordance with the rule stating that "a malefic planet occupying an Upachaya house brings excellent results to that house," the 3rd house of Sagittarius is empowered by its occupancy of the Sun even though, as the ruler of the 11th Upachaya house, it is an individually malefic planet. Due to the categorization of the 3rd and 11th houses as Kama, or desire, houses, she will eventually attain her goals by perseverance and hard work. Her fulfillment and income (11th house) will both be derived from photography, which she has been able to perfect due to her innovative mind and aptitude for the creative arts (3rd house). While the 3rd house Sun defines the successes of her sisters, the aspect the Sun, ruler of the 11th house (older sibling), receives from Saturn in the 1st house describes the friction Annemarie has experienced with her older sister from time to time.

As ruler of the 3rd house, Jupiter, an individual malefic in this chart, describes Annemarie's restless nature and adds to the difficulty she has in maintaining a successful long term relationship (Jupiter in the 7th house). Its conjunction with the Moon in the 7th house also brings inconsistency to her relationships.

Annemarie's 4th House

The 4th house has already been briefly discussed in connection with its ruler Saturn being placed in the 1st house and Venus as Ascendant ruler placed in the 4th house. Along with Venus, Kethu's placement in the 4th house is described as problematic for Annemarie's relationship with her mother—something that has already been seen. Conversely, Rahu's placement in the 10th house—accompanied by the full aspect from Venus— prompts Annemarie to take professional risks which work to her advantage. She has always been recognized by her peers and the public as a unique talent and has always been able to earn a good living though free-lance work.

Annemarie's 5th House

As ruler of the 5th house, Saturn's benefic rating has already been discussed. Its position in the 1st house brings great success in life through uniqueness and individuality. The occupant of the 5th house, Mars, is naturally malefic and individually benefic so difficulties will be somewhat eased. Mars in Aquarius in the 5th house represents intelligence, impetuosity, aggression, and a high-strung nature which may be a disadvantage. While providing exuberance, the occupancy of Aquarius and especially the naturally malefic Mars, will cause ambivalence about having children (the periods during which childbirth is most likely to occur are discussed in more detail in chapter 10).

Annemarie's 6th House

The 6th house has no occupants or aspects and, therefore, its condition will be assessed through the placement of Jupiter, its ruler, which is individually malefic. As already stated, this influence is one of work-related independence and, to this end, Annemarie has always been self-employed. As the indicator of illness, Pisces occupying the 6th house contributes to her excessive and indulgent nature which often triggers many of her ailments. Placed in the 7th house, Jupiter indicates that work will be with a partner or through the influence of her parents, the latter due to Jupiter's conjunction with the Moon, Karaka of mother and ruler of the 10th house (father) and Jupiter's aspect from Saturn, ruler of the 4th house (mother). Because Jupiter is a malefic influence in this horoscope, there will probably be friction with both partner and parents due to the nature of her work.

Annemarie's 7th House

The Moon and Jupiter, individually malefic planets, occupy the 7th house while Saturn, an individually benefic planet, aspects that house. Due to the fact that the Moon and Jupiter, two excessive planets, modify her relationships, it is not unusual that their excessive quality is once again reiterated. The Moon provides changeability, while Saturn indicates delay. Due to the complexity of the area of the chart which represents marriage, she spent her 20s and 30s in many short-lived relationships. With the 7th house representing residence or travel abroad, it is no wonder that she often travels to exhibit her photographs or to be with her trans-Atlantic relationships.

Mars, the ruler of the 7th house, has already been described through its role as ruler of the 2nd house. As the ruler of the 7th house, the position of Mars in the 5th house will lead to relationships which are excessive, passionate, fun-loving, but without the seriousness and forethought which would make them long-lasting. This placement will describe the fact that her partners share her interest in the arts, her passion for life, and her independent lifestyle. Her relationships have been with both men and women—a result of a provocative Mars in the 5th house of enjoyment and individuality.

Annemarie's 8th House

The occupancy of Venus-ruled Taurus in the 8th house is responsible for Annemarie's love of collectibles, such as books, antiques, paintings, art objects, etc. A need for companionship and financial stability may be reflected in her choice of a marriage partner. (Venus, the 8th house ruler, has already been discussed in the sections on the 1st and 4th houses.)

Annemarie's 9th House

As the ruler of the 9th house, Mercury, and Gemini, the sign it rules, typify the father as an intellectual whose restless nature and love of travel was satisfied by his role as international diplomat. As a benefic in this chart, Mercury's position in the 2nd house describes her positive earning potential as well as her restless childhood.

Annemarie's 10th House

Rahu's position in the 10th house reiterates an obsession to succeed professionally, and assertiveness in her chosen field. The aspect Rahu receives from Venus in the 4th house brings forth Annemarie's feeling for aesthetics and beauty expressed by means of her career as a photographer. In addition, her father's status, represented by the 10th house, is blessed with the harmony that only Venus bestows.

The ruler of the 10th house, the waxing moon, is naturally benefic but individually malefic. Placed in the 7th house and conjunct individually malefic Jupiter, the Moon brings a difficult influence to the 7th house. It indicates that Annemarie's partner may conflict with her career and/or her father—something already hinted at.

Annemarie's 11th House

There are no planets occupying the 11th house, but the sign of Leo (whose natural ruler is the Sun) defines Annemarie's hopes, dreams, friendships, and relationship to her community—all that is represented by the 11th house. With the individualistic Sun ruling this house, Annemarie's ambivalence toward having children is reaffirmed. The placement of her natal Sun in the 3rd house acknowledges that many of her goals and ideals revolve around communication and mobility. Although she will have harmonious relationships with her sisters, there will also be normal sibling rivalry from time to time.

Annemarie's 12th House

As ruler of the 9th and 12th houses, Mercury's placement in the 2nd house has already been discussed. Although it is inauspicious for a planet to rule the 12th house—a Dusthana house—its rulership of the 9th house contributes to Mercury's categorization as a benefic in this chart. Mercury-ruled Virgo lends Annemarie the ability to sustain the many solitary hours required to take and develop photographs. At times, however, Annemarie may get depressed and too self-deprecating due to the influence of Virgo in the 12th house. Since the ruler of the 12th house of expenditures is placed in the 2nd house of finances, Annemarie, as already stated, spends money as quickly as she earns it.

Barbara's Life

How an astrologer broaches interpretation is highly personal and his or her style was probably developed over many years of experimenting with numerous methods. Analyzing each house, as was just done with Annemarie's chart, is only one approach to chart interpretation. Beginning with a description of Barbara's early life and professional history, the following method summarizes some of the important aspects of her Rasi Chakra.

Barbara's family consists of her mother, father, and two older siblings; a comfortable home in the suburbs provided a typical American upbringing. Barbara, the youngest child, felt alienated from the rest of her family. Although she had an outgoing personality, she was often insecure and restless. Her favorite pastimes involved physical activities such as swimming, running, and bicycling. At an early age, Barbara developed an independent streak which enabled her to pursue a career and to make friends easily. For several years she was a professional nurse in a traditional hospital, later transferring to a hospice, a benevolent setting where terminally ill patients live out their remaining time with dignity. At present Barbara is a certified social worker who specializes in counseling dysfunctional families in which alcohol and/or drugs were used by one or more members. The attraction to working with this type of problem is a good outlet for Barbara, since the 8th-house emphasis gives her the tendency to be depressed and, at times, self-destructive. Compassionate outreach, however, will allow you to utilize that very intense energy for the benefit of helping others. She will, however, always battle the feeling that life is overwhelming due to the Kala Sarpa yoga which often makes her high-strung and unable to see her way out of seemingly hopeless situations.

The interpretation of Barbara's chart will be approached from a slightly different point of view. Her chart has a stellium (four or more planets) in the 8th house consisting of Venus, Mars, Jupiter, and Saturn in Sagittarius. Because of the overwhelming influence the 8th house exerts on Barbara's Rasi Chakra, the synopsis of her chart will begin by concentrating on each planet in that house.

Mars in Barbara's Chart

In its role as a natural malefic, Mars should ruin the affairs of the 8th house and, at the same time, be ruined by its placement in a Dusthana house. In Barbara's Rasi Chakra, however, Mars is not only individually benefic but works moderately well in the 8th house due to its mutual friendship with Jupiter, the lord and occupant of the 8th house. Venus and Saturn, the remaining 8th house planets, are neutral to Mars.

As ruler of Scorpio and the 7th house of partnership, Mars is indicative of Barbara's husband and the nature of their relationship. Because Scorpio is a passionate sign, it can be said that the union, which may present disagreements from time to time concerning money and mutual investments, will provide enough strength and happiness so that each crisis will be met head-on.

Mars' rulership of the 12th house, however, may mean that Barbara will have to temper her extravagant and devil-may-care attitude toward money to satisfy the need for financial security. Her Taurus Ascendant, however, should keep her in line and ensure that she always has material comforts.

As the ruler of both the 7th and the 12th houses, Mars' position in the 8th house describes her husband as emotional, hard-working, and shrewd concerning investments and business ventures. Because Mars is a passionate planet, Barbara has many emotional ups and downs which contribute to prolonged periods of listlessness. Although she also has stress-related digestive problems, Barbara discovered long ago that physical activity is an effective weapon to counter these and other potential ailments. The position of Mars, along with three other planets, in the 8th house (chronic illness) also gives her certain allergies and feminine-related hormonal problems.

Jupiter in Barbara's Chart

The ruler of the Sagittarian 8th house, Jupiter, is placed in its own sign/house. Although it is an individually malefic planet, Sagittarius is the sign of its rulership and moolatrikona, the two most fortunate placements for a planet. In addition, Jupiter's natural role as "the greater benefic" tempers most of its malefic qualities.

Since Jupiter (ruler of the 8th house of the partner's finances) conjoins Mars (ruler of the 7th partnership house), their shared attitude toward financial security and sound investments is what Barbara and her husband, an accountant, have in common. Sagittarius' occupancy of the 8th house indicates that there will either be a legacy at some time or, most likely, endowments from either Barbara's parents and/or her husband's family.

Because Jupiter is also the ruler of the 11th house in which Kethu is placed, her goals will eventually be fulfilled. Since Kethu's domain includes spirituality and addiction, it is not surprising that her fulfillment and income are related to working as an addiction therapist. She will also take an interest in spiritual and religious concerns at some time in her life. The 11th house occupancy of Jupiter-ruled Pisces also contributes to her popularity and penchant for working with groups who share her social and political ideals.

Venus in Barbara's Chart

Because Venus rules the 6th Upachaya house, its individual beneficence by virtue of its role as Lagna Lord is somewhat, though not completely, diminished. Although it is a natural benefic and conjoined with Jupiter, it still receives the influence of Mars and Saturn. In addition, an Aristha yoga in the 8th house is formed by the conjunction of Venus (ruler of the 6th house) and Mars (ruler of the 12th house) and Jupiter (ruler of the 8th house). While this will give her a melancholic nature, this placement also constitutes what Mantreswara considers to be a Vipareeta Raj yoga. Indeed, her husband's finances, as well as her ability to attract people and "lucky" circumstances, is borne out by the latter definition. Since there are four planets, there are also Raj and Dhana yogas in which Venus also partakes. The following definitions of Venus' influence in Barbara's Rasi Chakra, focus on the planet's more problematic sides.

To begin, Venus' rulership of the 1st house (appearance, personality, constitution) and the 6th house (health and work) indicates that her physical stamina is not always operating at its optimum level. Barbara has a tendency toward hormonal troubles and poor eyesight (both Venus-ruled). When she is ill, Barbara—like most Taureans—tends to be stoic and rarely asks for assistance. Because she distances herself during these times of need, it is difficult to recognize when she is sick or in pain.

The Taurus Ascendant endows her with a compulsive nature, which sometimes results in mood swings and erratic behavior. Her health may be affected by an inability to balance these patterns of her personality. The Ascendant ruler, Venus, does, however, provide her with an attractive appearance and a sensual, indulgent nature, similar to the effects of a Libra Ascendant. As 1st and 6th house ruler placed in the 8th house, Venus may indicate jealousy and power struggles between Barbara and her co-workers and/or supervisors.

Saturn in Barbara's Chart

Due to its rulership of the 9th Trikona house and the 10th Kendra house, Saturn is the Yogakaraka for a Taurus Ascendant and by far its most beneficial planet. Saturn's rulership of these two houses indicates the father's successful professional status in the publishing field. Not only was he a good provider and a hard worker, but a model of discipline and responsibility. With Saturn ruling the 9th house and placed in the 8th, Barbara is amazingly obstinate—also qualities of the fixed Taurus Ascendant. Once she forms an opinion, she is extremely inflexible and even those closest to her cannot penetrate her stubbornness. Conversely, Saturn-ruled Capricorn adds a serious and practical attitude toward her professional life, while her patience and the ability to listen makes her an excellent teacher and counselor. Aquarius' occupancy of the 10th house, representative of her career, corroborates the fact that she is a concerned social worker who takes the responsibilities of her position very seriously.

Saturn's position in the 8th house emits a need to be financially secure but, at the same time, presents her with irrational fears related to the pressures of everyday living. Taken to an extreme, these anxieties sometimes result in misunderstandings with friends due to differences of opinion and an inability to listen.

Though the 8th house may diminish the positive qualities of Saturn, it is still the yoga karaka in this chart, receiving the aspect of Venus and Jupiter which are friendly and neutral, respectively. The more problematic relationship is with Mars, which is a natural malefic and Saturn's enemy. With Mars ruling the 7th house of partnership and 12th house of expenditures, it is likely that her passionate, extravagant side is constantly at odds with her more prudent, conservative nature. Problematic areas may be resolved by calling on her reserve of Saturnian traits such as persistence and discipline. According to the scriptures, the placement of Saturn, karaka of longevity and 8th house, in the 8th house will strengthten the life span by denying (Saturn) death (8th house).

Mercury in Barbara's Chart

As the ruler of Gemini and Virgo, Mercury represents the affairs of the 2nd house (finances and assets) and the 5th house (creativity, romantic liaisons, and children). Since there are no planets posited in the 2nd house, its affairs will be judged primarily by Mercury's position in the horoscope. Because Mercury, an individual benefic, is placed in the auspicious 9th house, her financial situation will always be favorable. In addition, due to Mercury's conjunction with the individually benefic Sun (the ruler of the 4th house) in the 9th house (paternal line), there will always be substantial gifts from the family. This also stems from the fact that Mercury (ruler of the 2nd house and 5th Trikona house) placed in the 9th house constitutes a Dhana/Raj yoga, while its conjunction with the Sun (ruler of the 4th Kendra house) forms a Trikona Kendra Raj yoga. These two placements corroborate the theme of financial well-being which has already been touched upon. When a theme or pattern repeats itself throughout the horoscope, it is almost guaranteed that it will be a dominant factor in the person's life. The Raj/Dhana yoga placed in the 9th house (father, luck, and higher education) will not only endow her father with success, but Barbara will always be able to recognize advantageous circumstances and seize them. In addition to the Master's Degree which she already possesses, it would not be surprising if during her Mercury Dasa (planetary period) she decided to return to school to pursue another course of study.

Rahu and Kethu in Barbara's Chart

Rahu's placement in the 5th house reiterates Barbara's stomach troubles and indicates there will be difficulties either conceiving children or deciding on the appropriate time to have a baby. Kethu's placement in the 11th Upachaya house, however, fosters situations throughout her life in which her perseverance is tested. It is at these times that Barbara can muster her iron will and ultimately achieve her goals.

The Moon in Barbara's Chart

The naturally benefic Waxing Moon is the ruler of the 3rd Up-achaya house and contributes to its categorization as an individually malefic planet. As the ruler of Cancer in the 3rd house, the Moon describes her imaginative mind and ability to reflect upon what others have to say. Due to the nature of the Moon, however, Barbara is often insecure about the level of her intelligence and her ability to communicate ideas clearly.

Placed in the 10th house and aspected by Saturn, the Moon implies that Barbara will frequently travel for her work and that the desire to communicate with others will aid her career. Other definitions for the placement of the Moon in the 10th house focus on her popularity, her involvement with helping others, and working in a public service profession. The Moon, a symbol for femininity, also gives her an extremely close relationship with her mother and with women in general. Since the Moon is karaka of the Mother, she has been very influential in Barbara's choice of career.

At the same time, the Moon's individual malevolence, and aspect from Saturn, will give her a lack of self-esteem when it comes to her professional capabilities. Since the 3rd house governs one's desires and state of mind, the Moon's aspect from Saturn will cause depression, pessimism, and lack of aggression when it comes to fulfilling her goals. Coupled with a plethora of 8th house (behind the scenes) planets, Barbara is more comfortable taking orders than being placed in a supervisory position. She will, however, have to work hard in order to overcome these self-imposed restrictions.

The Sun in Barbara's Chart

As the ruler of the 4th Kendra house, the Sun represents the mother and family. It is, however, also the karaka for the father. Naturally malefic and individually benefic, it is positioned in the 9th house and conjoined with individually benefic Mercury. The Sun's placement in the 9th house and conjunction with Mercury indicates that her mother was a good teacher and perhaps a writer. Due to the Sun's natural malevolence, however, Barbara had difficulty communicating with her father and, as a child, spent time alone, alienated from the rest of the family. (We have already mentioned the influence of the Sun in the section pertaining to Mercury.)

• • •

The preceding descriptions merely touch upon the Rasi Chakras of Annemarie and Barbara using some of the principles of interpretation mentioned in chapters 5 through 8. It is never enough, however, to merely interpret a chart without viewing the accompanying planetary periods called dasas. While the aforementioned descriptions apply to Annemarie and Barbara as a general rule, the characteristics of a particular planet will manifest during that planet's period.

In my own chart, for example, Mars is the yogakaraka and by far my strongest planet. In addition, the Sun and Venus are exalted. While these planets will certainly manifest in a positive manner, their strongest application will come to fruition during the planetary periods of Mars, the Sun, and Venus. Since I will never experience the major periods of these planets in the course of my lifetime, they will give positive, but not maximum, results.

Part III
Forecasting

CHAPTER 9

PREDICTIVE ASTROLOGY:
VIMSHOTTARI DASA SYSTEM

TO UNDERSTAND THE BIRTH chart and the timing of events, it is imperative to interpret the Rasi Chakra, the Moon chart, and the navamsa chart in conjunction with the dasa system—a method of prediction unique to India whereby the life span is divided into nine planetary periods called dasas. *Dasa*, Sanskrit for "age," is an abbreviated form of the word *mahadasa*, whose prefix *maha* means "great," as in maha-rajah (great king) or maha-rani (great queen). Although there are literally *hundreds* of different dasa systems which apportion the periods of life according to different principles, the one most commonly utilized and noted for its accuracy is called Vimshottari dasa.[1]

At the heart of this system lie the 27 nakshatras, or fixed star clusters, which comprise the section of space known as the zodiacal belt (the 12 signs of the zodiac). Beginning at 0° of the actual constellation Aries, each of the 27 asterisms spans 13°20′ of the zodiac and is ruled by one of the nine grahas (see Table 9.1 on page 220). The nakshatras, more commonly known as Moon Mansions, are a fundamental feature of most lunar-based astrological systems, such as the Chinese, the Egyptian and, of course, the Indian.

The Moon, the most important heavenly body in Indian astrology and mythology, was regarded by most ancient cultures, including Sumer, Babylonia, China, and Greece, as a god and *not* as a goddess. Because the Moon's cycle of 27–28 days correlates with the number of days in a woman's menstrual cycle, the Moon has mistakenly been considered by modern followers of ancient myth to be a feminine deity. There were in-

---

[1] K.S. Krishnamurti, the late astrologer (whose books have guided much of my study), also maintains that Vimshottari dasa is the most straightforward and accurate. Other common dasa systems include Kalachakra, Ashtottari, and Jaimini-based systems such as Yogini and Chara, which are sign-based. In this book, we will only focus on Vimshottari.

Table 9.1. Nakshatras According to Vimshottari Dasa System.

NAKSHATRAS	ZODIACAL POSITION	RULING PLANET	PLANETARY PERIODS (IN YEARS)
1. Aswini	0° AR 00'—13° AR 20'	Kethu	7
2. Bharani	13° AR 20'—26° AR 40'	Venus	20
3. Krittika	26° AR 40'—10° TA 00'	Sun	6
4. Rohini	10° TA 00'—23° TA 20'	Moon	10
5. Mrigsira	23° TA 20'— 6° GE 40'	Mars	7
6. Ardra	6° GE 40'—20° GE 00'	Rahu	18
7. Punarvasu	20° GE 00'— 3° CN 20'	Jupiter	16
8. Pushya	3° CN 20'—16° CN 40'	Saturn	19
9. Aslesha	16° CN 40'— 0° LE 00'	Mercury	17
10. Magha	0° LE 00'—13° LE 20'	Kethu	7
11. Purvaphalguni	13° LE 20'—26° LE 40'	Venus	20
12. Uttraphalguni	26° LE 40'—10° V 00'	Sun	6
13. Hasta	10° VI 00'—23° VI 20'	Moon	10
14. Chitra	23° VI 20'— 6° LI 40'	Mars	7
15. Svati	6° LI 40'—20° LI 00'	Rahu	18
16. Vishakha	20° LI 00'— 3° SC 20'	Jupiter	16
17. Anuradha	3° SC 20'—16° SC 40'	Saturn	19
18. Jyeshtha	16° SC 40'— 0° SA 00'	Mercury	17
19. Mula	0° SA 00'—13° SA 20'	Kethu	7
20. Purvashadya	13° SA 20'—26° SA 40'	Venus	20
21. Uttrashadya	26° SA 40'—10° CP 00'	Sun	6
22. Shravana	10° CP 00'—23° CP 20'	Moon	10
23. Dhanishtha	23° CP 20'— 6° AQ 40'	Mars	7
24. Shatbisha	6° AQ 40'—20° AQ 00'	Rahu	18
25. Purvaphadrapada	20° AQ 00'— 3° PI 20'	Jupiter	16
26. Uttraphadrapada	3° PI 20'—16° PI 40'	Saturn	19
27. Revati	16° PI 40'— 0° AR 00'	Mercury	17

deed Moon goddesses, but they were either daughters of the Moon God (the Sumerian Inanna and Babylonian Ishtar, whose fathers were Nanna and Sin) or lovers and worshippers of the Moon (the Greek Artemis and Roman Diana, who worshipped Selene, the Greek Moon god). These goddesses were never manifestations of the Moon itself, which was considered to be male.

According to Hindu lore, Soma, the Moon God, considers the 27 nakshatras to be his resting places as he journeys through the zodiac. Still other legends personify the Moon mansions as his amorous satellites or wives—one lover for each day of the Moon's cycle. In this regard, several nakshatras have qualities very similar to the zodiacal signs they occupy, or to one of the fixed stars contained within that particular sign. A perfect example is Rohini, the fourth asterism, known throughout Indian mythology as the Moon's favorite and most jealous wife.[2] Meaning "red cow," Rohini spans 13-1/3° of Taurus the Bull, the most possessive and sensual sign of the zodiac. It's no wonder that the Moon's place of exaltation, or where He feels most exhilarated, is Taurus, the very sign he loves so much.

Reflecting on my days as a student of Dr. Muralil Sharma, my first Jyotish teacher, I recall my very first homework assignment was to memorize and recite the names of the 27 nakshatras. Since Sanskrit is spoken with different parts of the mouth than we use, pronouncing these terms correctly was no easy task. When I finally learned their names in correct sequential order, I proudly recounted them to my teacher. At that moment he knew I was a serious student of Jyotish.

• • •

Vimshottari Dasa is comprised of 120 years, man's ultimate lifespan according to the Hindu scriptures.[3] These 120 years are then divided into nine planetary periods of unequal duration which, when listed sequentially, correspond to the 27 different nakshatras (Table 9.1, page 220). There is no apparent logic or mathematical reasoning behind the unequal division of Vimshottari dasa. Many attempts, all unsuccessful, have been made by various astrologers to determine either numerically or philosophically why these periods are divided in this manner. In fact, one mathematician tried to prove this system's accuracy, basing his proof on Bode's Law, but found this, too, provided no rationale.[4]

---

[2] Wendy O' Flaherty, *Hindu Myths* (New York: Penguin, 1975) p. 351.
[3] There is a common Yiddish expression, "Zolst leben biz a hindit'n tzvantzik yurn"which, translated, means, "You should live to be 120 years."
[4] Grace Inglis, *Hindu Dasa System* (New Delhi: Sagar Publications, 1973), pp. 8–9.

Although there are reasonably priced computer programs and mail-order computer services which provide accurate dasa calculations (see Appendix, page 291), I feel that it is important to have a working knowledge of the mathematical calculations.[5] What follows, therefore, is an illustration of the steps involved in calculating planetary periods according to Vimshottari dasa.

Calculating Annemarie's Dasas

Annemarie's chart is the first example used to demonstrate these steps. She was born on December 26, 1952 at 5:50 A.M., Greenwich Mean Time. Her Nirayana (Sidereal) Moon position is 11° Aries 59′.

Step 1. *Finding the Nakshatra of the Natal Moon*
The initial step for calculating Vimshottari dasa is to identify which nakshatra the natal Moon occupied at the exact moment of birth. Table 9.1 (page 220) indicates that, in addition to being placed in the zodiacal sign of Aries, the Moon is also situated in the first constellation of Aswini, which runs from 0°–13° Aries 20′. This first nakshatra corresponds to Kethu's mahadasa, which lasts seven years.

Step 2. *Where the Birth Falls Within the Mahadasa*
Now that we know that Annemarie was born in Kethu mahadasa we must find out how many years, months, and days of that dasa preceded her birth and how much still remains. At the moment of birth, the Moon was 11° Aries 59′ and, according to Table 9.1 (page 220), only 1°21′, or 81 minutes, remained in Kethu's dasa before the onset of the Bharani naksha-

---

[5] Because of the absolute exactitude the computer will give for the starting date of a planetary period, there may be a discrepancy of a few days between this figure and the results obtained by manual calculations. For example, when Annemarie's chart is done by computer, most of her dasa periods begin on September 6th. When done manually, they begin on September 7th or 8th.

tra and entrance into Venus mahadasa. The following formula is used to see how many years of Kethu remain:

> The number of years, months, and days remaining in the Mahadasa will be proportionately equivalent to the difference between the exact degree the Moon occupies and the last degree of its Nakshatra.

Using minutes as the common denominator, the following equations illustrate the above formula. Remember that each Nakshatra spans 13°20′ (or 800′) and, in the equation for each horoscope, that number remains constant.

$$\frac{\text{Difference in Minutes between Moon Degree and Last Degree of Nakshatra}}{800' \text{ (Total Minutes in Nakshatra)}} \times \frac{\text{Years of Mahadasa}}{}$$

Let us now apply this formula to Annemarie's chart.

$$\frac{81}{800} \times 7 = 0.708$$

Eighty-one minutes are divided by 800 and then multiplied by 7 years, which gives us a total of 0.708. This decimal is a percentage of 365-1/4, the number of days in a year. Translating this into days, we arrive at approximately 255 days. At the time Annemarie was born, on December 26, 1952, there were approximately 255 days remaining in Kethu dasa which, as the first major period of Annemarie's life, lasted from the date of her birth, December 26, 1952 until September 6, 1953.

Step 3. *Listing the Mahadasas to Follow*
Table 9.2 illustrates the sequence of mahadasas in Annemarie's chart according to Table 9.1 (page 220). Going full circle, Vimshottari dasa always begins and ends with the same planetary period (in this case it is Kethu) and will always total 120 years. Venus follows Kethu, adding another 20 years to the birth date. The Sun then follows Venus, adding 6 more years; the Moon adds 10 more years, etc.

Table 9.2. Annemarie's Dasa Periods.

PLANET	DECEMBER 26, 1952 TO DECEMBER 26, 2072
Kethu	+ 255 days = September 6, 1953
Venus	+ 20 Years = September 6, 1953–September 5, 1973
Sun	+ 6 Years = September 6, 1973–September 5, 1979
Moon	+ 10 Years = September 6, 1979–September 5, 1989
Mars	+ 7 Years = September 6, 1989–September 5, 1996
Rahu	+ 18 Years = September 6, 1996–September 5, 2014
Jupiter	+ 16 Years = September 6, 2014–September 5, 2030
Saturn	+ 19 Years = September 6, 2030–September 5, 2049
Mercury	+ 17 Years = September 6, 2049–September 5, 2066
Balance	+ 6 Years, 3 months, 19 days
of Kethu	= September 6, 2066-December 25, 2072
	This totals 120 Years of Vimshottari Dasa.

Calculating Barbara's Dasas

Let's follow Barbara's dasa calculations. She was born on January 30, 1960 at 16:59 Greenwich Mean Time. Her nirayana Moon position is 19° Aquarius 2′.

Step 1. *Finding the Nakshatra of the Natal Moon*
It is very clear from the nakshatra table (Table 9.1, page 220) that Barbara's Moon is situated in the 24th constellation, Shatbisha, which extends from 6°40′ to 20° Aquarius and corresponds to Rahu mahadasa, which lasts 18 years.

Step 2. *Where the Birth Falls Within the Mahadasa*
Although we know that Barbara was born in Rahu mahadasa, we must learn exactly how many years, months, and days of that dasa had passed prior to her birth. According to Table 9.1 (page 220), the constellation of Purvaphadrapada commences at 20° Aquarius. With Barbara's Moon being positioned at 19° Aquarius 2′, there are only 58′ remaining in Shatbisha and Rahu mahadasa. Because there is so little time remaining in the mahadasa of her birth, it is not necessary to calculate pre-natal time. In order to determine when Jupiter's mahadasa will com-

mence, the same formula used for Annemarie is applied to Barbara's chart:

$$\frac{\text{Difference in Minutes between Moon Degree and Last Degree of Nakshatra}}{800' \text{ (Total Minutes in Nakshatra)}} \times \frac{\text{Years of}}{\text{Mahadasa}}$$

Applied to Barbara's chart, the equation is as follows:

$$\frac{58}{800} \times 18 = 1.3 \text{ years or 1 year, 3 months, 20 days.}$$

Rahu mahadasa, the first major period of life, lasts from January 30, 1960, the day of birth, until May 20, 1961, when Jupiter's mahadasa begins.

Step 3. *Listing the Mahadasas to Follow*
The following is a list of Barbara's mahadasas which begin and end with Rahu mahadasa and are taken from the figures in Table 9.1.

Since the planetary periods vary in length from 6 to 20 years, it is necessary to further divide the dasa into planetary sub-periods known as Antara dasas in Northern India and

Table 9.3 Barbara's Dasa Periods.

PLANET	JANUARY 30, 1960 TO JANUARY 30, 2080
Rahu	+ 1 year 3 months 20 days = May 20, 1961
Jupiter	+ 16 years = May 20, 1961—May 19, 1977
Saturn	+ 19 years = May 20, 1977—May 19, 1996
Mercury	+ 17 years = May 20, 1996—May 19, 2013
Kethu	+ 7 years = May 20, 2013—May 19, 2020
Venus	+ 20 years = May 20, 2020—May 19, 2040
Sun	+ 6 years = May 20, 2040—May 19, 2046
Moon	+ 10 years = May 20, 2046—May 19, 2056
Mars	+ 7 years = May 20, 2056—May 19, 2063
Balance of Rahu	+ 16 years, 8 months, 10 days = May 20, 2063—January 30, 2080

Bhukti dasas in the South.[6] Within the framework of each mahadasa, the nine sub-periods are listed in the same sequential
manner as the mahadasas and begin with the bhukti ruled by
the mahadasa ruler. For instance, in the breakdown of Annemarie's Moon mahadasa, the initial bhukti also belongs to
the Moon. The planets then follow in the same sequence as
listed in Table 9.1 (page 220), with Mars bhukti next, then
Rahu bhukti, then Jupiter bhukti, etc., all within the Moon's
mahadasa until the Moon's period ends with Sun bhukti.

Table 9.4 (page 227) displays the length of each sub-period
within the context of the dasa in which it is placed. The major
periods are proportionately divided into bhukties the same way
the 120 years of Vimshottari dasa are divided into the nine mahadasas. To determine the length of Mars bhukti with the
Moon mahadasa, multiply 7/120 (7 years in Mars mahadasa
out of the 120 years of Vimshottari dasa) by 10 years (length of
Moon's dasa). The following Rahu bhukti is 18/120 multiplied
by 10, Jupiter is 16/120 multiplied by 10, etc. If we actually
took the time to calculate all these, the result would be the
same as those shown in Table 9.4. While each sub-period will
vary in length according to the dasa in which it is placed, they
will always be proportionally divided; Venus will always be the
longest period and the Sun will always be the shortest.

This process continues in the same manner when calculating the sub-sub-period called Pratyantara dasa in the North and
Antara dasa in the South.[7] Each bhukti begins with the Antara
dasa whose planetary ruler is the same as the bhukti ruler after
which they continue in the same sequential order. Table
9.7–9.15 (pages 241–249) lists the sub-sub-periods within each
bhukti dasa in the same way that Table 9.4 lists the sub-periods
within each Mahadasa. Although most of us will not be calculating these periods by hand, it is important to view the relative
lengths of each planetary period in relation to one another.

Tables 9.5 (pages 228–232) and 9.6 (pages 233–237) show
the complete Dasa-Bhukti-Antara listings for Annemarie and

---

[6] Because it has become the popularized term, I will utilize *bhukti* for sub-period.
[7] Because it is the most known term for sub-sub-period, I will utilize "Antara
dasa."

Table 9.4. Bhukti Dasas.*

DASA LORD	KETHU		VENUS		SUN		MOON		MARS		RAHU		JUPITER		SATURN		MERCURY	
	MO.	D.	MO.	D.	MO.	D.	MO.	D.	MO.	D.	MO.	D.	MO.	D.	MO.	D.	MO.	D.
Kethu sub-period	4	27	40	0	3	18	10	0	4	27	32	12	25	18	36	3	28	27
Venus sub-period	14	0	12	0	6	0	7	0	12	18	28	24	30	12	32	9	11	27
Sun sub-period	4	6	20	0	4	6	18	0	11	6	34	6	27	6	13	9	34	0
Moon sub-period	7	0	14	0	10	24	16	0	13	9	30	18	11	6	38	0	10	6
Mars sub-period	4	27	36	0	9	18	19	0	11	27	12	18	32	0	11	12	17	0
Rahu sub-period	12	18	32	0	11	12	17	0	4	27	36	0	9	18	19	0	11	27
Jupiter sub-period	11	6	38	0	10	6	7	0	14	0	10	24	16	0	13	9	30	18
Saturn sub-period	13	9	34	0	4	6	20	0	4	6	18	0	11	6	34	6	27	6
Mercury sub-period	11	27	14	0	12	0	6	0	7	0	12	18	28	24	30	12	32	9
Total years of Dasa	7 yrs		20 yrs		6 yrs		10 yrs		7 yrs		18 yrs		16 yrs		19 yrs		17 yrs	

* Adapted from data provided in K. S. Krishnamurti's *Casting the Horoscope*, Vol. 1 (Madras: Mahabala, 1971), p. 90.

Table 9.5. Annemarie's Dasa-Bhukti-Antara Periods. *

KETU DASA (Read Bhuktis Across, Antardasas Down)

KETU Birth Bhukti	VENUS	SUN	MOON	MARS	RAHU	JUPITER	SATURN	MERCURY Birth Bhukti
KE Sep 6 46	VE Feb 3 47	SU Apr 4 48	MO Aug 10 48	MA Mar 11 49	RA Aug 7 49	JU Aug 25 50	SA Aug 1 51	ME Sep 9 52 A
VE Sep 15 46	SU Apr 15 47	MO Apr 10 48	MA Aug 27 48	RA Mar 19 49	JU Oct 3 49	SA Oct 10 50	ME Oct 4 51	KE Oct 30 52 N
SU Oct 10 46	MO May 6 47	MA Apr 21 48	RA Sep 9 48	JU Apr 11 49	SA Nov 23 49	ME Dec 3 50	KE Dec 1 51	VE Nov 20 52 T
MO Oct 17 46	MA Jun 10 47	RA Apr 28 48	JU Oct 11 48	SA May 1 49	ME Jan 23 50	KE Jan 20 51	VE Dec 24 51	SU Jan 20 53 A
MA Oct 30 46	RA Jul 5 47	JU May 17 48	SA Nov 8 48	ME May 24 49	KE Mar 18 50	VE Feb 9 51	SU Mar 1 52	MO Feb 7 53 R
RA Nov 8 46	JU Sep 7 47	SA Jun 3 48	ME Dec 12 48	KE Jun 14 49	VE Apr 10 50	SU Apr 7 51	MO Mar 21 52	MA Mar 9 53 D
JU Nov 30 46	SA Nov 3 47	ME Jun 24 48	KE Jan 11 49	VE Jun 23 49	SU Jun 13 50	MO Apr 24 51	MA Apr 24 52	RA Mar 30 53 A
SA Dec 20 46	ME Jan 9 48	KE Jul 12 48	VE Jan 23 49	SU Jul 18 49	MO Jul 2 50	MA May 22 51	RA May 17 52	JU May 24 53 S
ME Jan 12 47	KE Mar 10 48	VE Jul 19 48	SU Feb 28 49	MO Jul 25 49	MA Aug 3 50	RA Jun 11 51	JU Jul 17 52	SA Jul 11 53 A

VENUS DASA (Read Bhuktis Across, Antardasas Down)

VENUS 1 Yrs Old	SUN 4 Yrs Old	MOON 5 Yrs Old	MARS 7 Yrs Old	RAHU 8 Yrs Old	JUPITER 11 Yrs Old	SATURN 14 Yrs Old	MERCURY 17 Yrs Old	KETU 20 Yrs Old
VE Sep 6 53	SU Jan 6 57	MO Jan 6 58	MA Sep 2 59	RA Nov 6 60	JU Nov 7 63	SA Jul 8 66	ME Sep 6 69	KE Jul 7 72 A
SU Jan 28 54	MO Jan 24 57	MA Feb 26 58	RA Oct 2 59	JU Apr 19 61	SA Mar 16 64	ME Jan 7 67	KE Jan 31 70	VE Aug 1 72 N
MO May 28 54	MA Feb 23 57	RA Apr 2 58	JU Dec 5 59	SA Sep 12 61	ME Aug 17 64	KE Jun 20 67	VE Apr 1 70	SU Oct 11 72 T
MA Sep 6 54	RA Mar 17 57	JU Jul 3 58	SA Jan 30 60	ME Mar 5 62	KE Jan 2 65	VE Aug 26 67	SU Sep 21 70	MO Nov 1 72 A
RA Nov 17 54	JU May 11 57	SA Sep 22 58	ME Apr 7 60	KE Aug 7 62	VE Feb 28 65	SU Mar 6 68	MO Nov 12 70	MA Dec 1 72 R
JU May 18 55	SA Jun 28 57	ME Dec 27 58	KE Jun 6 60	VE Oct 10 62	SU Aug 9 65	MO May 3 68	MA Feb 6 71	RA Jan 1 73 D
SA Oct 27 55	ME Aug 25 57	KE Mar 23 59	VE Jul 1 60	SU Apr 11 63	MO Sep 27 65	MA Aug 14 68	RA Apr 7 71	JU Mar 6 73 A
ME May 7 56	KE Oct 16 57	VE Apr 28 59	SU Sep 10 60	MO Jun 4 63	MA Dec 17 65	RA Oct 17 68	JU Sep 9 71	SA May 2 73 S
KE Oct 27 56	VE Nov 6 57	SU Aug 7 59	MO Oct 1 60	MA Sep 4 63	RA Feb 12 66	JU Apr 5 69	SA Jan 25 72	ME Jul 8 73 A

Table 9.5. Annemarie's Dasa-Bhukti-Antara Periods* (continued).

SUN DASA (Read Bhuktis Across, Antardasas Down)

SUN	MOON	MARS	RAHU	JUPITER	SATURN	MERCURY	KETU	VENUS	
21 Yrs Old	21 Yrs Old	21 Yrs Old	22 Yrs Old	23 Yrs Old	24 Yrs Old	24 Yrs Old	25 Yrs Old	26 Yrs Old	
SU Sep 6 73	MO Dec 25 73	MA Jun 26 74	RA Oct 31 74	JU Sep 25 75	SA Jul 13 76	ME Jun 25 77	KE May 2 78	VE Sep 7 78	A
MO Sep 12 73	MA Jan 9 74	RA Jul 3 74	JU Dec 20 74	SA Nov 3 75	ME Sep 6 76	KE Aug 8 77	VE May 9 78	SU Nov 7 78	N
MA Sep 21 73	RA Jan 20 74	JU Jul 22 74	SA Feb 2 75	ME Dec 19 75	KE Oct 25 76	VE Aug 26 77	SU May 31 78	MO Nov 25 78	T
RA Sep 27 73	JU Feb 16 74	SA Aug 8 74	ME Mar 26 75	KE Jan 30 76	VE Nov 15 76	SU Oct 17 77	MO Jun 6 78	MA Dec 25 78	A
JU Oct 14 73	SA Mar 13 74	ME Aug 28 74	KE May 11 75	VE Feb 16 76	SU Jan 12 77	MO Nov 2 77	MA Jun 17 78	RA Jan 16 79	R
SA Oct 28 73	ME Apr 10 74	KE Sep 16 74	VE May 30 75	SU Apr 5 76	MO Jan 29 77	MA Nov 28 77	RA Jun 24 78	JU Mar 11 79	D
ME Nov 15 73	KE May 6 74	VE Sep 23 74	SU Jul 24 75	MO Apr 19 76	MA Feb 27 77	RA Dec 16 77	JU Jul 13 78	SA Apr 29 79	A
KE Nov 30 73	VE May 17 74	SU Oct 14 74	MO Aug 10 75	MA May 13 76	RA Mar 19 77	JU Jan 31 78	SA Jul 30 78	ME Jun 26 79	S
VE Dec 7 73	SU Jun 16 74	MO Oct 21 74	MA Sep 6 75	RA May 31 76	JU May 10 77	SA Mar 14 78	ME Aug 20 78	KE Aug 17 79	A

MOON DASA (Read Bhuktis Across, Antardasas Down)

MOON	MARS	RAHU	JUPITER	SATURN	MERCURY	KETU	VENUS	SUN	
27 Yrs Old	28 Yrs Old	28 Yrs Old	30 Yrs Old	31 Yrs Old	33 Yrs Old	34 Yrs Old	35 Yrs Old	36 Yrs Old	
MO Sep 7 79	MA Jul 7 80	RA Feb 5 81	JU Aug 7 82	SA Dec 7 83	ME Jul 8 85	KE Dec 7 86	VE Jul 8 87	SU Mar 8 89	A
MA Oct 2 79	RA Jul 20 80	JU Apr 29 81	SA Oct 11 82	ME Mar 8 84	KE Sep 19 85	VE Dec 19 86	SU Oct 18 87	MO Mar 17 89	N
RA Oct 20 79	JU Aug 21 80	SA Jul 11 81	ME Dec 27 82	KE May 29 84	VE Oct 19 85	SU Jan 24 87	MO Nov 17 87	MA Apr 1 89	T
JU Dec 5 79	SA Sep 18 80	ME Oct 5 81	KE Mar 6 83	VE Jul 1 84	SU Jan 13 86	MO Feb 4 87	MA Jan 7 88	RA Apr 12 89	A
SA Jan 14 80	ME Oct 22 80	KE Dec 22 81	VE Apr 4 83	SU Oct 6 84	MO Feb 8 86	MA Feb 21 87	RA Feb 11 88	JU May 9 89	R
ME Mar 2 80	KE Nov 21 80	VE Jan 23 82	SU Jun 24 83	MO Nov 4 84	MA Mar 23 86	RA Mar 6 87	JU May 13 88	SA Jun 3 89	D
KE Apr 15 80	VE Dec 3 80	SU Apr 24 82	MO Jul 18 83	MA Dec 22 84	RA Apr 22 86	JU Apr 7 87	SA Aug 2 88	ME Jul 2 89	A
VE May 2 80	SU Jan 8 81	MO May 22 82	MA Aug 28 83	RA Jan 25 85	JU Jul 9 86	SA May 5 87	ME Nov 6 88	KE Jul 27 89	S
SU Jun 22 80	MO Jan 19 81	MA Jul 6 82	RA Sep 25 83	JU Apr 21 85	SA Sep 16 86	ME Jun 8 87	KE Jan 31 89	VE Aug 7 89	A

Table 9.5. Annemarie's Dasa-Bhukti-Antara Periods* (continued).

MARS DASA (Read Bhuktis Across, Antardasas Down)

MARS 37 Yrs Old	RAHU 37 Yrs Old	JUPITER 38 Yrs Old	SATURN 39 Yrs Old	MERCURY 40 Yrs Old	KETU 41 Yrs Old	VENUS 42 Yrs Old	SUN 43 Yrs Old	MOON 43 Yrs Old
MA Sep 6 89	RA Feb 3 90	JU Feb 21 91	SA Jan 28 92	ME Mar 8 93	KE Mar 5 94	VE Aug 1 94	SU Oct 1 95	MO Feb 6 96 A
RA Sep 15 89	JU Apr 1 90	SA Apr 8 91	ME Apr 1 92	KE Apr 28 93	VE Mar 14 94	SU Oct 11 94	MO Oct 8 95	MA Feb 24 96 N
JU Oct 8 89	SA May 22 90	ME Jun 1 91	KE May 28 92	VE May 19 93	SU Apr 8 94	MO Nov 2 94	MA Oct 18 95	RA Mar 7 96 T
SA Oct 27 89	ME Jul 22 90	KE Jul 19 91	VE Jun 21 92	SU Jul 19 93	MO Apr 15 94	MA Dec 7 94	RA Oct 26 95	JU Apr 8 96 A
ME Nov 20 89	KE Sep 14 90	VE Aug 8 91	SU Aug 28 92	MO Aug 6 93	MA Apr 28 94	RA Jan 1 95	JU Nov 14 95	SA May 7 96 R
KE Dec 11 89	VE Oct 7 90	SU Oct 4 91	MO Sep 17 92	MA Sep 5 93	RA May 6 94	JU Mar 6 95	SA Dec 1 95	ME Jun 9 96 D
VE Dec 20 89	SU Dec 10 90	MO Oct 21 91	MA Oct 21 92	RA Sep 26 93	JU May 29 94	SA May 2 95	ME Dec 21 95	KE Jul 10 96 A
SU Jan 14 90	MO Dec 29 90	MA Nov 18 91	RA Nov 13 92	JU Nov 19 93	SA Jun 17 94	ME Jul 8 95	KE Jan 8 96	VE Jul 22 96 S
MO Jan 21 90	MA Jan 30 91	RA Dec 8 91	JU Jan 13 93	SA Jan 7 94	ME Jul 11 94	KE Sep 6 95	VE Jan 16 96	SU Aug 27 96 A

RAHU DASA (Read Bhuktis Across, Antardasas Down)

RAHU 44 Yrs Old	JUPITER 46 Yrs Old	SATURN 49 Yrs Old	MERCURY 52 Yrs Old	KETU 54 Yrs Old	VENUS 55 Yrs Old	SUN 58 Yrs Old	MOON 59 Yrs Old	MARS 61 Yrs Old
RA Sep 6 96	JU May 20 99	SA Oct 13 01	ME Aug 19 04	KE Mar 8 07	VE Mar 26 08	SU Mar 27 11	MO Feb 18 12	MA Aug 19 13 A
JU Feb 1 97	SA Sep 14 99	ME Mar 27 02	KE Dec 29 04	VE Mar 31 07	SU Sep 25 08	MO Apr 12 11	MA Apr 4 12	RA Sep 11 13 N
SA Jun 13 97	ME Jan 31 00	KE Aug 21 02	VE Feb 21 05	SU Jun 3 07	MO Nov 18 08	MA May 10 11	RA May 6 12	JU Nov 7 13 T
ME Nov 16 97	KE Jul 3 00	VE Oct 21 02	SU Jul 27 05	MO Jun 22 07	MA Feb 18 09	RA May 29 11	JU Jul 27 12	SA Dec 28 13 A
KE Apr 5 98	VE Jul 24 00	SU Apr 13 03	MO Sep 11 05	MA Jul 24 07	RA Apr 23 09	JU Jul 17 11	SA Oct 8 12	ME Feb 27 14 R
VE Jun 1 98	SU Dec 18 00	MO Jun 4 03	MA Nov 28 05	RA Aug 15 07	JU Oct 4 09	SA Aug 30 11	ME Jan 3 13	KE Apr 22 14 D
SU Nov 12 98	MO Jan 30 01	MA Aug 29 03	RA Jan 21 06	JU Oct 12 07	SA Feb 27 10	ME Oct 21 11	KE Mar 22 13	VE May 15 14 A
MO Jan 1 99	MA Apr 13 01	RA Oct 29 03	JU Jun 10 06	SA Dec 2 07	ME Aug 20 10	KE Nov 7 11	VE Apr 23 13	SU Jul 18 14 S
MA Mar 24 99	RA Jun 4 01	JU Apr 2 04	SA Oct 12 06	ME Feb 1 08	KE Jan 22 11	VE Dec 26 11	SU Jul 23 13	MO Aug 6 14 A

Table 9.5. Annemarie's Dasa-Bhukti-Antara Periods* (continued).

JUPITER DASA (Read Bhuktis Across, Antardasas Down)

JUPITER 62 Yrs Old	SATURN 64 Yrs Old	MERCURY 66 Yrs Old	KETU 69 Yrs Old	VENUS 70 Yrs Old	SUN 72 Yrs Old	MOON 73 Yrs Old	MARS 74 Yrs Old	RAHU 75 Yrs Old
JU Sep 7 14	SA Oct 25 16	ME May 8 19	KE Aug 13 21	VE Jul 20 22	SU Mar 20 25	MO Jan 6 26	MA May 8 27	RA Apr 13 28 A
SA Dec 20 14	ME Mar 21 17	KE Sep 3 19	VE Sep 2 21	SU Dec 30 22	MO Apr 4 25	MA Feb 16 26	RA May 28 27	JU Aug 23 28 N
ME Apr 22 15	KE Jul 30 17	VE Oct 21 19	SU Oct 29 21	MO Feb 16 23	MA Apr 28 25	RA Mar 16 26	JU Jul 18 27	SA Dec 18 28 T
KE Aug 11 15	VE Sep 22 17	SU Mar 7 20	MO Nov 15 21	MA May 8 23	RA May 15 25	JU May 28 26	SA Sep 2 27	ME May 6 29 A
VE Sep 25 15	SU Feb 23 18	MO Apr 17 20	MA Dec 13 21	RA Jul 4 23	JU Jun 28 25	SA Aug 1 26	ME Oct 26 27	KE Sep 7 29 R
SU Feb 2 16	MO Apr 10 18	MA Jun 25 20	RA Jan 2 22	JU Nov 27 23	SA Aug 6 25	ME Oct 18 26	KE Dec 13 27	VE Oct 28 29 D
MO Mar 12 16	MA Jun 26 18	RA Aug 13 20	JU Feb 23 22	SA Apr 5 24	ME Sep 21 25	KE Dec 26 26	VE Jan 2 28	SU Mar 23 30 A
MA May 16 16	RA Aug 19 18	JU Dec 15 20	SA Apr 9 22	ME Sep 6 24	KE Nov 2 25	VE Jan 23 27	SU Feb 28 28	MO May 6 30 S
RA Jun 30 16	JU Jan 5 19	SA Apr 4 21	ME Jun 2 22	KE Jan 22 25	VE Nov 19 25	SU Apr 14 27	MO Mar 16 28	MA Jul 18 30 A

SATURN DASA (Read Bhuktis Across, Antardasas Down)

SATURN 78 Yrs Old	MERCURY 81 Yrs Old	KETU 83 Yrs Old	VENUS 85 Yrs Old	SUN 88 Yrs Old	MOON 89 Yrs Old	MARS 90 Yrs Old	RAHU 91 Yrs Old	JUPITER 94 Yrs Old
SA Sep 7 30	ME Sep 10 33	KE May 20 36	VE Jun 29 37	SU Aug 28 40	MO Aug 10 41	MA Mar 12 43	RA Apr 20 44	JU Feb 25 47 A
ME Feb 28 31	KE Jan 27 34	VE Jun 13 36	SU Jan 8 38	MO Sep 15 40	MA Sep 28 41	RA Apr 4 43	JU Sep 23 44	SA Jun 28 47 N
KE Aug 3 31	VE Mar 25 34	SU Aug 19 36	MO Mar 6 38	MA Oct 14 40	RA Oct 31 41	JU Jun 4 43	SA Feb 9 45	ME Nov 21 47 T
VE Oct 6 31	SU Sep 5 34	MO Sep 8 36	MA Jun 11 38	RA Nov 3 40	JU Jan 26 42	SA Jul 28 43	ME Jul 23 45	KE Apr 1 48 A
SU Apr 6 32	MO Oct 24 34	MA Oct 12 36	RA Aug 17 38	JU Dec 25 40	SA Apr 13 42	ME Sep 30 43	KE Dec 18 45	VE May 24 48 R
MO May 31 32	MA Jan 14 35	RA Nov 5 36	JU Feb 7 39	SA Feb 9 41	ME Jul 14 42	KE Nov 26 43	VE Feb 17 46	SU Oct 26 48 D
MA Aug 30 32	RA Mar 13 35	JU Jan 7 37	SA Jul 7 39	ME Apr 5 41	KE Oct 4 42	VE Dec 20 43	SU Aug 5 46	MO Dec 11 48 A
RA Nov 2 32	JU Aug 7 35	SA Feb 27 37	ME Jan 10 40	KE May 24 41	VE Nov 6 42	SU Feb 26 44	MO Sep 30 46	MA Feb 26 49 S
JU Apr 16 33	SA Dec 16 35	ME May 2 37	KE Jun 22 40	VE Jun 14 41	SU Feb 11 43	MO Mar 17 44	MA Dec 26 46	RA Apr 21 49 A

Table 9.5. Annemaries Dasa-Bhukti-Antara Periods* (continued).

MERCURY DASA (Read Bhuktis Across, Antardasas Down)

MERCURY 97 Yrs Old	KETU 99 Yrs Old	VENUS 100 Yrs Old	SUN 103 Yrs Old	MOON 104 Yrs Old	MARS 105 Yrs Old	RAHU 106 Yrs Old	JUPITER 109 Yrs Old	SATURN 111 Yrs Old
ME Sep 7 49	KE Feb 4 52	VE Jan 31 53	SU Dec 2 55	MO Oct 7 56	MA Mar 9 58	RA Mar 6 59	JU Sep 22 61	SA Dec 29 63 A
KE Jan 9 50	VE Feb 25 52	SU Jul 22 53	MO Dec 17 55	MA Nov 19 56	RA Mar 30 58	JU Jul 23 59	SA Jan 11 62	ME Jun 2 64 N
VE Mar 2 50	SU Apr 25 52	MO Sep 12 53	MA Jan 12 56	RA Dec 19 56	JU May 23 58	SA Nov 25 59	ME May 22 62	KE Oct 19 64 T
SU Jul 26 50	MO May 13 52	MA Dec 7 53	RA Jan 30 56	JU Mar 7 57	SA Jul 10 58	ME Apr 20 60	KE Sep 16 62	VE Dec 15 64 A
MO Sep 8 50	MA Jun 12 52	RA Feb 6 54	JU Mar 17 56	SA May 15 57	ME Sep 6 58	KE Aug 30 60	VE Nov 3 62	SU May 28 65 R
MA Nov 21 50	RA Jul 3 52	JU Jul 11 54	SA Apr 27 56	ME Aug 5 57	KE Oct 27 58	VE Oct 23 60	SU Mar 21 63	MO Jul 16 65 D
RA Jan 11 51	JU Aug 27 52	SA Nov 26 54	ME Jun 15 56	KE Oct 17 57	VE Nov 17 58	SU Mar 28 61	MO May 2 63	MA Oct 6 65 A
JU May 23 51	SA Oct 14 52	ME May 9 55	KE Jul 29 56	VE Nov 16 57	SU Jan 16 59	MO May 13 61	MA Jul 10 63	RA Dec 3 65 S
SA Sep 17 51	ME Dec 10 52	KE Oct 2 55	VE Aug 16 56	SU Feb 11 58	MO Feb 4 59	MA Jul 30 61	RA Aug 27 63	JU Apr 29 66 A

MAHADASA SUMMARY

Ketu	: Sep 6, 1946
Venus	: Sep 6, 1953
Sun	: Sep 6, 1973
Moon	: Sep 7, 1979
Mars	: Sep 6, 1989
Rahu	: Sep 6, 1996
Jupiter	: Sep 7, 2014
Saturn	: Sep 7, 2030
Mercury	: Sep 7, 2049

DASA AT BIRTH:

Dasa	: Ketu
Bhukti	: Mercury
Antardasa	: Venus
Sookshma	: Jupiter

* 1 minute error in the birth time = 2 day error in dasa periods.
Table reproduced by permission of C & D Scientific Software.

Table 9.6. Barbara's Dasa-Bhukti-Antara Periods. *

RAHU DASA (Read Bhuktis Across, Antardasas Down)

RAHU	JUPITER	SATURN	MERCURY	KETU	VENUS	SUN	MOON (Birth Bhukti)	MARS (0 Yrs Old)
RA May 20 43	JU Jan 30 46	SA Jun 25 48	ME May 2 51	KE Nov 18 53	VE Dec 7 54	SU Dec 7 57	MO Oct 31 58	MA May 1 60 A
JU Oct 15 43	SA May 27 46	ME Dec 7 48	KE Sep 11 51	VE Dec 11 53	SU Jun 7 55	MO Dec 23 57	MA Dec 16 58	RA May 24 60 N
SA Feb 24 44	ME Oct 13 46	KE May 3 49	VE Nov 4 51	SU Feb 13 54	MO Aug 1 55	MA Jan 19 58	RA Jan 17 59	JU Jul 20 60 T
ME Jul 29 44	KE Feb 14 47	VE Jul 3 49	SU Apr 7 52	MO Mar 4 54	MA Nov 1 55	RA Feb 8 58	JU Apr 9 59	SA Sep 9 60 A
KE Dec 15 44	VE Apr 6 47	SU Dec 23 49	MO May 24 52	MA Apr 5 54	RA Jan 3 56	JU Mar 29 58	SA Jun 21 59	ME Nov 9 60 R
VE Feb 11 45	SU Aug 30 47	MO Feb 13 50	MA Aug 10 52	RA Apr 27 54	JU Jun 16 56	SA May 12 58	ME Sep 16 59	KE Jan 2 61 D
SU Jul 25 45	MO Oct 13 47	MA May 11 50	RA Oct 3 52	JU Jun 24 54	SA Nov 9 56	ME Jul 3 58	KE Dec 3 59	VE Jan 25 61 A
MO Sep 13 45	MA Dec 25 47	RA Jul 11 50	JU Feb 20 53	SA Aug 14 54	ME May 1 57	KE Aug 18 58	VE Jan 4 60	SU Mar 30 61 S
MA Dec 4 45	RA Feb 14 48	JU Dec 14 50	SA Jun 24 53	ME Oct 14 54	KE Oct 4 57	VE Sep 7 58	SU Apr 4 60	MO Apr 18 61 A

JUPITER DASA (Read Bhuktis Across, Antardasas Down)

JUPITER (1 Yrs Old)	SATURN (3 Yrs Old)	MERCURY (6 Yrs Old)	KETU (8 Yrs Old)	VENUS (9 Yrs Old)	SUN (12 Yrs Old)	MOON (13 Yrs Old)	MARS (14 Yrs Old)	RAHU (15 Yrs Old)
JU May 20 61	SA Jul 8 63	ME Jan 18 66	KE Apr 25 68	VE Apr 1 69	SU Dec 1 71	MO Sep 18 72	MA Jan 18 74	RA Dec 25 74 A
SA Sep 1 61	ME Dec 1 63	KE May 16 66	VE May 15 68	SU Sep 10 69	MO Dec 16 71	MA Oct 29 72	RA Feb 7 74	JU May 6 75 N
ME Jan 2 62	KE Apr 11 64	VE Jul 1 66	SU Jul 11 68	MO Oct 29 69	MA Jan 9 72	RA Nov 26 72	JU Mar 30 74	SA Aug 31 75 T
KE Apr 22 62	VE Jun 4 64	SU Nov 18 66	MO Jul 28 68	MA Jan 18 70	RA Jan 26 72	JU Feb 7 73	SA May 15 74	ME Jan 16 76 A
VE Jun 7 62	SU Nov 5 64	MO Dec 29 66	MA Aug 25 68	RA Mar 16 70	JU Mar 10 72	SA Apr 13 73	ME Jul 8 74	KE Jul 20 76 R
SU Oct 15 62	MO Dec 21 64	MA Mar 8 67	RA Sep 14 68	JU Aug 9 70	SA Apr 18 72	ME Jun 29 73	KE Aug 25 74	VE Jul 10 76 D
MO Nov 23 62	MA Mar 8 65	RA Apr 26 67	JU Nov 4 68	SA Dec 17 70	ME Jun 3 72	KE Sep 6 73	VE Sep 14 74	SU Dec 3 76 A
MA Jan 27 63	RA May 1 65	JU Aug 28 67	SA Dec 20 68	ME May 20 71	KE Jul 15 72	VE Oct 5 73	SU Nov 10 74	MO Jan 16 77 S
RA Mar 13 63	JU Sep 17 65	SA Dec 16 67	ME Feb 12 69	KE Oct 5 71	VE Aug 1 72	SU Dec 25 73	MO Nov 27 74	MA Mar 30 77 A

Table 9.6. Barbara's Dasa-Bhukti-Antara Periods* [continued].

SATURN DASA (Read Bhuktis Across, Antardasas Down)

SATURN 17 Yrs Old	MERCURY 20 Yrs Old	KETU 23 Yrs Old	VENUS 24 Yrs Old	SUN 27 Yrs Old	MOON 28 Yrs Old	MARS 30 Yrs Old	RAHU 31 Yrs Old	JUPITER 34 Yrs Old
SA May 20 77	ME May 23 80	KE Jan 31 83	VE Mar 11 84	SU May 11 87	MO Apr 22 88	MA Nov 22 89	RA Dec 31 90	JU Nov 6 93 A
ME Nov 10 77	KE Oct 9 80	VE Feb 23 83	SU Sep 19 84	MO May 29 87	MA Jun 9 88	RA Dec 15 89	JU Jun 6 91	SA Mar 10 94 N
KE Apr 14 78	VE Dec 5 80	SU May 2 83	MO Nov 16 84	MA Jun 27 87	RA Jul 13 88	JU Feb 14 90	SA Oct 22 91	ME Aug 3 94 T
VE Jun 18 78	SU May 18 81	MO May 22 83	MA Feb 21 85	RA Jul 17 87	JU Oct 8 88	SA Apr 9 90	ME Apr 4 92	KE Dec 12 94 A
SU Dec 18 78	MO Jul 6 81	MA Jun 25 83	RA Apr 29 85	JU Sep 7 87	SA Dec 24 88	ME Jun 12 90	KE Aug 30 92	VE Feb 4 95 R
MO Feb 11 79	MA Sep 26 81	RA Jul 18 83	JU Oct 20 85	SA Oct 23 87	ME Mar 26 89	KE Aug 8 90	VE Oct 29 92	SU Jul 9 95 D
MA May 13 79	RA Nov 23 81	JU Sep 17 83	SA Mar 23 86	ME Dec 17 87	KE Jun 16 89	VE Sep 1 90	SU Apr 21 93	MO Aug 24 95 A
RA Jul 16 79	JU Apr 19 82	SA Nov 10 83	ME Sep 22 86	KE Feb 4 88	VE Jul 19 89	SU Nov 7 90	MO Jun 12 93	MA Nov 9 95 S
JU Dec 28 79	SA Aug 28 82	ME Jan 13 84	KE Mar 5 87	VE Feb 24 88	SU Oct 24 89	MO Nov 28 90	MA Sep 7 93	RA Jan 2 96 A

MERCURY DASA (Read Bhuktis Across, Antardasas Down)

MERCURY 36 Yrs Old	KETU 39 Yrs Old	VENUS 40 Yrs Old	SUN 43 Yrs Old	MOON 43 Yrs Old	MARS 45 Yrs Old	RAHU 46 Yrs Old	JUPITER 48 Yrs Old	SATURN 51 Yrs Old
ME May 20 96	KE Oct 16 98	VE Oct 16 99	SU Aug 13 02	MO Jun 20 03	MA Nov 18 04	RA Nov 16 05	JU Jun 4 08	SA Sep 10 10 A
KE Sep 21 96	VE Nov 6 98	SU Apr 3 00	MO Aug 29 02	MA Aug 2 03	RA Dec 10 04	JU Apr 4 06	SA Sep 22 08	ME Feb 13 11 N
VE Nov 12 96	SU Jan 6 99	MO May 25 00	MA Sep 24 02	RA Sep 1 03	JU Feb 2 05	SA Aug 7 06	ME Jan 31 09	KE Jul 2 11 T
SU Apr 7 97	MO Jan 24 99	MA Aug 19 00	RA Oct 12 02	JU Nov 18 03	SA Mar 22 05	ME Jan 1 07	KE May 29 09	VE Aug 28 11 A
MO May 21 97	MA Feb 23 99	RA Oct 18 00	JU Nov 28 02	SA Jan 26 04	ME May 18 05	KE May 13 07	VE Jul 16 09	SU Feb 8 12 R
MA Aug 3 97	RA Mar 16 99	JU Mar 23 01	SA Jan 8 03	ME May 18 04	KE Jul 1 05	VE Jul 6 07	SU Dec 1 09	MO Mar 28 12 D
RA Sep 23 97	JU May 10 99	SA Aug 8 01	ME Feb 26 03	KE Jul 1 04	VE Jul 30 05	SU Dec 8 07	MO Jan 11 10	MA Jun 18 12 A
JU Feb 2 98	SA Jun 27 99	ME Jan 18 02	KE Apr 11 03	VE Jul 29 04	SU Sep 28 05	MO Jan 24 08	MA Mar 21 10	RA Aug 15 12 S
SA May 30 98	ME Aug 23 99	KE Jun 14 02	VE Apr 29 03	SU Oct 24 04	MO Oct 16 05	MA Apr 11 08	RA May 9 10	JU Jan 9 13 A

Table 9.6. Barbara's Dasa-Bhukti-Antara Periods* (continued).

KETU DASA (Read Bhuktis Across, Antardasas Down)

KETU 53 Yrs Old	VENUS 54 Yrs Old	SUN 55 Yrs Old	MOON 55 Yrs Old	MARS 56 Yrs Old	RAHU 56 Yrs Old	JUPITER 57 Yrs Old	SATURN 58 Yrs Old	MERCURY 59 Yrs Old
KE May 20 13	VE Oct 16 13	SU Dec 16 14	MO Apr 23 15	MA Nov 22 15	RA Apr 19 16	JU May 8 17	SA Apr 14 18	ME May 24 19 A
VE May 29 13	SU Dec 26 13	MO Dec 23 14	MA May 11 15	RA Dec 1 15	JU Jun 16 16	SA Jun 22 17	ME Jun 17 18	KE Jul 14 19 N
SU Jun 23 13	MO Jan 17 14	MA Jan 2 15	RA May 23 15	JU Dec 23 15	SA Aug 6 16	ME Aug 15 17	KE Aug 13 18	VE Aug 4 19 T
MO Jun 30 13	MA Feb 21 14	RA Jan 10 15	JU Jun 24 15	SA Jan 12 16	ME Oct 6 16	KE Oct 3 17	VE Sep 6 18	SU Oct 3 19 A
MA Jul 13 13	RA Mar 18 14	JU Jan 29 15	SA Jul 23 15	ME Feb 5 16	KE Nov 29 16	VE Oct 23 17	SU Nov 12 18	MO Oct 22 19 R
RA Jul 21 13	JU May 21 14	SA Feb 15 15	ME Aug 25 15	KE Feb 26 16	VE Dec 21 16	SU Dec 18 17	MO Dec 3 18	MA Nov 21 19 D
JU Aug 13 13	SA Jul 17 14	ME Mar 7 15	KE Sep 25 15	VE Mar 6 16	SU Feb 23 17	MO Jan 4 18	MA Jan 5 19	RA Dec 12 19 A
SA Sep 1 13	ME Sep 22 14	KE Mar 25 15	VE Oct 7 15	SU Mar 31 16	MO Mar 15 17	MA Feb 2 18	RA Jan 29 19	JU Feb 4 20 S
ME Sep 25 13	KE Nov 21 14	VE Apr 2 15	SU Nov 12 15	MO Apr 7 16	MA Apr 16 17	RA Feb 22 18	JU Mar 31 19	SA Mar 24 20 A

VENUS DASA (Read Bhuktis Across, Antardasas Down)

VENUS 60 Yrs Old	SUN 64 Yrs Old	MOON 65 Yrs Old	MARS 66 Yrs Old	RAHU 67 Yrs Old	JUPITER 70 Yrs Old	SATURN 73 Yrs Old	MERCURY 76 Yrs Old	KETU 79 Yrs Old
VE May 20 20	SU Sep 19 23	MO Sep 19 24	MA May 20 26	RA Jul 21 27	JU Jul 20 30	SA Mar 20 33	ME May 20 36	KE Mar 21 39 A
SU Dec 9 20	MO Oct 8 23	MA Nov 8 24	RA Jun 14 26	JU Jan 1 28	SA Nov 27 30	ME Sep 19 33	KE Oct 14 36	VE Apr 15 39 N
MO Feb 8 21	MA Nov 7 23	RA Dec 14 24	JU Aug 17 26	SA May 26 28	ME Apr 30 31	KE Mar 2 34	VE Dec 13 36	SU Jun 25 39 T
MA May 20 21	RA Nov 28 23	JU Mar 15 25	SA Oct 13 26	ME Nov 15 28	KE Sep 15 31	VE Mar 9 34	SU Jul 3 37	MO Jul 16 39 A
RA Jul 30 21	JU Jan 22 24	SA Jun 4 25	ME Dec 19 26	KE Apr 20 29	VE Nov 11 31	SU Nov 18 34	MO Jul 25 37	MA Aug 21 39 R
JU Jan 29 22	SA May 11 24	ME Sep 9 25	KE Feb 18 27	VE Jun 23 29	SU Apr 22 32	MO Jan 14 35	MA Oct 19 37	RA Sep 14 39 D
SA Jul 10 22	ME May 28 24	KE Dec 8 25	VE Mar 25 27	SU Dec 22 29	MO Jun 9 32	MA Apr 21 35	RA Dec 19 37	JU Nov 15 39 A
ME Jan 19 23	KE Jun 28 24	VE Jan 9 26	SU May 15 27	MO Feb 15 30	MA Aug 29 32	RA Jun 27 35	JU May 23 38	SA Jan 13 40 S
KE Jul 10 23	VE Jul 20 24	SU Apr 20 26	MO Jun 15 27	MA May 17 30	RA Oct 25 32	JU Dec 18 35	SA Oct 8 38	ME Mar 21 40 A

Table 9.6. Barbara's Dasa-Bhukti-Antara Periods* (continued).

SUN DASA (Read Bhuktis Across, Antardasas Down)

SUN 80 Yrs Old	MOON 81 Yrs Old	MARS 81 Yrs Old	RAHU 81 Yrs Old	JUPITER 82 Yrs Old	SATURN 83 Yrs Old	MERCURY 84 Yrs Old	KETU 85 Yrs Old	VENUS 85 Yrs Old	
SU May 20 40	MO Sep 7 40	MA Mar 8 41	RA Jul 14 41	JU Jun 8 42	SA Mar 27 43	ME Mar 21 44	KE Jan 12 45	VE May 20 45	A
MO May 25 40	MA Sep 22 40	RA Mar 16 41	JU Sep 1 41	SA Jul 17 42	ME May 21 43	KE Apr 21 44	VE Jan 20 45	SU Jul 20 45	N
MA Jun 4 40	RA Oct 2 40	JU Apr 4 41	SA Oct 15 41	ME Sep 1 42	KE Jul 9 43	VE May 9 44	SU Feb 10 45	MO Aug 7 45	T
RA Jun 10 40	JU Oct 30 40	SA Apr 21 41	ME Dec 6 41	KE Oct 12 42	VE Jul 29 43	SU Jun 30 44	MO Feb 17 45	MA Sep 7 45	A
JU Jun 26 40	SA Nov 23 40	ME May 11 41	KE Jan 22 42	VE Oct 29 42	SU Sep 25 43	MO Jul 15 44	MA Feb 27 45	RA Sep 28 45	R
SA Jul 11 40	ME Dec 22 40	KE May 29 41	VE Feb 10 42	SU Dec 17 42	MO Oct 12 43	MA Aug 10 44	RA Mar 7 45	JU Nov 22 45	D
ME Jul 28 40	KE Jan 17 41	VE Jun 6 41	SU Apr 6 42	MO Jan 1 43	MA Nov 10 43	RA Aug 28 44	JU Mar 26 45	SA Jan 10 46	A
KE Aug 13 40	VE Jan 28 41	SU Jun 28 41	MO Apr 22 42	MA Jan 25 43	RA Dec 1 43	JU Oct 14 44	SA Apr 12 45	ME Mar 8 46	S
VE Aug 19 40	SU Feb 27 41	MO Jul 3 41	MA May 20 42	RA Feb 11 43	JU Jan 22 44	SA Nov 24 44	ME May 2 45	KE Apr 29 46	A

MOON DASA (Read Bhuktis Across, Antardasas Down)

MOON 86 Yrs Old	MARS 87 Yrs Old	RAHU 88 Yrs Old	JUPITER 89 Yrs Old	SATURN 91 Yrs Old	MERCURY 92 Yrs Old	KETU 94 Yrs Old	VENUS 94 Yrs Old	SUN 96 Yrs Old	
MO May 21 46	MA Mar 21 47	RA Oct 20 47	JU Apr 20 49	SA Aug 20 50	ME Mar 20 52	KE Aug 20 53	VE Mar 21 54	SU Nov 19 55	A
MA Jun 15 46	RA Apr 2 47	JU Jan 10 48	SA Jun 24 49	ME Nov 19 50	KE Jun 1 52	VE Sep 1 53	SU Jun 30 54	MO Nov 29 55	N
RA Jul 3 46	JU May 4 47	SA Mar 23 48	ME Sep 9 49	KE Feb 9 51	VE Jul 1 52	SU Oct 7 53	MO Jul 31 54	MA Dec 14 55	T
JU Aug 17 46	SA Jun 2 47	ME Jun 18 48	KE Dec 15 49	VE Mar 2 51	SU Sep 26 52	MO Oct 17 53	MA Sep 19 54	RA Dec 24 55	A
SA Sep 27 46	ME Jul 5 47	KE Sep 4 48	VE Mar 6 50	SU Jun 19 51	MO Oct 22 52	MA Nov 4 53	RA Oct 25 54	JU Jan 21 56	R
ME Nov 14 46	KE Aug 5 47	VE Oct 6 48	SU Apr 27 50	MO Jul 18 51	MA Dec 4 52	RA Nov 16 53	JU Jan 24 55	SA Feb 14 56	D
KE Dec 27 46	VE Aug 17 47	SU Jan 5 49	MO May 10 50	MA Sep 9 51	RA Jan 3 53	JU Dec 18 53	SA Apr 15 55	ME Mar 24 56	A
VE Jan 14 47	SU Sep 22 47	MO Feb 1 49	MA May 31 50	RA Oct 8 51	JU Mar 22 53	SA Jan 16 54	ME Jul 21 55	KE Apr 9 56	S
SU Mar 6 47	MO Oct 2 47	MA Mar 19 49	RA Jun 8 50	JU Jan 3 52	SA May 30 53	ME Feb 19 54	KE Oct 15 55	VE Apr 20 56	A

Table 9.6. Barbara's Dasa-Bhukti-Antara Periods* [continued].

MARS DASA (Read Bhuktis Across, Antardasas Down)

MARS 96 Yrs Old	RAHU 97 Yrs Old	JUPITER 98 Yrs Old	SATURN 99 Yrs Old	MERCURY 100 Yrs Old	KETU 101 Yrs Old	VENUS 101 Yrs Old	SUN 102 Yrs Old	MOON 103 Yrs Old	
MA May 20 56	RA Oct 16 56	JU Nov 4 57	SA Oct 11 58	ME Nov 19 59	KE Nov 16 60	VE Apr 14 61	SU Jun 14 62	MO Oct 20 62	A
RA May 29 56	JU Dec 13 56	SA Dec 19 57	ME Dec 14 58	KE Jan 10 60	VE Nov 24 60	SU Jun 24 61	MO Jun 20 62	MA Nov 7 62	N
JU Jun 20 56	SA Feb 2 57	ME Feb 11 58	KE Feb 9 59	VE Jan 31 60	SU Dec 19 60	MO Jul 15 61	MA Jul 1 62	RA Nov 19 62	T
SA Jul 10 56	ME Apr 4 57	KE Mar 31 58	VE Mar 5 59	SU Mar 31 60	MO Dec 27 60	MA Aug 20 61	RA Jul 8 62	JU Dec 21 62	A
ME Aug 3 56	KE May 28 57	VE Apr 20 58	SU May 11 59	MO Apr 18 60	MA Jan 8 61	RA Sep 14 61	JU Jul 28 62	SA Jan 18 63	R
KE Aug 24 56	VE Jun 19 57	SU Jun 16 58	MO May 31 59	MA May 19 60	RA Jan 17 61	JU Nov 16 61	SA Aug 14 62	ME Feb 21 63	D
VE Sep 1 56	SU Aug 22 57	MO Jul 3 58	MA Jul 4 59	RA Jun 9 60	JU Feb 8 61	SA Jan 12 62	ME Sep 3 62	KE Mar 23 63	A
SU Sep 26 56	MO Sep 10 57	MA Aug 1 58	RA Jul 28 59	JU Aug 2 60	SA Feb 28 61	ME Mar 21 62	KE Sep 21 62	VE Apr 5 63	S
MO Oct 4 56	MA Oct 12 57	RA Aug 21 58	JU Sep 27 59	SA Sep 19 60	ME Mar 24 61	KE May 20 62	VE Sep 29 62	SU May 10 63	A

```
DASA AT BIRTH:
    Dasa      : Rahu
    Bhukti    : Moon
    Antardasa : Venus
    Sookshma  : Moon
```

```
         MAHADASA SUMMARY
    Rahu    : May 20, 1943
    Jupiter : May 20, 1961
    Saturn  : May 20, 1977
    Mercury : May 20, 1996
    Ketu    : May 20, 2013
    Venus   : May 20, 2020
    Sun     : May 20, 2040
    Moon    : May 21, 2046
    Mars    : May 20, 2056
```

* 1 minute error in the birth time = 5 day error in dasa periods.
Reproduced courtesy of C & D Scientific Software.

Barbara. Using Annemarie's chart, we must first determine what portion of the mahadasa sub-period has passed, as we did when we calculated the portion of the mahadasa which had passed at birth. Keeping in mind that Annemarie was born during Kethu's mahadasa, refer to Table 9.4 to see in which bhukti of Kethu's mahadasa her birth falls. Since Annemarie's Moon is 11° Aries 59' and Kethu's mahadasa runs from 0° to 13°Aries 20', a great portion of Kethu dasa had already passed, leaving 255 days before moving into Venus mahadasa on September 6, 1953. It is apparent from Table 9.4 that Mercury bhukti, the final bhukti in Kethu's dasa, lasts 11 months, 27 days and was, therefore, in progress at the moment of birth.

Barbara's chart provides our next example. As we did with Annemarie's chart, we must first study her birth mahadasa to see what portion has passed in order to divide the balance of the mahadasa into bhuktis. Since Barbara's Moon is 19° Aquarius 1', and Rahu's Mahadasa runs from 6° Aquarius 40' to 20° Aquarius, she was born in the latter part of this dasa. Since Barbara had 1 year, 3 months, 20 days before Jupiter's mahadasa began on May 20, 1961, her birth, according to Table 9.4, was during Rahu mahadasa, Moon bhukti. Subtracting the duration of the following Mars bhukti (1 year 18 days) from the total remaining portion of Rahu mahadasa (1 year 3 months 20 days) produces a difference of 3 months 2 days, which is the duration of Rahu mahadasa, Moon bhukti—the first period of her life.

We will not be delving into the symbolism of the nakshatras in this particular volume,[8] but it is necessary to impart how important a role they actually play. Planets are not only modified by the sign and house they occupy, but by the particular nakshatra in which they are situated. Because it takes approximately one month for the Moon to travel through the entire zodiac, the nakshatra which the Moon transits is used extensively for setting up the electional, or event, chart. Known

---

[8] A more thorough treatment of nakshatras may be found in *Myths and Symbols in Vedic Astrology* by Bepin Behari (Salt Lake City: Passage Press, 1990), *The Circle of Stars* by Valerie Roebuck (Shaftesbury, England: Element, 1991), and *Muhurtha*, by B. V. Raman (Bangalore: IBH Prakashana, 1986).

in Sanskrit as *Muhurta*, the event chart favors certain nakshatras over others for marriages, contract signing, automobile or home purchases, journeys, and even surgery.

In general, Jyotishis utilize the Moon's nakshatra position for short-term planning and the dasa system for long term predictions. The Hindu dasa system is used to forecast planetary cycles the same way that Western astrologers use different progression techniques. Common to both progressions and the dasa system is the fact that they are both defined by the interaction of two planets and by what those two planets symbolically represent. The major difference between these two systems is the fact that we are not always under the influence of a major planetary configuration by progression, while planetary periods and sub-periods prevail at all times.

What the two systems do have in common, however, is the utilization of *Gochara* (Sanskrit for "transits") to trigger events within the framework of the Western progressions and Eastern dasas. In Jyotish, a transiting planet is said to influence a natal planet from the moment it enters the sign/house the natal planet occupies. For example, if natal Venus is posited at 26° Sagittarius in the 3rd house, Saturn is said to be transiting natal Venus the entire 2½ years it travels through Sagittarius. Of course, the transit is still considered to be at its peak when Saturn actually conjoins the planet within one degree.

In addition to influencing the house through which it passes, the transiting planet also affects the houses which it aspects. This means that any transiting planet will naturally aspect the seventh house from it, just as the planet would in a natal chart. In addition, transiting Mars aspects the 4th and 8th house from it, transiting Jupiter aspects the 5th and 9th house from it, and transiting Saturn aspects the 3rd and 10th house from it.

Let's use Annemarie's chart as an example. On January 1, 1997, Saturn transits the 6th house of Pisces. In addition to the 6th house, it affects the 8th house of Taurus (3rd from Pisces), the 12th house of Virgo (7th from Pisces), and the Sun in the 3rd house of Sagittarius (10th from Pisces). Jupiter, on the other hand, transits Venus and Rahu in the 4th house of Capricorn, the 8th house of Taurus (5th from Capricorn), the 10th house of Cancer (7th from Capricorn), and Kethu in the 12th house of Virgo (9th from Capricorn).

In Barbara's chart, Saturn transits Kethu in the 11th house of Pisces and, therefore, affects the 1st house of Taurus (3rd from Pisces), Rahu in the 5th house of Virgo (7th from Pisces), and Venus, Mars, Jupiter, and Saturn in the 8th house of Sagittarius (10th from Pisces). Jupiter transits the Sun and Mercury in the 9th house of Capricorn and, therefore, affects the 1st house of Taurus (5th from Capricorn), 3rd house of Cancer (7th from Capricorn), and 5th house of Virgo (9th from Capricorn). Because Saturn will affect six grahas for the entire 2½ years the planet remains in Pisces, Barbara must be alerted as to when the transit will be precise.

Although many Westerners mistakenly believe that the dasa system is the only predictive tool used by Jyotishis, no self-respecting Hindu astrologer will forecast the trends of a particular dasa-bhukti period unless the transit supports the findings. For instance, Saturn dasa, Venus bhukti lasts approximately three years. In general, this may indicate the formation of a longlasting romantic union or the breakup of one. However, the actual manifestation may not take place until there is an actual Saturn transit in the horoscope. If there is no Saturn transit, the influence may not be as all encompassing. By the same token, if there is a Jupiter transit, the event may be particularly positive. It is also of utmost importance to use the sub-sub-periods during longer dasa-bhukti periods, such as Saturn Dasa, Venus Bhukti, which lasts approximately three years.

Table 9.7. Kethu Mahadasa.*

1.KETHU BHUKTI			2. VENUS BHUKTI			3. SUN BHUKTI		
Antara	M	D	Antara	M	D	Antara	M	D
Kethu	0	8	Venus	2	10	Sun	0	6
Venus	0	24	Sun	0	21	Moon	0	10
Sun	0	7	Moon	1	5	Mars	0	7
Moon	0	12	Mars	0	24	Rahu	0	18
Mars	0	8	Rahu	2	3	Jupiter	0	16
Rahu	0	22	Jupiter	1	26	Saturn	0	19
Jupiter	0	19	Saturn	2	6	Mercury	0	17
Saturn	0	23	Mercury	1	29	Kethu	0	7
Mercury	0	20	Kethu	0	24	Venus	0	21
Total	4	27	Total	14	0	Total	4	6
4. MOON BHUKTI			5. MARS BHUKTI			6. RAHU BHUKTI		
Antara	M	D	Antara	M	D	Antara	M	D
Moon	0	17	Mars	0	8	Rahu	1	26
Mars	0	12	Rahu	0	22	Jupiter	1	20
Rahu	1	1	Jupiter	0	19	Saturn	1	29
Jupiter	0	28	Saturn	0	23	Mercury	1	23
Saturn	1	3	Mercury	0	20	Kethu	0	22
Mercury	0	29	Kethu	0	8	Venus	2	3
Kethu	0	12	Venus	0	24	Sun	0	18
Venus	1	5	Sun	0	7	Moon	1	1
Sun	0	10	Moon	0	12	Mars	0	22
Total	7	0	Total	4	27	Total	12	18
7. JUPITER BHUKTI			8. SATURN BHUKTI			9. MERCURY BHUKTI		
Antara	M	D	Antara	M	D	Antara	M	D
Jupiter	1	14	Saturn	2	3	Mercury	1	20
Saturn	1	23	Mercury	1	26	Kethu	0	20
Mercury	1	17	Kethu	0	23	Venus	1	29
Kethu	0	19	Venus	2	6	Sun	0	17
Venus	1	26	Sun	0	19	Moon	0	29
Sun	0	16	Moon	1	3	Mars	0	20
Moon	0	28	Mars	0	23	Rahu	1	23
Mars	0	19	Rahu	1	29	Jupiter	1	17
Rahu	1	20	Jupiter	1	23	Saturn	1	26
Total	11	6	Total	13	9	Total	11	27

*Tables 9.7 through 9.15 are adapted from data provided in *Hindu Dasa System* by Grace Inglis (New Delhi: Sagar Publications, 1973), pp. 205–218.

Table 9.8. Venus Mahadasa.

1. VENUS BHUKTI			2. SUN BHUKTI			3. MOON BHUKTI		
Antara	M	D	Antara	M	D	Antara	M	D
Venus	6	20	Sun	0	18	Moon	1	20
Sun	2	0	Moon	1	0	Mars	1	5
Moon	3	10	Mars	0	21	Rahu	3	0
Mars	2	10	Rahu	1	24	Jupiter	2	20
Rahu	6	0	Jupiter	1	18	Saturn	3	5
Jupiter	5	10	Saturn	1	27	Mercury	2	25
Saturn	6	10	Mercury	1	21	Kethu	1	5
Mercury	5	20	Kethu	0	21	Venus	3	10
Kethu	2	10	Venus	2	0	Sun	1	0
Total	40	0	Total	12	0	Total	20	0

4. MARS BHUKTI			5. RAHU BHUKTI			6. JUPITER BHUKTI		
Antara	M	D	Antara	M	D	Antara	M	D
Mars	0	24	Rahu	5	12	Jupiter	4	8
Rahu	2	3	Jupiter	4	24	Saturn	5	2
Jupiter	1	26	Saturn	5	21	Mercury	4	16
Saturn	2	6	Mercury	5	3	Kethu	1	26
Mercury	1	29	Kethu	2	3	Venus	5	10
Kethu	0	24	Venus	6	0	Sun	1	18
Venus	2	10	Sun	1	24	Moon	2	20
Sun	0	21	Moon	3	0	Mars	1	26
Moon	1	5	Mars	2	3	Rahu	4	24
Total	14	0	Total	36	0	Total	32	0

7. SATURN BHUKTI			8. MERCURY BHUKTI			9. KETHU BHUKTI		
Antara	M	D	Antara	M	D	Antara	M	D
Saturn	6	0	Mercury	4	24	Kethu	0	24
Mercury	5	11	Kethu	1	29	Venus	2	10
Kethu	2	6	Venus	5	20	Sun	0	21
Venus	6	10	Sun	1	21	Moon	1	5
Sun	1	27	Moon	2	25	Mars	0	24
Moon	3	5	Mars	1	29	Rahu	2	3
Mars	2	6	Rahu	5	3	Jupiter	1	26
Rahu	5	21	Jupiter	4	16	Saturn	2	6
Jupiter	5	2	Saturn	5	11	Mercury	1	29
Total	38	0	Total	34	0	Total	14	0

Table 9.9. Sun Mahadasa.

1. SUN BHUKTI			2. MOON BHUKTI			3. MARS BHUKTI		
Antara	M	D	Antara	M	D	Antara	M	D
Sun	0	6	Moon	0	15	Mars	0	7
Moon	0	9	Mars	0	10	Rahu	0	19
Mars	0	6	Rahu	0	27	Jupiter	0	16
Rahu	0	17	Jupiter	0	24	Saturn	0	20
Jupiter	0	14	Saturn	0	28	Mercury	0	18
Saturn	0	17	Mercury	0	25	Kethu	0	7
Mercury	0	15	Kethu	0	10	Venus	0	21
Kethu	0	6	Venus	1	0	Sun	0	6
Venus	0	18	Sun	0	9	Moon	0	10
Total	3	18	Total	6	0	Total	4	6
4. RAHU BHUKTI			**5. JUPITER BHUKTI**			**6. SATURN BHUKTI**		
Antara	M	D	Antara	M	D	Antara	M	D
Rahu	1	18	Jupiter	1	8	Saturn	1	24
Jupiter	1	13	Saturn	1	15	Mercury	1	18
Saturn	1	21	Mercury	1	10	Kethu	0	19
Mercury	1	15	Kethu	0	16	Venus	1	27
Kethu	0	18	Venus	1	18	Sun	0	17
Venus	1	24	Sun	0	14	Moon	0	28
Sun	0	16	Moon	0	24	Mars	0	19
Moon	0	27	Mars	0	16	Rahu	1	21
Mars	0	18	Rahu	1	13	Jupiter	1	15
Total	10	24	Total	9	18	Total	11	12
7. MERCURY BHUKTI			**8. KETHU BHUKTI**			**9. VENUS BHUKTI**		
Antara	M	D	Antara	M	D	Antara	M	D
Mercury	1	13	Kethu	0	7	Venus	2	0
Kethu	0	17	Venus	0	21	Sun	0	18
Venus	1	21	Sun	0	6	Moon	1	0
Sun	0	15	Moon	0	10	Mars	0	21
Moon	0	25	Mars	0	7	Rahu	1	24
Mars	0	17	Rahu	0	18	Jupiter	1	18
Rahu	1	15	Jupiter	0	16	Saturn	1	27
Jupiter	1	10	Saturn	0	19	Mercury	1	21
Saturn	1	18	Mercury	0	17	Kethu	0	21
Total	10	6	Total	4	6	Total	12	0

Table 9.10. Moon Mahadasa.

1. MOON BHUKTI			2. MARS BHUKTI			3. RAHU BHUKTI		
Antara	M	D	Antara	M	D	Antara	M	D
Moon	0	25	Mars	0	12	Rahu	2	21
Mars	0	17	Rahu	1	1	Jupiter	2	12
Rahu	1	15	Jupiter	0	28	Saturn	2	25
Jupiter	1	10	Saturn	1	3	Mercury	2	16
Saturn	1	17	Mercury	0	29	Kethu	1	1
Mercury	1	12	Kethu	0	12	Venus	3	0
Kethu	0	17	Venus	1	5	Sun	0	27
Venus	1	20	Sun	0	10	Moon	1	15
Sun	0	15	Moon	0	17	Mars	1	1
Total	10	0	Total	7	0	Total	18	0

4. JUPITER BHUKTI			5. SATURN BHUKTI			6. MERCURY BHUKTI		
Antara	M	D	Antara	M	D	Antara	M	D
Jupiter	2	4	Saturn	3	0	Mercury	2	12
Saturn	2	16	Mercury	2	20	Kethy	0	29
Mercury	2	8	Kethu	1	3	Venus	2	25
Kethu	0	28	Venus	3	5	Sun	0	25
Venus	2	20	Sun	0	28	Moon	1	12
Sun	0	24	Moon	1	17	Mars	0	29
Moon	1	10	Mars	1	3	Rahu	2	16
Mars	0	28	Rahu	2	25	Jupiter	2	8
Rahu	2	12	Jupiter	2	16	Saturn	2	20
Total	16	0	Total	19	0	Total	17	0

7. KETHU BHUKTI			8. VENUS BHUKTI			9. SUN BHUKTI		
Antara	M	D	Antara	M	D	Antara	M	D
Kethu	0	12	Venus	3	10	Sun	0	9
Venus	1	5	Sun	1	0	Moon	0	15
Sun	0	10	Moon	1	20	Mars	0	10
Moon	0	17	Mars	1	5	Rahu	0	27
Mars	0	12	Rahu	3	0	Jupiter	0	24
Rahu	1	1	Jupiter	2	20	Saturn	0	28
Jupiter	0	28	Saturn	3	5	Mercury	0	25
Saturn	1	3	Mercury	2	25	Kethu	0	10
Mercury	0	29	Kethu	1	5	Venus	1	0
Total	7	0	Total	20	0	Total	6	0

Table 9.11. Mars Mahadasa.

1. MARS BHUKTI			2. RAHU BHUKTI			3. JUPITER BHUKTI		
Antara	M	D	Antara	M	D	Antara	M	D
Mars	0	8	Rahu	1	26	Jupiter	1	14
Rahu	0	22	Jupiter	1	20	Saturn	1	23
Jupiter	0	19	Saturn	1	29	Mercury	1	17
Saturn	0	23	Mercury	1	23	Kethu	0	19
Mercury	0	20	Kethu	0	22	Venus	1	26
Kethu	0	8	Venus	2	3	Sun	0	16
Venus	0	24	Sun	0	18	Moon	0	28
Sun	0	7	Moon	1	1	Mars	0	19
Moon	0	12	Mars	0	22	Rahu	1	20
Total	4	27	Total	12	18	Total	11	2
4. SATURN BHUKTI			**5. MERCURY BHUKTI**			**6. KETHU BHUKTI**		
Antara	M	D	Antara	M	D	Antara	M	D
Saturn	2	3	Mercury	1	20	Kethu	0	8
Mercury	1	26	Kethu	0	20	Venus	0	24
Kethu	0	23	Venus	1	29	Sun	0	7
Venus	2	6	Sun	0	17	Moon	0	12
Sun	0	19	Moon	0	29	Mars	0	8
Moon	1	3	Mars	0	20	Rahu	0	22
Mars	0	23	Rahu	1	23	Jupiter	0	19
Rahu	1	29	Jupiter	1	17	Saturn	0	23
Jupiter	1	23	Saturn	1	26	Mercury	0	20
Total	13	9	Total	11	27	Total	4	27
7. VENUS BHUKTI			**8. SUN BHUKTI**			**9. MOON BHUKTI**		
Antara	M	D	Antara	M	D	Antara	M	D
Venus	2	10	Sun	0	6	Moon	0	17
Sun	0	21	Moon	0	10	Mars	0	12
Moon	1	5	Mars	0	7	Rahu	1	1
Mars	0	24	Rahu	0	18	Jupiter	0	28
Rahu	2	3	Jupiter	0	16	Saturn	1	3
Jupiter	1	26	Saturn	0	19	Mercury	0	29
Saturn	2	6	Mercury	0	17	Kethu	0	12
Mercury	1	29	Kethu	0	7	Venus	1	5
Kethu	0	24	Venus	0	21	Sun	0	10
Total	14	0	Total	4	6	Total	7	0

Table 9.12. Rahu Mahadasa.

1. RAHU BHUKTI			2. JUPITER BHUKTI			3. SATURN BHUKTI		
Antara	M	D	Antara	M	D	Antara	M	D
Rahu	4	25	Jupiter	3	25	Saturn	5	12
Jupiter	4	9	Saturn	4	16	Mercury	4	25
Saturn	5	3	Mercury	4	2	Kethu	1	29
Mercury	4	17	Kethu	1	20	Venus	5	21
Kethu	1	26	Venus	4	24	Sun	1	21
Venus	5	12	Sun	1	13	Moon	2	25
Sun	1	18	Moon	2	12	Mars	1	29
Moon	2	21	Mars	1	20	Rahu	5	3
Mars	1	26	Rahu	4	9	Jupiter	4	16
Total	32	12	Total	28	24	Total	34	6

4. MERCURY BHUKTI			5. KETHU BHUKTI			6. VENUS BHUKTI		
Antara	M	D	Antara	M	D	Antara	M	D
Mercury	4	10	Kethu	0	22	Venus	6	0
Kethu	1	23	Venus	2	3	Sun	1	24
Venus	5	3	Sun	0	18	Moon	3	0
Sun	1	15	Moon	1	1	Mars	2	3
Moon	2	16	Mars	0	22	Rahu	5	12
Mars	1	23	Rahu	1	26	Jupiter	4	24
Rahu	4	17	Jupiter	1	20	Saturn	5	21
Jupiter	4	2	Saturn	1	29	Mercury	5	3
Saturn	4	25	Mercury	1	23	Kethu	2	3
Total	30	18	Total	12	18	Total	36	0

7. SUN BHUKTI			8. MOON BHUKTI			9. MARS BHUKTI		
Antara	M	D	Antara	M	D	Antara	M	D
Sun	0	16	Moon	1	15	Mars	0	22
Moon	0	27	Mars	1	1	Rahu	1	26
Mars	0	18	Rahu	2	21	Jupiter	1	20
Rahu	1	18	Jupiter	2	12	Saturn	1	29
Jupiter	1	13	Saturn	2	25	Mercury	1	23
Saturn	1	21	Mercury	2	16	Kethu	0	22
Mercury	1	15	Kethu	1	1	Venus	2	3
Kethu	0	18	Venus	3	0	Sun	0	18
Venus	1	24	Sun	0	27	Moon	1	1
Total	10	24	Total	18	0	Total	12	18

Table 9.13. Jupiter Mahadasa.

1. JUPITER BHUKTI			2. SATURN BHUKTI			3. MERCURY BHUKTI		
Antara	M	D	Antara	M	D	Antara	M	D
Jupiter	3	12	Saturn	4	24	Mercury	3	25
Saturn	4	1	Mercury	4	9	Kethu	1	17
Mercury	3	18	Kethu	1	23	Venus	4	16
Kethu	1	14	Venus	5	2	Sun	1	10
Venus	4	8	Sun	1	15	Moon	2	8
Sun	1	8	Moon	2	16	Mars	1	17
Moon	2	4	Mars	1	23	Rahu	4	2
Mars	1	14	Rahu	4	16	Jupiter	3	18
Rahu	3	25	Jupiter	4	1	Saturn	4	9
Total	25	18	Total	30	12	Total	27	6

4. KETHU BHUKTI			5. VENUS BHUKTI			6. SUN BHUKTI		
Antara	M	D	Antara	M	D	Antara	M	D
Kethu	0	19	Venus	5	10	Sun	0	14
Venus	1	26	Sun	1	18	Moon	0	24
Sun	0	16	Moon	2	20	Mars	0	16
Moon	0	28	Mars	1	26	Rahu	1	13
Mars	0	9	Rahu	4	24	Jupiter	1	8
Rahu	1	20	Jupiter	4	8	Saturn	1	15
Jupiter	1	14	Saturn	5	2	Mercury	1	10
Saturn	1	23	Mercury	4	16	Kethu	0	16
Mercury	1	17	Kethu	1	26	Venus	1	18
Total	11	6	Total	32	0	Total	9	8

7. MOON BHUKTI			8. MARS BHUKTI			9. RAHU BHUKTI		
Antara	M	D	Antara	M	D	Antara	M	D
Moon	1	10	Mars	0	19	Rahu	4	9
Mars	0	28	Rahu	1	20	Jupiter	3	25
Rahu	2	12	Jupiter	1	14	Saturn	4	16
Jupiter	2	4	Saturn	1	23	Mercury	4	2
Saturn	2	16	Mercury	1	17	Kethu	1	20
Mercury	2	8	Kethu	0	19	Venus	4	24
Kethu	0	28	Venus	1	26	Sun	1	13
Venus	2	20	Sun	0	16	Moon	2	12
Sun	0	24	Moon	0	28	Mars	1	20
Total	16	0	Total	11	6	Total	28	24

Table 9.14. Saturn Mahadasa.

1. SATURN BHUKTI			2. MERCURY BHUKTI			3. KETHU BHUKTI		
Antara	M	D	Antara	M	D	Antara	M	D
Saturn	5	21	Mercury	4	17	Kethu	0	23
Mercury	5	3	Kethu	1	26	Venus	2	6
Kethu	2	3	Venus	5	11	Sun	0	19
Venus	6	0	Sun	1	18	Moon	1	3
Sun	1	24	Moon	2	20	Mars	0	23
Moon	3	0	Mars	1	26	Rahu	1	29
Mars	2	3	Rahu	4	25	Jupiter	1	23
Rahu	5	12	Jupiter	4	9	Saturn	2	3
Jupiter	4	24	Saturn	5	3	Mercury	1	26
Total	36	3	Total	32	9	Total	13	9

4. VENUS BHUKTI			5. SUN BHUKTI			6. MOON BHUKTI		
Antara	M	D	Antara	M	D	Antara	M	D
Venus	6	10	Sun	0	17	Moon	1	17
Sun	1	27	Moon	0	28	Mars	1	3
Moon	3	5	Mars	0	19	Rahu	2	25
Mars	2	6	Rahu	1	21	Jupiter	2	16
Rahu	5	21	Jupiter	1	15	Saturn	3	0
Jupiter	5	2	Saturn	1	24	Mercury	2	20
Saturn	6	0	Mercury	1	18	Kethu	1	3
Mercury	5	11	Kethu	0	19	Venus	3	5
Kethu	2	6	Venus	1	27	Sun	0	28
Total	38	0	Total	11	12	Total	19	0

7. MARS BHUKTI			8. RAHU BHUKTI			9. JUPITER BHUKTI		
Antara	M	D	Antara	M	D	Antara	M	D
Mars	0	23	Rahu	5	3	Jupiter	4	1
Rahu	1	29	Jupiter	4	16	Saturn	4	24
Jupiter	1	23	Saturn	5	12	Mercury	4	9
Saturn	2	3	Mercury	4	25	Kethu	1	23
Mercury	1	26	Kethu	1	29	Venus	5	2
Kethu	0	23	Venus	5	21	Sun	1	15
Venus	2	6	Sun	1	21	Moon	2	16
Sun	0	19	Moon	2	25	Mars	1	23
Moon	1	3	Mars	1	29	Rahu	4	16
Total	13	5	Total	34	6	Total	30	12

Table 9.15. Mercury Mahadasa.

1. MERCURY BHUKTI			2. KETHU BHUKTI			3. VENUS BHUKTI		
Antara	M	D	Antara	M	D	Antara	M	D
Mercury	4	2	Kethu	0	20	Venus	5	20
Kethu	1	20	Venus	1	29	Sun	1	21
Venus	4	24	Sun	0	17	Moon	2	25
Sun	1	13	Moon	0	29	Mars	1	29
Moon	2	12	Mars	0	20	Rahu	5	3
Mars	1	20	Rahu	1	23	Jupiter	4	16
Rahu	4	10	Jupiter	1	17	Saturn	5	11
Jupiter	3	25	Saturn	1	26	Mercury	4	23
Saturn	4	17	Mercury	1	20	Kethu	1	29
Total	28	27	Total	11	27	Total	34	0
4. SUN BHUKTI			5. MOON BHUKTI			6. MARS BHUKTI		
Antara	M	D	Antara	M	D	Antara	M	D
Sun	0	15	Moon	1	12	Mars	0	20
Moon	0	25	Mars	0	29	Rahu	1	23
Mars	0	17	Rahu	2	16	Jupiter	1	17
Rahu	1	15	Jupiter	2	8	Saturn	1	26
Jupiter	1	10	Saturn	2	20	Mercury	1	20
Saturn	1	18	Mercury	2	12	Kethu	0	20
Mercury	1	13	Kethu	0	29	Venus	1	29
Kethu	0	17	Venus	2	25	Sun	0	17
Venus	1	21	Sun	0	25	Moon	0	29
Total	10	6	Total	17	0	Total	11	27
7. RAHU BHUKTI			8. JUPITER BHUKTI			9. SATURN BHUKTI		
Antara	M	D	Antara	M	D	Antara	M	D
Rahu	4	17	Jupiter	3	18	Saturn	5	3
Jupiter	4	2	Saturn	4	9	Mercury	4	17
Saturn	4	25	Mercury	3	25	Kethu	1	26
Mercury	4	10	Kethu	1	17	Venus	5	11
Kethu	1	23	Venus	4	16	Sun	1	18
Venus	5	3	Sun	1	10	Moon	2	20
Sun	1	15	Moon	2	8	Mars	1	26
Moon	2	16	Mars	1	17	Rahu	4	25
Mars	1	23	Rahu	4	2	Jupiter	4	9
Total	30	18	Total	27	6	Total	32	9

CHAPTER 10

INTERPRETING THE
DASAS AND BHUKTIS

EASTERN AND WESTERN FORECASTING techniques (Hindu dasa system versus transits and progressions) are as dissimilar in their methodologies as they are in their mathematical calculations. Rather than predict actual events, contemporary Western astrologers tend to describe future trends and behavior patterns which recur throughout life. They encourage clients to make their own choices based on a thorough understanding of the self (their horoscope) and an awareness of their planetary life cycles (transits and progressions).

While the Jyotishi also guides his[1] clients by helping them reach their own conclusions through an understanding of individual cycles, there is a narrower framework than in the West, and clients' decisions are made, due, in part, to a firmer acceptance of fate and the law of karma (see chapter 11). As a result, there is a greater emphasis on the timing of events than on a deep grasp of their psychological significance.

In order to facilitate the accuracy of their lifetime predictions, Hindu astrologers employ the dasa system in combination with the current transits. Traditionally, their first task is to calculate whether the client will live to an early, middle, or late age. While astrologers do not usually relay the results to a client, they will nonetheless use this information to assess the degree of seriousness during certain obstacle-ridden periods. Although several chapters in many of the ancient astrological texts are devoted to the determination of life expectancy, I advise using them cautiously, if at all. Since these texts were written in an era when there was little medical knowledge, the application of principles regarding illness and death can be irrelevant and/or misleading.

---

[1] Most "professional" astrologers in the Hindu community are men. However, many women are recipients of astrological knowledge which has been transmitted to them by members of their family and which they often pass on to their children.

In analyzing the mahadasas and bhukti dasas for Anne-marie and Barbara, I have included only those traditional interpretations which are either relevant or can be translated into modern terminology.

Mahadasa Rulers

The favored method for assessing each mahadasa is to evaluate the strength or weakness of its planetary ruler. Rather than merely determining whether the dasa will bring either "good" or "bad" results, I advocate defining the quality of each mahadasa based on its ruler's general description and individual significance.

General Description of Dasa Rulers

Based on the characteristics of each planet (see chapter 4), the following delineations emphasize the general issues which will be important during each mahadasa.

Sun Mahadasa—During the Sun dasa, there will be involvement with public life and the focus will be on finances, career, travel, education, and acquisition of land. The affairs of the house the Sun rules and/or occupies in the birth chart will be emphasized in this period.

If the Sun occupies the 6th, 8th, or 12th house in the birth chart or is otherwise poorly placed, there may be loss of position, illnesses related to the eyes or teeth and difficulties with the authority figures, the father or anything connected with the paternal line including inheritances.

Moon Mahadasa—If the Moon is well-placed in the natal chart, this mahadasa will be fortunate for one's mother, partner, and children. It is a good time to begin a new business or commercial venture, attain literary success, and achieve relative harmony.

If the Moon is not well-placed in the horoscope, there may be vacillation as to professional ventures, emotional ups and downs, and misunderstandings between friends and relatives.

The sign and house position of the Moon will also affect these issues.

Mars Mahadasa—With Mars positively positioned in the birth chart, there is the opportunity to apply strong will, action, and determination to any project undertaken. Health will be excellent and this will be the perfect opportunity to develop an exercise program or engage in a sport or hobby involving physical skills. It may be a time for travel or any other new enterprise or adventure. Friends will be helpful during this period.

Conversely, a poorly placed Mars will bring fevers, colds, chronic ailments, and accidents if one is not careful. There may be marital problems, misunderstandings between friends and colleagues, general impatience, argumentativeness, as well as restlessness and independence which could lead to changing jobs and/or residences.

Rahu Mahadasa—Although the malefic Rahu has no opportunity of becoming individually benefic, it may be well-placed in the horoscope nonetheless. Annemarie's chart has already revealed that Rahu is positively placed in a Kendra house and receives a 7th house aspect from Venus. If Rahu is positively positioned in the chart, Rahu mahadasa will set up conditions whereby the native may be successful, acquire money, and travel frequently. Otherwise, one may expect professional setbacks, loss of work or friends and the possible breakup of a marriage.

Jupiter Mahadasa—Jupiter's dasa will often be a period of excess. If it is well-placed, one will attract people and generally fortuitous circumstances. There will be luck and harmony, marriage, the births of children, and success in one's chosen profession. There may also be interest in Jupiterian subjects such as the law, philosophy, theology, and teaching during this period. If Jupiter is well-aspected in the horoscope, there will be unlimited success and prosperity in this period.

If, however, Jupiter is not well-placed, there will be extravagance, greed and laziness which may result in the loss of opportunities, job or finances.

Saturn Mahadasa—If Saturn is well-placed, this period may bring the success one has worked so hard to achieve. With continued patience and efforts, this period may also see the successful conclusion of action begun in another cycle.

If Saturn is poorly placed or aspected, there will be illness, depression, loneliness, and obstacles which may be beyond control or jurisdiction.

Mercury Mahadasa—Mercury's period lends itself to changes of residences, jobs, or partners. This dasa is extremely conducive to returning to school, pursuing a degree, starting a business, or embarking on a career in writing, communications, accounting, or sales. If well-placed, Mercury Dasa will bring successful business ventures, and expanded horizons through writing, reading, and traveling. It is a good time to consider seeing a therapist and/or participating in those activities which may lead to self-understanding.

If Mercury is not well-placed, there will be a period of depression, anxiety, pessimism, disappointments, and delayed business ventures.

Kethu Mahadasa—Like Rahu, Kethu cannot become individually benefic by virtue of house rulership. If, however, it is well-placed, new career opportunities may present themselves or there may be a promotion at your present job. This may also be a time of spiritual awareness and meditation.

If Kethu is ill-placed by aspect or house position, the affairs of the house it occupies may suffer dramatic losses. There may be monetary setbacks, personal unhappiness, and/or a feeling of alienation which can result in a need to withdraw.

Venus Mahadasa—It is obvious that, in addition to influencing whatever Venus represents in the birth chart, this period will be one that focuses on love and the attainment of desires. Relationships with spouses, lovers, siblings, friends, and/or colleagues should command undivided attention. If Venus is well-placed, there will be successful relationships, acquisitions, travels, births of children, and generally harmonious times when social life is fulfilling.

If it is ill-placed, Venus mahadasa will be a period when one may spend too much money, be taken advantage of, and quarrel with family and friends.

Individual Significance of Dasa Rulers

The significant issues which may arise during a particular Mahadasa are influenced by the house(s) the dasa lord occupies and rules in the Rasi Chakra. The relative strength and weakness of the planet determines whether the issues at stake during these periods will reap rewards or present difficulties. The following represent some of the concerns of the dasa when the planetary lord rules or occupies:

Lagna: Professional and personal fulfillment, adjustments to health and appearance.

2nd House: Addition to the family, earning power, eloquence in speech, early educational matters.

3rd House: Brothers and sisters, risk-taking, recognition for attempts, travel, literary efforts, change.

4th House: Family matters, mother, acquisition of land or purchase of home, promotion.

5th House: Children, indulgence, creative projects, sports, taxes, higher education, investments.

6th House: Health, daily job, service to others, domestic animals, litigation, marital woes.

7th House: Marriage, contracts, forming partnerships.

8th House: Debts, quarrels with friends, anxiety, partner's finances, business ventures, investments, interpersonal relationships.

9th House: Prosperity, higher education, travel, publishing, rewards for efforts, timely opportunities.

10th House: Complete undertakings, professional success or failure, father, political concerns.

11th House: Happiness, prosperity, ideals and goals fulfilled, community service, social concerns.

12th House: Extravagances, isolation, alienation, foreign travel, emigration, spiritual practice, research.

One of the most important functions of the dasa system for the Hindu astrologer has traditionally been to see which periods are most conducive to marriage and, ultimately, childbearing. As unofficial matchmaker, the Hindu astrologer is responsible for advising the best time to marry and approving prospective brides and grooms. Since many parents heed the astrologer's advice, it's not certain if most marriages would have indeed occurred on the predicted dates had they not been arranged by an astrologer.

The following method is one of many which an astrologer utilizes to determine a marriage date. Before the time can be set, the nature of the relationship must be assessed by thoroughly examining the 7th house, the 7th house ruler, and Venus, the karaka for relationships.[2] In addition, the navamsa chart must be evaluated before reaching a final decision. According to *Phaladeepika*, marriage may take place during the dasa of one of the following planets:

1. Planet in the 7th house;

2. Planet aspecting the 7th house;[3]

3. Planet owning the 7th house;

4. When lord of Lagna transits the 7th house.[4]

---

[2] Traditionally, Venus represents the wife in a man's chart while Jupiter signifies the husband in a woman's chart. However, I have always used Venus as indicator of relationships regardless of sexual orientation.

[3] Although I only use the full aspect for determining strength or weakness, this rule also refers to the weaker aspects including three-quarter aspect (four and eight houses apart); half-aspect (five and nine houses apart); and quarter-aspect (three and ten houses apart).

[4] Mantreswara, *Phaladeepika* (Bangalore: K. Subrahmanyam, 1981), p. 137.

It's quite common for the Hindu astrologer to arrange a marriage during a dasa which is conducive for childbirth. He has a wide span of years from which to choose this date, since many Hindu women marry when still in their teens to men at least ten years older than they are. Like choosing a marriage date, there is more than one method of calculation used to determine periods conducive for childbirth. Before a date can even begin to be considered, the 5th house, the 5th house ruler, and Jupiter (karaka for children) must be painstakingly assessed along with an evaluation of the septamsa chart. According to *Phaladeepika*, the birth of a child may be expected during the dasa of one of the following planets:

1. Lord of Lagna;

2. Lord of the 7th house;

3. Lord of the 5th house;

4. Jupiter;

5. Planet aspecting or occupying the 5th house.[5]

Though this method is still practiced in India, predicting pregnancy and the birth of a child is extremely difficult in the East as well as in the West. Due to sophisticated methods of birth control and the added possibility of choosing legal abortions, contemporary women have mastery over their biological destinies. Even if the exact moment of conception and pregnancy *could* be predicted, the use of birth control precludes this from occurring. If the chart does point to delay in childbirth or the possibility of infertility, advances in corrective surgery and an infinite variety of fertilization techniques available to promote pregnancies make it almost impossible to predict conception based on natural cycles.

I recommend using the Hindu dasa system to suggest, rather than predict, various periods which may be conducive for marriage and childbirth, applying common sense and logic to planetary indications.

---

[5] Mantreswara, *Phaladeepika*, p. 159.

Bhukti Rulers

Like the mahadasa ruler, the planetary ruler of each bhukti is also judged according to its general definitions and to:

1. The house it rules;

2. The house it occupies;

3. Its relative strength or weakness;

4. Relationship to dasa lord: a) whether it is friendly, inimical, or neutral to the Mahadasa Lord; and b) the number of houses between dasa lord and bhukti lord. (This is easily done by placing the planetary lord as the Ascendant of a new chart in much the same way as we did for Chandra Lagna.)

In order to actually pinpoint precisely what to expect during a given planetary period, it is also necessary to assess the condition of the dasa lord in the divisional charts and to evaluate the effect of particular transits. Since there is not room to list all of these factors in this particular volume, what follows is a delineation of the issues at hand during each period, rather than the actual timing of events.

Annemarie's Cycles

The following is a description of the trends and cycles in Annemarie's life according to Vimshottari dasa (see Table 9.5, page 228). I was introduced to Annemarie in 1978 by a mutual friend shortly before the beginning of the Moon's mahadasa in September 1979. Over the next several years we occasionally met at various functions, and became increasingly interested in each other's skills and talents. After some time, we began to exchange services—she provided me with slides for a workshop I was leading and I rendered advice based on her horoscope. As our relationship continued, she began to consult me professionally about once a year. The focus of the readings were the subjects which concerned her the most: her fluctuating romantic liaisons and the nature of her rising career.

Although Annemarie had been a moderately successful photographer, it wasn't until 1980 that her work was publicly recognized and she gained hard-earned respect from her peers. She traveled to London, Lisbon, and Buenos Aires where her photographs were exhibited to critical acclaim and completed a book of photographic studies (appropriately titled *Life Studies*) based on an ongoing photographic series of the same name. With hindsight, let's review the ten-year period of the Moon's mahadasa using some of the interpretive techniques previously discussed.

Annemarie's Moon Mahadasa (1979–1989)

In general, the Moon's period places an emphasis on public life, emotional fluctuations, business ventures, changes of residence, and familial relationships. Because the Moon goes through monthly phases, if not well-placed, there will be instability affecting the affairs of the house the Moon occupies and rules. During her Moon mahadasa, Annemarie entered into several relationships and experienced professional ups and downs. There were more successes than failures, however, thus enhancing her reputation as a free-lance photographer.

In Annemarie's Rasi Chakra, the Moon, an individual malefic, and ruler of the 10th house, is placed in the 7th house. The Moon's mahadasa, therefore, brought a concentration on Annemarie's career (10th house) and countless opportunities for success through both professional and romantic partnerships (7th house). Fame was almost guaranteed during this period, since the 10th house relates to public recognition rather than to earning money (2nd house) or developing skills (6th house). The aspect the Moon receives from Saturn (the planet of work) in the 1st house, however, indicates that Annemarie had to work diligently to attain her professional goals. Since Saturn is the Yogakaraka for a Libra ascendant, her efforts will usually be rewarded although the Moon's conjunction with individually malefic Jupiter often causes opportunities which are overlooked or even wasted.

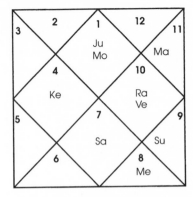 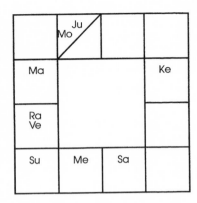

Figure 10.1. Annemarie's Dasa as Lagna chart. Left: North Indian model; Right: South Indian model.

Annemarie's Bhuktis

Let's continue by focusing on each bhukti dasa as calculated in the previous chapter (see Table 9.5, page 228). It is important to note that the Moon has no enemies and will, therefore, never be in a difficult relationship with a bhukti lord. Figure 10.1 illustrates Annemarie's "dasa as ruler" chart with Aries, the sign of the Moon, the dasa ruler, situated in the Ascendant position. The following descriptions of Annemarie's sub-periods incorporate the relationship between dasa and bhukti lord.

Moon Mahadasa, Moon Bhukti
(September 7, 1979–July 7, 1980)
The first bhukti of each mahadasa always shares its planetary lord with the dasa ruler and is generally considered inauspicious. Because the Moon is individually malefic, and aspected by both Jupiter and Saturn, this period will not be as productive as Annemarie may have hoped. With the Moon ruling the 10th house and placed in the 7th house, the Moon bhukti reflects the same concerns as the Moon mahadasa—the 7th house of partnership and the 10th house of profession. According to Annemarie, there was indeed tension with her live-in relationship although her career was, in fact, on the rise.

Moon Mahadasa, Mars Bhukti
(July 7, 1980–February 5, 1981)

Mars, which is somewhat neutral for a Libra Ascendant, is natally placed in the 5th house and rules both the 2nd house (Scorpio) and the 7th house (Aries). In the Dasa as Lagna chart, Mars is placed in the 11th house. As the ruler of the 2nd and 7th houses, Mars provides the opportunity to earn money through the formation of a partnership and its placement in the 5th house indicates that the partnership is likely to be indulgent and romantic. Since the 5th house represents speculation, and the 11th house signifies profits, this period should be one of impulsive spending and/or financial risk-taking.

During this time, Annemarie and her lover, also a photographer, formed an artistic partnership marketing a series of greeting cards and postcards for which Annemarie was both photographer and model. Due to Mars' influence, this venture was challenging and creative but also involved financial speculation. As it turned out, the business lost money but the artistic aspect of the project was enormously successful. The couple was asked to exhibit their work, they co-authored a book, and their photographs appeared in international publications. Although the partnership temporarily revitalized their relationship, the pair would eventually go their separate ways in the next sub-period of Rahu.

Moon Mahadasa, Rahu Bhukti
(February 5, 1981–August 7, 1982)

A glimpse of the natal chart shows that Rahu is in the 4th house conjoined with Venus. As Rahu cannot rule a particular house, its influence is considered to be that of the 4th house (the house it occupies natally) and the 10th house (the house it is placed in according to the Dasa as Lagna chart). Rahu will also take on the qualities of Venus, the aspecting planet, and Saturn, its dispositor.

Emblematic of the combination of Venus and Saturn, Annemarie's relationship with her partner/lover ended during Rahu's bhukti, resulting in a period of depression when she doubted her ability to be independently creative. She literally spent most of her time at home (4th house) rethinking her career (10th house) and contemplated the direction her work should take to maintain the prestige she'd acquired during the previous period of Mars. Since Rahu behaves, according to the scriptures, much like Saturn, it is no wonder that she felt limited in her creativity. Annemarie discontinued the self-portraits which comprised a significant portion of the work she'd done with her ex-partner. Rahu,[6] however, also needs to rebuild that which has failed and, as a result, she began experimenting with new photographic techniques and subject matter aimed at cultivating a "more humanistic and less self-centered approach to her work."

Moon Mahadasa, Jupiter Bhukti
(August 7, 1982–December 7, 1983)

As the ruler of the natal 3rd and 6th houses, Jupiter, an individually malefic planet, is aspected by both the Moon and Saturn, bringing with it mixed results. It was during this period that the more problematic face of Jupiter reared its ugly head and, along with the fame and recognition Annemarie acquired, came the carelessness and tendency toward excess that Jupiter so readily brings. Ignoring health and work (6th house) led to excessive spending, whose consequences were felt during the next Saturn bhukti, which literally swept up the debris left behind by Jupiter.

Moon Mahadasa, Saturn Bhukti
(December 7, 1983–July 8, 1985)

In Annemarie's natal horoscope, Saturn's auspiciousness is seen through its role as Yogakaraka and individual benefic (Ruler of the 4th and 5th houses), its exalted position in Libra in the 1st house, its aspect from the Moon and Jupiter, and its placement in its Vargottama, which strengthens Saturn's beneficence. Its position in the 7th house from the Moon made this period one which pertained to partnerships and other 7th house concerns.

At this time, a new relationship entered Annemarie's life. Since the indulgent Moon and Jupiter both aspect Saturn, and because Saturn is in Libra, this union had many excesses, pas-

---

[6] I have found Rahu to act very much like Pluto does in the Western chart. Oftentimes, Rahu's influence relates to a complete restructuring of one's resources while Kethu's influence, like Neptune, is often one of complete obliteration.

sions, and other insurmountable obstacles. Though it ended rather abruptly, Annemarie considered it a worthwhile learning experience. Since the natal 5th house, which Saturn rules, is the significator of taxes, and the 7th house (Saturn's position from the Moon) is an indicator of disputes, it was no wonder that problems resulting from unpaid taxes surfaced during this time. These financial difficulties were incurred during the excessive and careless period of the previous Jupiter bhukti. Because of the beneficial nature of Saturn which tends to reap what Jupiter sows, these problems were resolved. It was also in this period that Annemarie applied for a government grant to further her Life Studies photography project.

Moon Mahadasa, Mercury Bhukti
(July 8, 1985–December 7, 1986)
In her natal chart, Mercury, the ruler of the 9th and 12th houses, is individually benefic, but somewhat weakened by its association with the 12th house. As ruler of the 9th and 12th placed in Scorpio in the 2nd house, Mercury bhukti also involves generating revenue from educational studies (9th house), working abroad or research projects (12th house). Since Mercury is eighth from the Moon, gains through business propositions, and matters involving life and death were extremely important.

It was in this period that Annemarie actually received the subsidy (8th house) she had applied for. Her Life Studies project (8th and 9th house) included portraits of people related to one another (i.e. siblings, parent/child, cousins, etc.) and culminated in an exhibition during the autumn of 1986 and a book published in 1990. She was also hired to teach (9th house) a few short courses. But despite her professional accomplishments, this was not a successful time for relationships and, as one would surmise, Mercury's 8th house position from the Moon caused a great deal of personal unhappiness despite financial gains.

Moon Mahadasa, Kethu Bhukti
(December 7, 1986–July 8, 1987)
Unless they are associated with benefic planets, Rahu and Kethu are quite often the least favorable periods in any ma-

hadasa. With both Saturn and Venus aspecting Kethu, both positive and negative influences can be expected. Since Kethu is placed in the natal 10th house (aspecting the 4th house) and is additionally placed 4th from the Moon, home and family should be an extremely important focus in this period.

During this time her father became ill and Annemarie considered leasing a home with an option to buy, which combined studio and living space, and which would become vacant in September 1987, during the sub-period of Venus. With the emphasis on the 4th and 10th houses, it is no wonder that she should find a house which combined living and working space. At the time I advised her that a new home/work space accompanied by a stable relationship with her current lover would certainly be an appropriate beginning for the Venus bhukti.

It was at this time that Annemarie began contemplating the idea of having a baby and asked me if were possible to predict if and when this could possibly happen. By applying the rules set out in the beginning of the chapter, it is possible, in theory, to determine which dasa and sub-dasa periods would be most auspicious. In the first place, an examination of the 5th house indicates that Mars is placed there. Saturn, the ruler of the 5th house, is aspected by the Moon and Jupiter (individual malefics), and Jupiter, karaka for childbirth, is aspected by Moon and Saturn. This indicates that while Annemarie would probably be quite fertile, having a child will not be without its obstacles.

If we follow the methods set out in this chapter for predicting the time, the first step would be to calculate which dasas fall between the ages of 15 and 52—the absolute maximum of years during which a woman may can conceive a child. Table 9.5 (see page 228) shows that this period would encompass 1967–2004, the dasas of Venus, the Sun, the Moon, Mars, and Rahu.

The next step would be to determine which of those years fit the description according to Mantreswara's guidelines. Applying these principles to Annemarie's chart, the dasas during which she is likely to give birth are:

1. Lord of Lagna—Venus mahadasa;

2. Lord of the 7th house—Mars mahadasa;

3. Lord of the 5th house—Saturn mahadasa;

4. Jupiter mahadasa;

5. Planet aspecting or occupying the 5th house—Mars mahadasa.

Since the Dasas of Jupiter and Saturn take place after the age of 52, Venus and Mars Mahadasa would be the two periods most feasible. Venus Mahadasa ended in 1973 when Annemarie was 21 years old. Had Annemarie been a typical young Hindu woman, it would not have been unusual for the astrologer to arrange a marriage so she could, indeed, give birth before Venus mahadasa ended. Since Annemarie's Venus mahadasa has already passed, the most likely period for childbearing strictly using the Vimshottari dasa system would be any Mars bhukti or Mars mahadasa beginning in 1989 and ending in 1996, or between the ages of 36 and 43. Because Mars mahadasa spans her 36th–43rd years, she will either have a child during this time or not at all, based on the Vimshottari dasa system and her fertility cycle.

Moon Mahadasa, Venus Bhukti
(July 8, 1987–March 8, 1989)
As the lord of the 1st and 8th houses, Venus is both naturally and individually benefic though its rulership of the 8th house somewhat weakens its beneficent quality. It is placed in the natal 4th house, the 10th house from the Moon, and is aspected by Rahu and Kethu. Due to Venus' rulership of the natal 1st and 8th houses, her highly sexual and passionate nature was tested in Venus' sub-period while the 8th house influence caused her to spend more time promoting and selling her work than immersing herself in the creative process. During September-December 1987, Annemarie exhibited in Lisbon, London, and Buenos Aires. Although her reputation as a photographer continued to soar throughout Venus bhukti, the aspects natal Venus receives from Rahu and Kethu presented conflict regarding 4th and 10th house matters.

In September 1987 Annemarie rented the house she had found during Kethu's sub-period, unifying home and career. Her primary concerns were: 1) striking the balance between her profession and relationships; and 2) maintaining the professional standards which would enable her to buy the house. At this time, she applied for an additional subsidy to increase the number of photographs in her *Life Studies* series and contracted to produce a book based on these portraits.

Moon Mahadasa, Sun Bhukti
(March 8, 1989–September 6, 1989)
As the ruler of the 11th house of profit, the Sun is in Sagittarius in the 3rd house, and receives aspects from Saturn in the 1st house (3rd house aspect) and Jupiter in the 7th house (9th house aspect). Since the Sun is situated in the 9th house from the Moon, Annemarie received offers to travel and she even resided abroad for a short time. With the 9th house representing publishing, her book appeared to positive reviews.

Barbara's Cycles

The following is an interpretation of the trends and cycles in Barbara's life according to the Vimshottari dasa system (Table 9.6 page 233). When she first consulted me in 1984, Barbara was contemplating a career change from nursing and was enrolled in a graduate program to become a certified social worker. Presently a supervisor in an out-patient treatment center, Barbara counsels and instructs recovering substance abusers.

Before analyzing her present Saturn mahadasa, which comprises the 19 years between 1977 and 1996, let's assess her previous Jupiter mahadasa which spanned 1961 until 1977 (Barbara was 1–17 years old). Ruling this youthful period, Jupiter, individually malefic as the ruler of the 8th and 11th houses, is placed in the 8th house and conjoined with Mars and Saturn. Its saving grace is that Jupiter is naturally benefic, conjoined with Venus and well-placed in Sagittarius—its rulership and moolatrikona sign. These very powerful positions will somewhat soften the despair and pessimism resulting from the influence of the 8th house and Jupiter's malefic associations.

Although Barbara had a very stable, loving upbringing, she developed an inferiority complex sometime during puberty which stemmed from the fact that she was the youngest in a family of achievers and was underaverage in height. During her adolescence, she became preoccupied with death, displaying what would later become a tendency towards melancholia and depression. Though adolescence is very often a period of confusion and estrangement from family who don't ever seem to "understand," some teenagers suffer varying degrees of depression, while others are not affected at all. We cannot, therefore, attribute Barbara's moods solely to adolescence, but must assume it was partially due to the enormous influence of the 8th house—the realm of matters concerning life, death, anxiety, and chronic illness.

During this time, a significant concern was her height since, due to a hormonal imbalance, she was significantly shorter than most girls her age and was worried she would not grow. My Jyotish teacher assured me that Barbara would experience a profound change when Saturn's mahadasa began. Jupiter, he explained, both ruled and was placed in the inauspicious 8th house surrounded by two malefics, Saturn and Mars. As the ruler of the 9th and 10th houses, Saturn, whose mahadasa follows that of Jupiter, is a yogakaraka for a Taurus Ascendant. As the astrologer predicted, Barbara grew three inches during the early period of Saturn's mahadasa, and her hormonal imbalance ceased to be a problem.

One of the more fascinating facets of the Vimshottari dasa system is the uncanny timing of events which sometimes cannot be explained by using progressions or transits. This does not mean, however, that either system is foolproof since, in the final analysis, we always have a hand in directing our destinies.

Barbara's Saturn Mahadasa

Let us review Saturn's mahadasa until the present. As we have just seen, Saturn is an individual benefic which rules the 9th and 10th houses yet is situated in the 8th house. Since Barbara has four planets in the eighth house, Saturn is conjoined with Jupiter, Mars, and Venus. With Saturn related to the 8th, 9th and 10th houses, the emphasis of this dasa will focus on business partnerships, interpersonal relationships, depression, chronic illness, higher education, travel, and profession—not unusual for anyone between the ages of 17 and 36. Saturn's po-

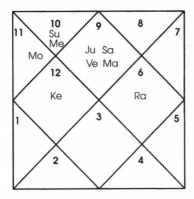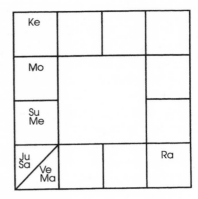

Figure 10.2. Barbara's Dasa as Lagna chart. Left: North Indian model; Right: South Indian model.

sition in the 8th house ensures that, throughout all this activity, there will always be intermittent periods of worry, anxiety and general melancholia.

Figure 10.2 illustrates Barbara's "dasa as lagna" chart with Sagittarius, the sign of Saturn, the dasa Ruler, situated in the Ascendant position. The following descriptions of Barbara's Bhukti periods incorporate the relationship between dasa and bhukti lord. The following interpretation of the bhukti Dasas enables us to pinpoint more specifically when these issues will be most significant. It is important to remember that Mercury and Venus are Saturn's friends; the Sun, Moon, and Mars are its enemies; and Jupiter[7] is neutral to Saturn.

Saturn Mahadasa, Saturn Bhukti
(May 18, 1977–May 21, 1980)

Though the first sub-period of any dasa is always considered detrimental, Saturn's rulership of the 9th and 10th houses lends its positive influence. As already stated, however, the murky background of the 8th house forever seems to be standing in the way of achieving total success and/or happiness. During this bhukti, Barbara's father received a promotion which

---

[7] Just as the Moon does not have enemies, Jupiter cannot be an enemy to any other planet.

changed the course of his professional life and affected Barbara in that there was more money available for the entire family. (Because Barbara was young, she could not experience the 10th house as her own profession. As the 2nd from the 9th, the 10th house also represents the father's income.) During this period, Barbara attended college (9th house) and took her first steps toward selecting a career. Before finally deciding on nursing, she attended three universities in an attempt to select the one which would best serve her professional needs.

Although she no longer suffered from extremely low self-esteem or insecurity per se, there were still periodic bouts with depression. Additionally, the deaths of several family members had a profound effect (Saturn in the 8th). With four planets natally placed in the 8th house, death will always surround her in one way or another. Even her work with drug addicts is overshadowed by the possibility they may overdose or commit suicide. It was in this period that she experienced her first "mature" relationship, which lasted from her teenage years into early adulthood with someone who, himself, had addiction problems.

Saturn Mahadasa, Mercury Bhukti
(May 21, 1980–January 30, 1983)
As the ruler of the 2nd and 5th houses, Mercury, which represents intellectual pursuits, is conjoined with the Sun, the ruler of the 4th house, in the 9th house forming a Raj yoga (ruler of the 4th conjunct ruler of the 5th). Mercury's placement also constitutes a Dhana yoga since it links the rulers of the 2nd, 5th, and 9th houses. Because Mercury is friendly to Saturn, exalted in the navamsa, and is individually benefic, Mercury bhukti was extremely beneficial.

Not surprisingly, this period saw college graduation, Barbara's first trip abroad, and her first nursing position. She found an apartment and ended the relationship which had begun in Saturn's bhukti. Looking at Mercury as representative of financial success and professional satisfaction, it's safe to say that during Mercury's mahadasa, between the ages of 36 and 53, Barbara will probably reach her financial peak and fulfill many of her personal and professional goals.

270 ⟩ VEDIC ASTROLOGY

Saturn Mahadasa, Kethu Bhukti
(January 30, 1983–March 10, 1984)

Natally, Kethu is positioned in Pisces in the 11th house of profits, disposited by Jupiter, and aspected by Mars. With Kethu
situated in the 4th house from the dasa lord, Saturn, Barbara
moved into a centrally located, affordable apartment (4th
house) which gave her the opportunity of becoming involved in
community-sponsored activities promoting artists and writers
(11th house). She had a beneficial job change but, due to the
depressive influence of Kethu, she spent many lonely hours in
an effort to adjust to living alone.

Saturn Mahadasa, Venus Bhukti
(March 10, 1984–May 10, 1987)

Although Venus is the Lagna Lord, its rulership of the 6th
house gives it a somewhat malefic flavor, especially since it is
situated in the 8th house and conjoined by Mars and Saturn.
As already discussed in chapter 8, Barbara's afflicted Venus indicates a tendency toward precarious mental and physical
health. Barbara had to contend with lingering illnesses, allergies, and continued depression during this period.

As 6th house ruler, Venus bhukti was also a time of extremely hard work, constant self-examination, and a reorienta-
tion of her skills. Barbara returned to school to earn a Master's
degree in social work which would enable her to switch professions. Another 6th house matter—domestic animals—reared its
ugly head in the form of the death of a beloved pet. The 1st
house, ruled by Venus, is the 8th house (death) from the 6th
house (pets).

In its favor, Venus is a friend to Saturn and is aspected by
Jupiter, the male partner in a female's chart. Due to Venus'
mundane meaning as indicator of love and partnership, Barbara met her future husband during this bhukti.

Saturn Mahadasa, Sun Bhukti
(May 10, 1987–April 22, 1988)

In the Rasi Chakra, the Sun is conjoined with Mercury (Ruler
of 2nd and 5th houses) in the auspicious 9th house, and is classified as a benefic planet due to its rulership of the 4th house.
The concentration on higher education (9th house) shone

through as Barbara obtained her Master's degree in social work in June 1987 and began her first job as a certified social worker. Since the Sun is placed in the 2nd house from Saturn, she was able to earn money through her profession with an eye toward a practice of her own. During this bhukti, she moved in with her boyfriend whom she planned to marry.

Since the Sun is an enemy of Saturn, this period still had its pitfalls. Although living together was a move in the right direction, Barbara's 8th house would not allow her to adjust easily to yet another change in her life. The pressures of her first position as a case worker responsible for the welfare of many clients, along with sharing a small apartment, caused her a great deal of stress and anxiety. This period was, however, pivotal for her personal growth and did, indeed, prepare her for the pressures inherent in her profession and the positive and negative facets of married life.

Saturn Mahadasa, Moon Bhukti
(April 22, 1988–November 22, 1989)
In the Rasi Chakra, the Moon, individually malefic, is the ruler of the 3rd house and is placed in Aquarius in the 10th house. As an enemy of Saturn, the Moon also receives a 3rd house aspect from Saturn, making this period one of tremendous difficulty, depression, and limitation. Since the malefic ruler of the 3rd house is situated in the 8th house from it, it clearly accentuates a depressed and obstacle-ridden (8th house) mental attitude (3rd house).

Because there is an emphasis on the 3rd house, this period was a very active time for her siblings. During the Moon's bhukti, her oldest sister dissolved a live-in relationship, moved into her own apartment, and switched careers. Her middle sister married and began to look for a home to purchase. Due to the changeable Moon's individually malefic influence on the 10th house of career, however, Barbara began a new social work job which turned out to be a source of unhappiness and frustration. Before the bhukti was over, she resigned that short-lived position and was rehired by the organization which she had originally left behind.

Whereas her father had received a promotion during the Moon's bhukti in the Jupiter dasa, the Moon's bhukti in the present Saturn dasa brought an offer of early retirement which he readily accepted.

Despite the fact that this period was filled with constant self-doubt, endless obstacles, and personal unhappiness, Barbara married the person she had been living with in August 1989. While she was very confident that marriage was right for her, she was skeptical whether getting married in this period would serve her best interests due to work pressures. Her horoscope indicated that, given the stress factor, the following Mars bhukti might have been more conducive. Let's see how Mantreswara's guidelines for prediction of marriage (p. 256) may be applied to Barbara's decision. The dasas of the following planets indicate possible times for marriage:

1. Planet in the 7th house—none;

2. Planet aspecting the 7th house—none;

3. Planet owning the 7th house—Mars;

4. When lord of Lagna transits the 7th house—whenever Venus as ruler of Taurus Lagna transits Scorpio.

If, however, we look at the navamsa chart, the divisional chart which specifically represents marriage, we can see why marriage took place in the Saturn mahadasa, Moon bhukti even though Mars bhukti may have indeed been less stressful.

It is important to look at the third level of Dasas during a longer period such as Saturn, whose sub-periods sometimes entail up to three years. Her life did improve during the Venus Antaradasa, which lasted from July 25, 1989 to October 30, 1989. Barbara got married—quite an appropriate planetary influence under which one would form a lasting relationship—and she got a new job, which she had wanted to do for the previous months.

Let us apply the above rules to the navamsa chart:

1. Planet in the 7th house—Mars and Saturn;

2. Planet aspecting the 7th house—Moon;

3. Planet owning the 7th house—Mercury;

4. When lord of Lagna transits the 7th house—whenever Jupiter as ruler of Pisces Lagna transits Virgo.

Since Saturn, Mars, and the Moon are all related to the 7th house in the navamsa, both the Moon and Mars bhuktis fit into the above rules. Utilizing the navamsa chart for an understanding of marriage is an example of how divisional charts are used to clarify the particular issues which each represents (i.e., dasamsa for career, septamsa for children, etc.).[8]

Although marriage is still difficult to predict in the West due to the increased number of couples living together without actually "tying the knot," these guidelines often indicate the planetary dasa or bhukti in which an actual wedding, or legal contract, takes place.

Saturn Mahadasa, Mars Bhukti
(November 22, 1989–December 30, 1990)
Mars, an individually benefic planet, is conjoined with Saturn, Venus, and Jupiter in Sagittarius in the 8th house. Due to its conjunction with other benefic and malefic planets, it forms both a Raj and Aristha yoga, providing both auspicious and in-auspicious results. While it did relieve some of the tensions and pressures of the Moon's period, Mars, still an enemy of Saturn, continued to create obstacles regarding education (9th house) and career (10th house) due to Saturn's rulership of the 9th and 10th houses.

Because the 7th and 12th houses are ruled by Mars, there was tension and unhappiness in her marriage due to her own feeling of alienation (12th house). At the time, I had also cautioned Barbara to pay more attention to her expenditures (12th house) and warned her regarding bouts of depression due to the influence of the introspective and sometimes alienating 12th house.

---

[8] Unfortunately, there is not enough space in this particular volume to explore the varga or divisional charts. They will, however, be dealt with in a future volume.

Saturn Mahadasa, Rahu Bhukti
(December 31, 1990–November 6, 1993)

Since Saturn aspects Rahu by 10th house aspect, the present Saturn Rahu period will accentuate this combination of two malefic planets. Since Rahu, natally aspected by Saturn, has, according to the Scriptures, Saturnine qualities, this particular sub-period should display difficulties, delays, and obstacles—qualities of the greater malefic. However, Saturn's position as Yogakaraka, the most individually beneficent planet by virtue of house rulership, will bring the rewards of Saturn's patience and hard work.

Although this period was one of emotional ups and downs and constant introspection, Rahu is placed in Virgo in the 5th house of children, auspicious deeds, and speculation. Rahu is additionally disposited by Mercury, which rules the 2nd house of finances along with the 5th, and is placed in the 10th house (profession) of the "Dasa as Lagna" chart. To this end, Barbara received a noteworthy promotion, and continued to gain confidence in her professionalism. She also received another degree, which would entitle her to a supervisory position and substantial raise in salary. Both of these came in October, a month before the Jupiter bhukti began.

Saturn Mahadasa, Jupiter Bhukti
(November 16, 1993–May 26, 1996)

In the Rasi Chakra, Jupiter, the ruler of the 8th (financial transactions and husband's finances) and 11th (profit) houses is placed in its rulership and moolatrikona sign of Sagittarius, making it quite fortunate regarding 8th house affairs. Of course, it is also conjoined with Venus, Mars, and the dasa ruler, Saturn, so that 8th house matters such as death may also be something that she will have to confront during this period. Furthermore, Jupiter is in the house of Saturn, its enemy, so that this period will have its highs and lows.

It was during this period that her husband received a substantial promotion and, in November 1995, when Jupiter entered Sagittarius and began its transit through the 8th house of inheritances, the rewards of Jupiter's bhukti were ensured. At that time, Barbara's aunt informed her that she would be receiving a sizeable monetary gift. On the other hand, Barbara was devastated by the death of someone very close to her in February 1995, and this trauma, with its accompanying psychological effects, lasted through the transition from her Saturn dasa to her Mercury dasa.

• • •

At the time of the writing of this book (August 1996), Barbara has recently entered her Mercury dasa and is finally recovering from the grieving process. Whenever a major dasa change occurs, especially between long periods such as Saturn to Mercury, the transition, which is often difficult since it signifies completely new energies at work, is usually felt from six months to a year prior to the new dasa's commencement. The transition may even continue throughout the entire first bhukti of the new mahadasa.

In Barbara's case, there are many unresolved issues and decisions to be made over the next few years which she is not quite ready to confront at the present time. Change is never easy, especially for someone like Barbara with a plethora of 8th house planets which often bring depression and obstacles, whether real or self-created. But once Barbara accepts that finances, assets (2nd house), and children (5th house) must be addressed during the initial Mercury bhukti, I believe that Mercury's dasa spanning the ages of 36–53 should be prosperous and emotionally fulfilling. As the ruler of the 2nd and 5th houses, Mercury's placement in the 9th house constitutes a Dhana yoga which reiterates the fact that this will be a successful period.

Given the fact that the timing of conception is exceedingly difficult in these modern times, let's speculate on which period might be conducive for having children, following the terms already laid out in *Phaladeepika*. As stated, conception will take place during the dasa of one of the following planets:

1. Lord of Lagna—Venus;

2. Lord of the 7th House—Mars;

3. Lord of the 5th House—Mercury;

4. Jupiter;

5. The occupying planet of the 5th house—Rahu.

Her childbearing years are framed by the Saturn and Mercury mahadasas, which span her 17th-53rd years. Of course, it is possible for her to have a child during the sub-periods related to these planets, but if we were to judge this based on major periods alone, we see that Saturn is not included in the afore-mentioned indications. Mercury, lord of the 5th house, is mentioned and, in light of the fact that Saturn occupies the obstacle-ridden 8th house, it is more likely that Barbara will begin a family after the age of 36, at which time she is apt to be financially secure.

More than predicting actual events, it is my hope that this chapter has illustrated which issues may be paramount during a particular period. As with interpretation, everything always makes perfect sense when viewing it with hindsight. It is important to refrain from making any definitive judgments unless the accompanying transits are analyzed and the antaradasas are examined, especially during the longer dasas of Venus, Saturn, Rahu, Mercury, and Jupiter.

It is important to remember that the transitional time between the ending of one dasa and the beginning of another one is crucial in that an individual must learn to adapt to completely different influences. A case in point is Carly, a client whose life dramatically changed when Rahu mahadasa ended and Jupiter mahadasa began.

During Carly's Rahu mahadasa, which lasted from 1971 until 1988, she was involved in a series of failed relationships. In the summer of 1988, when Jupiter's mahadasa began, Carly met someone purely by chance whom she married the following year. Unless Rahu and Kethu are in Upachaya houses, or aspected by benefics, its periods are often marked by obstacles and projects which are unable to get off the ground. Once Jupiter's dasa began, all the difficulties and worries inherent in Rahu's period dissipated, and her life worked out exactly as she had always hoped, replete with husband, children, and a home in the suburbs. Of course, it did not hurt that Jupiter, the ruler of her 5th (and 8th house), is placed in the 1st house of destiny, forming both a simple Raj and Dhana Yoga.

Another client, Mark, experienced exactly the opposite effect once his Jupiter mahadasa ended and Saturn mahadasa began. With four planets in their rulership and exaltation signs,

Mark led a charmed life during his Jupiter mahadasa, which lasted from 1970–1986, coinciding with the economic boom years of the 1980's. Not only did he own a successful multimillion dollar business but, like many others who thought the good times would never end, he invested large amounts of money which he eventually lost once the Saturn mahadasa began. It is important to remember that, regardless of the condition of natal Jupiter and Saturn, Jupiter always represents expansion, opportunity, and extravagance, while Saturn constitutes restriction, discipline, and frugality. I explained this to my client and recommended that he downsize and discontinue expanding as he had done in his Jupiter dasa. Since Jupiter is his ruling planet with a Sagittarius Lagna, Mark did not heed Saturn's warning and, ultimately, his business went bankrupt. To accentuate matters, Saturn is fallen in his navamsa chart, which always presents the possibility that, during the fallen planet's dasa, a project will come to an end.

The following chapter is devoted to the influence and authority of the Hindu astrologer, and will illustrate how his insights and decision-making abilities affect the community.

CHAPTER 11

THE ROLE OF THE ASTROLOGER

A BOOK ABOUT JYOTISH would be incomplete without a more definitive description of Indian astrologers and the invaluable service they provide. The influential and multi-functional roles of advisor, therapist, medical practitioner and—at times—priest have earned Indian astrologers the utmost praise and respect within the Hindu community.

In order to maintain a commercial practice, astrologers are not required, but may decide nonetheless, to obtain a higher degree in Jyotish, which can sometimes take up to eight years to complete. In addition to reading the ancient religious and astrological texts, the course of study includes a thorough understanding of the intricate, precise mathematical and astronomical principles of the movement of the heavenly bodies. Although they may never utilize every facet of this complex study, the vast knowledge and deep spirituality gained should help them to convey the horoscope's subtleties and intricacies to their clientele both clearly and compassionately.

Since it is common for professions to be handed down through generations, most *consulting* astrologers learn their craft from a family member and then apprentice for many years in order to gain first-hand experience in applying the astronomical principles to the art of interpretation. The apprenticeship, usually served in the practice or shop of the father, an uncle, or another relative, must be completed before any astrologer can share or take over a practice.

It is customary to have a chart constructed by an astrologer when a child is born. During the time I studied with my second teacher, the astrologer Deoki Nandan Shastri, I was present on many occasions when parents brought their children to his office for horoscope readings—a common practice in India tantamount to a check-up by the pediatrician. The horoscope is often presented to the parents in booklet form and always includes diagrams of the Rasi Chakra, the Shodasavarga charts (including the navamsa chart), and the planetary periods of Vimshotthari dasa. These drawings are accompanied by written or typed explanations of character traits, learning capabilities, parental descriptions, possible illness(es), possible profession (though many times it is that of the father), the most suitable marriage partner, and a general summary describing how the child's life will proceed. Also included are prognostications for auspicious and inauspicious time periods most conducive for education, marriage, children, residence and/or travel.

After the initial information about the child's destiny is relayed to the parents, the astrologer often advises the parents periodically as to the child's eating habits, behavior patterns, upbringing, education, and, ultimately, marriage arrangements. It is quite common for Hindus not only to have their charts constructed at birth but to consult the same astrologer throughout their lives, seeking medical and developmental guidance from one usually knowledgeable in medicine and child psychology. In fact, astrologers are often called upon by doctors and teachers to render a second opinion, as medical astrology is a very important branch of Hindu astrology practiced by most astrologers in varying degrees. By assessing the planets in terms of their physical correspondences, astrologers can easily see which part or parts of the body are weak and the periods during which they will be most problematic. They may suggest that a gemstone or amulet which corresponds to the Ascendant or current dasa lord be worn close to the afflicted part of the body in order to revive it or merely to improve the general constitution. Most importantly, they will usually prescribe a mantra which not only strengthens a particular planet, but invokes the protection of the deity which corresponds with the afflicted planet.

Though there is a wide variety of reasons why people visit astrologers, their advice is most often sought when making important decisions, whether they be long-term (i.e., change of residence, choosing a career, marriage) or short-term (signing a document or purchasing a car or house). If the client so requests, astrologers may choose the precise moment when an event should take place (Muhurtha, or electional astrology) based on the Nakshatra the Moon occupies and the nature of any transiting planets. If a client requires short-term counsel, needs to chat, or requires comfort, he or she may simply drop in without an appointment. Though their advice is based on precise mathematical calculations, the astrologers' real ability to counsel is predicated on an unselfish concern for others, objective insight and experiential wisdom. Because so many people heed astrologers' advice in terms of setting marriage dates and other major decisions, it is often difficult to judge whether predictive techniques actually work as accurately as Jyotishis insist they do.

An example is the story of the late Shivanath, an Indian friend of mine, whose business took him to Europe several times a year. Since Shiva lived in Benares (where I studied Hindu astrology), I had asked that he give my regards to my astrology teacher, Pandit Shastri. Although Shiva's parents had his horoscope drawn up as a child, he had never himself consulted an astrologer and saw this as a perfect opportunity to do so. At their first meeting my friend inquired whether it would be feasible to expand his import business in Western Europe. He was advised to repeat a certain mantra each morning and wear a gemstone around his neck 24 hours a day. After following my teacher's advice for two weeks, Shiva was encouraged to proceed with the business. He was warned, however, to start slowly, patiently, and frugally, and was told that within five years business would soar. Shiva heeded the astrologer's advice and began by importing a limited supply of Indian artifacts and selling them to many different storekeepers. Ten years later he was the operator of three extremely successful shops located in two different countries. It is very probable that Shiva's excellent business instincts brought him the success he enjoyed. His humility, however, dictated that credit for his success also be given to the wearing of the amulet, the singing of the mantra, and the advice and blessing of Pandit Shastri.

In addition to their position in the community as general seers, confidantes, and therapists, astrologers are also the source of sacred knowledge. In ancient times astrologers believed they had a direct line to the gods, that their words had a divine source and that they were intermediaries who transmitted secret teachings. Like the priest, minister, rabbi, or other religious figure, it is the astrologer who provides nonjudgmental, wise counsel. Astrological sessions are, at times, "confessionals" furnishing comfort, hope, and encouragement in bleak moments. Unlike their Western counterparts, Hindu astrologers serve the community and are available for advice whenever needed. Modern young Indians may not always visit astrologers for accurate lifelong predictions as their parents do, but they often seek them for unbiased advice or simply to discuss their problems. If they leave less burdened, their visit was worthwhile.

Perhaps the astrologer's most significant function is sanctioning marriages which, among traditional Hindu society, are still prearranged by the parents. One of the most important decisions to be made, matrimony is not merely the coming together of two individuals but the union of two families. More often than not, it is part of a business merger or other profitable exchange in which each family, as a result of the wedding, receives something the other needs. If a business transaction is not the criterion, the parents will seek out a prospective son or daughter-in-law from a family of appropriate caste who promises to be a good provider. To ensure her financial security and happiness, the bride's family will present the future bridegroom with the traditional dowry—"the money, goods, or estate[1] that a woman brings to her husband in marriage."[2]

Those families who do not have prospective partners in mind must search for a family with whom to unite. They may consult an astrologer who will advise them as to profession, age, caste, and in which direction to search. For example, if the child's chart reveals that the potential marriage partner lives to the East, the astrologer advises the parents to search to the east of the child's birthplace. If the West is indicated, they are advised to look in that direction. The search for a suitable marriage partner may take place by word of mouth, business or family connections, or by means of a newspaper advertisement, a very common practice both in India and in Indian communities in the West.

Figure 11.1 is a reproduction of several authentic advertisements from the Sunday edition of *The Hindu*, an English-language newspaper published in India. (Advertisements are also placed in Indian language newspapers.) Placed by the prospective bride or groom's family or by the interested parties themselves, the ads contain a description of the person seeking

---

[1] This estate may consist of land, animals, or a business offer from her father.
[2] *Webster's Ninth New Collegiate Dictionary*, p. 379.

BRIDEGROOMS WANTED

Vathima Bharadwaja Maham, 22/160 M.C.A., L & T. employed, beautiful. Subsect acceptable. Decent marriage. Reply horoscope Box No. 4710, C/o THE HINDU, Madras-600002.

Alliance invited for good-looking Kammawar Naidu Graduate, 29/166/1100, State Government employed. Send horoscope family details Box No. 4478, C/o THE HINDU, Madras-600002.

Alliance from Iyer widower/ divorcee employed in Central Bank around 42 years for Iyer girl Vadama Kousika Barani divorcee no children aged 37 employed Central Govt. earning 2500. Reply with horoscope. Box No. 4694, C/o THE HINDU, Madras-600002.

Well educated and well placed groom around 38 years for a Garga double graduate Vadama girl, Chitrai. Send horoscope with biodata to Box. No. 4714, C/o THE HINDU, Madras-600002.

Saiva Vellala Pillai Doctor 24/156 cm slim fair non-veg seeks good alliance Doctor, Engineer same caste Mudaliar respectable family. Reply with horoscope Box No. 4722, C/o THE HINDU, Madras-600002.

Alliance for Srivatsa Vadama Avittam, Iyer girl. B. Tech., 22/163, from professionally qualified well settled boys of respectable family. Reply with horoscope to Box No. 4526, C/o THE HINDU, Madras-600002.

BRIDES WANTED

USA Greencard M.S. Engineer, 28/172, only son affluent

Srivaishnavite Iyengar family seeks Iyengar/Iyer/Telugu brahmin, below 23, beautiful tall accomplished well educated bride. Send horoscope. Box No. 7358, C/o THE HINDU, Madras 600002.

Wanted Graduate girl with transferable employment for graduate, Kousika Rohini, insurance employed, Tamil Iyer Boy, 28/170. Write details with horoscope. Box No. 7353, C/o THE HINDU, Madras-600002.

Telugu Yadava fair complexion girl, below 22 for boy, M. Com. 26/170 cm doing business. Reply with horoscope Box No. 4497, C/o THE HINDU, Madras-600002.

Alliance for Graduate, Brahacharanam, Kashyapa Aayilyam, 34/170/2500 Kerala Iyer employed in Multinational Co., in Bangalore from employed girls. Send horoscope. Box No. BA6217, C/o THE HINDU, Bangalore-560001.

Vaadyama Boy, Bharathwaja Gothram, Swathi, PUC, 30 age, 165 cms, only son, fair, well to do, self employed, defective vision but not blind, requires fair good looking plus Two, sincere, accommodative, respectable, home loving girl. Subsect no bar. Reply with horoscope: M. Ramamurthi, 40, I Main Road, CIT Colony, Mylapore, Madras-600004.

Alliance sought for well built, Propertied, Mudaliar groom, B.Sc., F.I.I.I. officer in General Insurance, 27/180/4000 with Chevvai Dosham from Pretty tall homely, intelligent, graduate/postgraduate Mudaiar girls, Reply Bio-data horoscope Box No. 4276, C/o THE HINDU, Madras-600002.

Figure 11.1. Matrimonial advertisement taken from *The Hindu*, Sunday, April 16, 1989.

a partner, accompanied by specific requirements as to age, caste, family background, education level, and profession. It is also interesting to note the frequency of requests for birth information which means that both parties either have a relationship with astrology or, at least, believe in its reliability. If an advertisement requests birth information, it is very likely that the family was informed by an astrologer that the current planetary period is appropriate for marriage. And when the family receives responses to the ad, they will oftentimes ask the astrologer to compare the two horoscopes (including the Nakshatras and the navamsa charts) to verify compatibility and to ensure that each party is in the correct "marriage" dasa. If the astrologer sanctifies the union, the families will plan the wedding in accordance with the time and date set by the astrologer.

On the other hand, if the astrologer discourages the union, the families may either seek a second opinion or dissolve the match and resume their search—depending, of course, on how much value they place on the astrologer's opinion. If the family cannot find a suitable partner, the astrologer may assume the role of matchmaker by contacting families who, in his or her opinion, will "pass the litmus test." Once a candidate is found, chart analyses begin anew.

Because marriage is the most important decision to be made, astrologers inform families in no uncertain terms how they feel about a possible union. If they approve, their enthusiasm is boundless. If, however, they are adamant that an impending marriage would bring disastrous results, they strongly discourage the union from taking place. I observed a few of my teacher's consultations with disappointed families. Although I could not understand his literal words, the flailing and waving of his arms and the defiant, commanding tone of voice clearly displayed disapproval. His actions also illustrate the power he wields over lives, a quality which, ironically, endears him to the community in which he resides.

Although many younger Indians, especially those living abroad, do not always subscribe to arranged marriages, some prefer to obtain the astrologer's approval nevertheless, either to please their parents or to hear an opinion about what may be in store should the marriage take place. They may not necessarily take the advice, but will, nonetheless, listen to what the as-

trologer has to say. (Most Western astrologers will not advise
two people whether they *should* be together, but will instead
point out what they have in common and examine the difficulties which may arise.)

Often, when my astrology lesson was over, I lingered on in
my teacher's one-room storefront office to witness a typical
working day. People with and without appointments continu-
ally strolled in and out seeking advice on marriage prospects,
business, and children, or picking up their prepared horoscopes.[3] Though they conversed in Hindi (the language spoken
in Benares), by observing facial expressions and body language,
and by listening to the tone of their voices, I was able to follow
the conversation. Sometimes shop owners, colleagues, and
friends came by and we would all sit cross-legged on the car-
peted floor drinking tea and conversing intellectually or discussing neighborhood gossip. At other times, serious Jyotish
students stopped by and audited Pandit Shastri's consultations
in an effort to experience first-hand the application of astrological theory to horoscope interpretation.

Although astrologers' offices reflect their individuality,
there are certain objects which remain constant. What I remember most about Pandit Shastri's office is the books in every corner of the room dealing with astrology, healing rituals, medicine, child development, and other related subjects. Atop his
miniature devotional altar were a photo of his spiritual guru
and patron god/goddess, flowers, and burning incense. Cover-
ing the walls were murals and pictures of various deities, myth-
ical heroes, and Vedic sages, all of which illustrate the extent to
which spirituality and religion are tied to the study of astrology.
Most important, somewhere in most every astrologer's room or
office there is a photograph or reproduction of the Elephant
God Ganesh, the guardian of all secret knowledge, including
astrology—one of the highest forms of knowledge that the gods
and goddesses are said to have bestowed upon the Earth.

---

[3] These recollections are based on my stay in Benares from 1976–1977. While there
are many astrologers who use computerized horoscopes and interpretations, the astrologers in the smaller towns and villages still do many of the calculations by
hand.

Glossary

Antara dasa: In South India, one of nine planetary sub-sub-periods into which a Bhukti Dasa is divided. In North India, the name for the sub-periods into which a Mahadasa is divided.

Autumn equinox: The opposite point of the vernal equinox; September 21st or 22nd; the first day of Autumn and the first degree of Libra, when there are an equal number of daylight and nighttime hours.

Ayanamsa: The numerical difference in degrees and minutes between the actual 0° Aries and the equinoctial point, the Tropical Zodiac's symbolic 0° Aries.

Benefic: A naturally auspicious planet, i.e., Venus, Jupiter, waxing Moon.

Bhava: Sanskrit for one of the 12 houses or arbitrary divisions of the zodiac.

Bhukti: In South India, one of nine planetary sub-periods into which a Mahadasa is divided.

Budha: Sanskrit for Mercury.

Caste: One of the five socio-economic classes into which one is born based on the deeds and actions of the previous life.

Chandra: Sanskrit for the Moon.

Dasa: An abbreviated form of Mahadasa.

Dhanus: Sanskrit for Sagittarius.

Dharma: One's mission or predetermined work that is supposed to be carried out in this lifetime based on one's caste and seen through one's horoscope.

Dreccan: One third of a zodiacal sign.

Drishti: Sanskrit for aspect.

Dusthana House: 6th, 8th or 12th house; considered to be inauspicious.

Equinoctial point: See Vernal Equinox.

Gochara: Sanskrit for transit.

Grahas: Sanskrit for "rotating bodies," including the Sun, Moon, planets, and Moon's Nodes.

Guru: Sanskrit for the planet Jupiter; literally "one who transmits knowledge."

Harmonics: System of degree divisional charts founded by John Addey.

Hinduism: Religion of four-fifths of the population of India.

Hora: One half of a zodiacal sign.

Jyotish: The discipline of Hindu astrology comprising mathematical, astronomical, and interpretive principles.

Kanya: Sanskrit for Virgo.

Karma: Accumulated actions from former lifetimes that help to create one's present life.

Kataka: Sanskrit for Cancer.

Kendra House: Angular House, or 1st, 4th, 7th or 10th house.

Kethu: Sanskrit for Dragon's Tail or South Node.

Kuja: Sanskrit for Mars.

Kumbha: Sanskrit for Aquarius.

Lagna: Sanskrit for Ascendant.

Mahadasa: One of nine major planetary periods.

Makara: Sanskrit for Capricorn.

Malefic: A naturally inauspicious planet i.e., Mars, Saturn, Sun, waning Moon.

Mantra: Sacred song that is recited as part of one's daily prayers.

Meena: Sanskrit for Pisces.

Mesha: Sanskrit for Aries.

Mithuna: Sanskrit for Gemini.

Moolatrikona: A set of degrees within a zodiacal sign considered to be the most favorable position for a certain planet to occupy.

Nakshatra: One of the 27 asterisms or fixed star clusters each of which span 13° 20′ of the zodiacal belt.

Navamsa: One ninth of a zodiacal sign.

Neecha: Degree and sign of planetary fall.

Nirayana Zodiac: Sidereal Zodiac based on actual position of the constellations of the zodiac.

Occidental astrology: Western Astrology.

Pratyantar Dasa: In North India, one of nine planetary sub-sub-periods into which a Mahadasa is divided.

Precession of the equinoxes: The retrograde movement of the equinoctial point (and, therefore, the four cardinal points) through the constellations of the zodiac.

Rahu: Sanskrit for Dragon's Head or North Node.

Rasi: Sanskrit for one of the 12 signs of the zodiac.

Rasi Chakra: Sanskrit for "zodiacal wheel"; Rasi Chakra is the horoscope itself.

Ravi: Sanskrit for Sun.

Sani: Sanskrit for Saturn.

Sanskrit: The ancient written language of India.

Sayana Zodiac: Tropical zodiac based on symbolic position of the constellations of the zodiac.

Septamsa: One seventh of a zodiacal sign.

Shad Bala: The six sources—position, aspect, natural strength, motion, direction, and time—from which a planet draws its strength.

Shodasavarga: Different sub-divisional charts.

Simha: Sanskrit for Leo.

Spring Equinox: See Vernal Equinox.

Sukra: Sanskrit for Venus.

Summer Solstice: The longest day of the year; June 21st or 22nd; the first day of summer and the first degree of Cancer.

Surya: Sanskrit for Sun.

Surya Siddhanta: One of the Siddhantas, the five scientific astronomical treatises written around A.D. 400.

Swakshetra: Sign of planetary rulership.

Thula: Sanskrit for Libra.

Tithi: Indian lunar day, which is measured by the length of time it takes for the Moon to travel 12°, 1/30 of a lunar month or 360°.

Trikona House: 5th or 9th house.

Uchcha: Degree and sign of planetary exaltation.

Upachaya House: 3rd, 6th, 10th, or 11th house.

Varga: Short for Shodasavarga.

Vargottama: A position of planetary strength which occurs when the planet's zodiacal sign is identical to its corresponding Navamsa sign.

Vedas: The series of religious books comprising sacred hymns and poems which map out myths, legends, and tenets of Hinduism.

Vernal or spring equinox: Also called the vernal or equinoctial point; the point at which the celestial equator intersects with the ecliptic. Occurring on March 20th–21st, it indicates the first day of Spring, the first degree of Aries, and is a day when there are an equal number of daylight and nighttime hours.

Vimshottari dasa: Totaling 120 years, this system maps out the planetary periods and sub-periods which define a person's life.

Vrischika: Sanskrit for Scorpio.

Winter Solstice: The shortest day of the year; December 21st or 22nd; the first day of winter and the first degree of Capricorn.

Yuga: One of four planetary eras which, when added together, make up the Maha Yuga, literally "great year."

Appendix

Schools and Organizations

American Council of Vedic Astrology (ACVA)
P.O. Box 2149
Sedona, AZ 86339
Tel. 1-800-900-6595
Sponsors conferences, tutorials, certification program, journals, provides list of resources.

British Association for Vedic Astrology
2 Tee Court
Romsey, Hants. SO51 8GY
England
Tel. 011-44-1794-524178
Monthly meetings, workshops.

Indian Council of Astrological Sciences
64 Gowdiamutt Road
Royapeeta
Madras-600 014
India

Computer Software

Visual Jyotish
C&D Scientific Software
One Ford Avenue
Lynnfield, MA 01940-1838
Tel/Fax 1-800-RAJYOGA
http://www.jyotish.com[1]

Parasara's Light
Geovision Software
P.O. Box 2152
Fairfield, IA 52556
1-800-4JYOTISH
http://www.fairfield.com/jyotish

---

[1] Tables 9.5 and 9.6 have been generated by Visual Jyotish Software, courtesy of C & D Scientific Software.

Goravani Jyotish
Goravani Astrological Services
211 Crest Drive
Eugene, OR 97405
Tel. (541) 485-8453
Fax (541) 343-0344
http://www.vedic-astrology.com[2]

PC Jyotish
Passage Press
8180 S. Highland Drive
Sandy, UT 84093
1-800-873-0075

Haydn's Jyotish
c/o James Braha
P.O. Box 552
Longboat Key, FL 34228
Tel. (941) 387-9101 or (305) 555-1212 directory information

Mail Order Computer Services

Astro Computing Services, Inc.
5521 Ruffin Road
San Diego, CA 92123
Tel. (619) 492-9919

Vedic Gemstones

King Enterprises
1305 N. H St./A-289-M
Lompoc, CA 93436
Tel. (805) 693-0911

Miriam Kaplan
Box 508
Fallsburg, NY 12733
1-800-969-0611

Jay Boyle Company
P.O. Box 2333
Fairfield, IA 52556
Tel. (515) 472-5090

---

[2] If you wish to utilize the Krishnamurti Ayanamsa listed in this book, you must use the User-defined options and *not* the Krishnamurti Ayanamsa option in Goravani Jyotish and Parasara's Light.

Yagyas

Biswa Kalyan Foundation
c/o James Braha
P.O. Box 552
Longboat Key, FL 34228
Tel. (941) 387-9101

Yagyas can also be obtained
at local Hindu temples.

Publications

ACVA Journal
P.O. Box 2149
Sedona, AZ 86339
Tel. 1-800-900-6595

Star Teller
Express Estates
Mount Road
Chennai 600002
India
Tel. 852-3055

The Astrological Magazine
Sri Rajeshwari
115-1 New Extension
Seshadripuram Bangalore
560 020
India
Tel. 080-334-8646

Vedic Astrology
A-199 Okhla Ind.
Area-1
New Delhi 110020
India
Tel. 681-1195
Fax 681-7017

Astrological Services by Ronnie Gale Dreyer

Natal Chart Interpretation

A thorough examination of one's emotional, physical, psychological, and spiritual strengths and weaknesses in the context of the Western and Vedic Horoscopes. Attention will be given to life cycles and trends for the coming year. Ronnie specializes in but is not limited to the horoscopes of women and their unique issues. Sessions are taped and conducted via the telephone if you are not within the immediate area. Please call or write for information about consultations, private lessons, and Ronnie's lecture and teaching schedule:

Ronnie Gale Dreyer
P.O. Box 8034
FDR Station
New York, NY 10150-8034
Tel. (212) 799-9187 Fax (212) 799-2748
E-Mail: RGDreyer@AOL.com
Web page: http://members.aol.com/RGDreyer

Bibliography

Addey, John. *Harmonics in Astrology*. Romford, England: Urania Trust, 1996.

Armstrong, Braha, de Fouw, Erlewine, Flaherty, Houck, Grasse and Watson, *Eastern Systems for Western Astrologers*. York Beach: Samuel Weiser, 1997.

Baigent, Michael, Nicholas Campion, and Charles Harvey. *Mundane Astrology*. London: Aquarian Press, 1984.

Behari, Bepin. *Fundamentals of Vedic Astrology*. Salt Lake City: Passage Press, 1992.

———. *Myths and Symbols of Vedic Astrology*. Salt Lake City: Passage Press, 1990.

———. *Planets in the Signs and Houses*. Salt Lake City: Passage Press, 1992.

Braha, James. *Ancient Hindu Astrology for the Modern Western Astrologer*. Longboat Key, FL: Hermetician Press, 1986.

———. *Astro-Logos: Revelations of a Hindu Astrologer*. Longboat Key, FL: Hermetician Press, 1996.

———. *How to Predict Your Future*. Longboat Key, FL: Hermetician Press, 1994.

Chakravarty, Apurba Kumar. *Origin and Development of Indian Calendrical Science*. Calcutta: Indian Studies Past and Present, 1975.

Charak, Dr. K. S. *Elements of Vedic Astrology*. New Delhi: Vision Wordtronic, 1994.

———. *Essentials of Medical Astrology*. New Delhi: Vision Wordtronic, 1994.

———. *Varshaphala*. New Delhi: Vision Wordtronic, 1993.

———. *Yogas in Astrology*. New Delhi: Vision Wordtronic, 1995.

Council of Scientific and Industrial Research. *Report of the Calendar Reform Committee*. New Delhi: Government of India Publications, 1955.

Cumont, Franz. *Astrology and Religion Among the Greeks and Romans*. New York: Dover Publications, 1960.

DeFouw, Hart. *Light on Life: An Introduction to the Astrology of India*. London: Arkana Books, 1996.

DeLuce, Robert. *Constellational Astrology*. Los Angeles: DeLuce Publishing Co., 1963.

Dreyer, Ronnie Gale. *Venus: The Evolution of the Goddess and Her Planet*. London: Aquarian Press, 1994.

Frawley, David. *The Astrology of the Seers*. Salt Lake City: Passage Press, 1990.

Houck, Richard. *The Astrology of Death*. Gaithersburg, MD: Groundswell Press, 1994.

_____, ed. *Hindu Astrology Lessons: 36 Teachers Share Their Wisdom*. Gaithersburg, MD: Groundswell Press, 1997.

Inglis, Grace. *Hindu Dasa System*. New Delhi: Sagar Publications, 1973.

Kannan, S. *Fundamentals of Hindu Astrology*. New Delhi: Sagar Publications, 1981.

Krishnamurti, K. S. *Casting the Horoscope*, Vol. I. Madras: Mahabala, 1971.

_____. *Fundamental Principles of Astrology*, Vol. II. Madras: Mahabala, 1971.

Kublin, Hyman. *India*. Boston: Houghton Mifflin, 1968.

Leadbeater, C. W. *The Chakras*. Wheaton: Theosophical Publishing House, 1972.

McIntosh, Christopher. *Astrologers and their Creed*. London: Century Hutchinson Publishing Group, Ltd., 1969.

MacLaine, Shirley. *Don't Fall off the Mountain*. New York: Bantam, 1985.

Mantreswara. *Phaladeepika*. Bangalore: K. Subrahmanyam, 1981.

_____. *Phaladeepika*. New Delhi: Ranjan Publications, 1991.

Mayo, Jeff. *The Astrologer's Astronomical Handbook*. Romford, England: L.N. Fowler, 1965.

Monier-Williams, Sir Monier. *A Sanskrit-English Dictionary: Etymologically and Philologically Arranged*. New Delhi: Motilal Banarsidass, 1974.

O'Flaherty, Wendy. *Hindu Myths*. London: Penguin Books, 1975.

O'Neill, W. M. *Time and the Calendars*. Sydney: Sydney University Press, 1973.

Parasara. *Hora Sastra*. New Delhi: Ranjan Publications, 1991.

Pattie, T. S. *Astrology*. London: British Library Publications, 1980.

Raman, B.V. *Graha and Bhava Balas*. Bangalore: IBH Prakashana, 1984.

———. *Hindu Predictive Astrology*. New Delhi: UBS Publishers' Distributors List, 1992.

———. *Muhurtha or Electional Astrology*. Banagalore: IBH Prakashana, 1986.

———. *Planetary Influences on Human Affairs*. Bangalore: IBH Prakashana, 1982.

———. *Three Hundred Important Combinations*. Bangalore: IBH Prakashana, 1983.

Rao, K. N. *Astrology, Destiny and the Wheel of Time*. New Delhi: Vision Wordtronic, 1993.

———. *Learn Vedic Astrology Without Tears*. New Delhi: Ranjan Publications, 1994.

———. *Planets and Children*. New Delhi: Vision Wordtronic, 1993.

———. *Predicting through Jaimini's Chara Dasha*. New Delhi: Vision Wordtronic, 1995.

———. *Timing Events through Vimshottari Dasha*. New Delhi: Vision Wordtronic, 1995.

Roebuck, Valerie. *The Circle of Stars*. Shaftesbury: Element Books, 1991.

Rule, Ann. *The Stranger Beside Me*. New York: Norton, 1980.

Schocken, Wolfgang Alexander. *The Calculated Confusion of Calendars*. New York: Vantage Press, 1976.

Sharma, Viswanath Deva. *Astrology and Jyotirvidya: The Fundamental Principles and the Systems of Prognosis*. Calcutta: Viswa Jyotirvid Samgha, 1973.

Stone, Anthony Philip. *Hindu Astrology, Myths, Symbols and Realities*. New Delhi: Select Books, 1981.

Tester, S. J. *A History of Western Astrology*. New York: Ballantine Books, 1987.

Varahamihira. *Brihat Jataka*. New Delhi: Sagar Publications, 1985.

Varma, Kalyana. *Saravali*. New Delhi: Ranjan Publications, 1983.

Walters, Derek. *Chinese Astrology*. London: Aquarian Press, 1987.

Wolkstein, Diane and Samuel Noah Kramer. *Inanna: Queen of Heaven and Earth*. New York: HarperCollins, 1983.

Wolpert, Stanley. *A New History of India*. New York: Oxford University Press, 1993.

Index

Capricorn in 5th, 115
Gemini in 5th, 132
Jupiter in 5th, 197
Kethu in 5th, 201
Leo in 5th, 97
Libra in 5th, 104
Mars in 5th, 195
Mercury in 5th, 196
Moon in 5th, 194
Pisces in 5th, 122
Rahu in 5th, 200
Sagittarius in 5th, 111
Saturn in 5th, 199
Scorpio in 5th, 108
Sun in 5th, 192
Taurus in 5th, 128
Venus in 5th, 198
Virgo in 5th, 101
6th house, 88
Aquarius in 6th, 115
Aries in 6th, 122
Cancer in 6th, 132
Capricorn in 6th, 111
Gemini in 6th, 128
Jupiter in 6th, 197
Kethu in 6th, 201
Leo in 6th, 135
Libra in 6th, 101
Mars in 6th, 195
Mercury in 6th, 196
Moon in 6th, 194
Pisces in 6th, 119
Rahu in 6th, 200
Sagittarius in 6th, 108
Saturn in 6th, 199
Scorpio in 6th, 104
Sun in 6th, 192
Taurus in 6th, 125
Venus in 6th, 198
Virgo in 6th, 97
7th house, 89
Aquarius in 7th, 112
Aries in 7th, 119
Cancer in 7th, 129
Capricorn in 7th, 108
Gemini in 7th, 126
Jupiter in 7th, 197
Kethu in 7th, 201

Leo in 7th, 132
Libra in 7th, 98
Mars in 7th, 195
Mercury in 7th, 196
Moon in 7th, 194
Pisces in 7th, 115
Rahu in 7th, 200
Sagittarius in 7th, 105
Saturn in 7th, 199
Scorpio in 7th, 101
Sun in 7th, 193
Taurus in 7th, 122
Venus in 7th, 198
Virgo in 7th, 135
8th house, 89
Aquarius in 8th, 109
Aries in 8th, 116
Cancer in 8th, 126
Capricorn in 8th, 105
Gemini in 8th, 123
Jupiter in 8th, 197
Kethu in 8th, 201
Leo in 8th, 129
Libra in 8th, 136
Mars in 8th, 195
Mercury in 8th, 196
Moon in 8th, 194
Pisces in 8th, 112
Rahu in 8th, 200
Sagittarius in 8th, 102
Saturn in 8th, 199
Scorpio in 8th, 98
Sun in 8th, 193
Taurus in 8th, 119
Venus in 8th, 198
Virgo in 8th, 132
9th house, 90
Aquarius in 9th, 105
Aries in 9th, 112
Cancer in 9th, 123
Capricorn in 9th, 102
Gemini in 9th, 119
Jupiter in 9th, 197
Kethu in 9th, 201
Leo in 9th, 126
Libra in 9th, 132
Mars in 9th, 195
Mercury in 9th, 196

306 𝄞 Vedic Astrology

Inanna, 220
income, 91
India, 4
India's Golden Age, 16
indications, general, 56
Indo-Aryans, 10
Indo-European tribes, 4
infections, bleeding, 70
influence, neutral, 141
Inglis, Grace, 221
instability, mental, 69
intelligence, 88
Iraq, 4, 8
Ishtar, 220
itchiness, 71

J

jade, 70
Jakata, 37
Jupiter, 5, 16, 71, 142, 153, 170,
    190, 196
   Mahadasa, 247
Jyotish, 14, 20, 27, 37

K

Kalabala, 155
Kali, 30
Kalyana Varma, 21
Kama, 75
Kamara, 66, 69
Kannan, S., 39
Kanya, 70, 81
   Lagna, 113
kapha, 92
karaka, 67, 71, 185
karma, 12, 19
   law of, 11
   previous, 88
Kataka, 68, 80
   Lagna, 106
Kendra, 42
   house, 146, 165
Kethu, 37, 39, 77, 170, 201
   Mahadasa, 241
Khavedamsa, 56
kidneys, 66, 74
kinsmen, 88

knees, 90
   weak, 76
knowledge, 88, 90
Krishnamurti, K. S., 31, 32, 96, 100,
    103, 107, 110, 114, 117, 121,
    124, 127, 130, 134, 155, 219,
    227
Krittika, 13
Kshatrias, 12
Kuja, 69
Kumbha, 75, 84
   Lagna, 130
Kusana regime, 15

L

Lagna, 40, 41, 85
Lahiri, 27, 33
Lakshmi, 66, 74, 180
land, 87
lapis lazuli, 75
Leadbeater, C. W., 39
learning, 86
legs, 91
Leo, 65, 81, 110
   Jupiter in, 190
   Mars in, 188
   Mercury in, 189
   Moon in, 187
   Saturn in, 191
   Sun in, 186
   Venus in, 191
liberation, 85
Libra, 74, 82, 117
   Jupiter in, 190
   Mars in, 188
   Mercury in, 189
   Moon in, 187
   Saturn in, 191
   Sun in, 186
   Venus in, 190
life, duration of, 89
limbs, 85
liver, 71
   ailments, 73
loss, 91
luck, 90
   good or bad, 56

Ronnie Gale Dreyer is an internationally known astrological consultant, lecturer and teacher. She is the author of *Indian Astrology: A Western Approach to the Ancient Hindu Art* (1990), which is the original version of this revised and updated volume. She has also written *Venus: The Evolution of the Goddess and Her Planet* (1994), *Your Sun and Moon Guide to Love and Life* (1997) and is a contributor to *Astrology for Women: Roles and Relationships* (1997), *Hindu Astrology Lessons: 36 Teachers Share Their Wisdom* (1997) and Llewellyn's 1998 Sun and Moon Sign books. She is currently working on a book about astrology and alternative health which will be published by Prentice-Hall in 1998.

Ronnie holds a Bachelor of Arts in English/Theater Arts from the University of New Mexico, and studied Jyotish (Vedic Astrology) both privately and at Sanskrit University in Benares, India. She co-founded the first astrological computer service in the Netherlands where she lived for ten years, was the official Dutch representative for Astro*Carto*Graphy and was an editorial consultant for several publishing companies. She is currently the secretary of the Association for Astrological Networking (AFAN) and is on the staff of the New York Astrology Center. In 1994 Ronnie was one of the recipients of the Jyotish Kovid award from the Indian Council of Astrological Sciences for "promoting the cause of astrology through writings and lectures." Ronnie's goal is to use ancient Hindu interpretive techniques alongside traditional Western horoscope analysis, bridging the gap between East and West.

Ronnie lectures extensively for astrology groups and national conferences including United Astrology Congress (UAC '95), and conducts ongoing courses and workshops in Vedic Astrology throughout the country. She has also lectured in Canada, Germany, Holland, and the United Kingdom. Ronnie lives and practices in New York City.